ANAHITA

ANCIENT PERSIAN GODDESS AND ZOROASTRIAN YAZATA

ANAHITA

ANCIENT PERSIAN GODDESS AND ZOROASTRIAN YAZATA

Edited by Payam Nabarz

Papers and Contributions by:

*Dr. Israel Campos Méndez, Dr. Kaveh Farrokh,
Dr. Matteo Compareti, Sheda Vasseghi, D.M. Murdock, Dr. Sam Kerr,
Rahele Koulabadi, Dr. Seyyed Rasool Mousavi Haji, Morteza Ataie,
Seyed Mehdi Mousavi Kouhpar, Seyyed Sadrudin Mosavi Jashni,
Farhang Khademi Nadooshan, Hassan Nia, Masoud Sabzali,
Dr. Masato Tojo, Behzad Mahmoudi, Amir Mansouri, Dr Kamyar Abdi,
Dr Gholamreza Karamian, Maryam Zour, Saman Farzin,
Babak Aryanpour, Reza MehrAfarin, Akashanath,
Shapour Suren-Pahlav, Ana C. Jones, Katherine Sutherland,
and Dr. Payam Nabarz.*

Published By Avalonia

www.avaloniabooks.co.uk

Published by Avalonia

BM Avalonia

London

WC1N 3XX

England, UK

www.avaloniabooks.co.uk

Anahita: Ancient Persian Goddess and Zoroastrian Yazata

> *A special issue of Mithras Reader: An Academic and Religious Journal of Greek, Roman and Persian Studies.*

Copyright © 2012 Payam Nabarz

ISBN (10)   1-905297-30-0

ISBN (13) 978-1-905297-30-6

First Edition, February 2013

Design by Satori

Front Cover Image is of the *Sasanian stucco discovered in the Barz-e-qawela in Lorestan provenance of Iran, by Behzad Mahmoudi, Amir Mansouri, Dr Kamyar Abdi, Dr Gholamreza karamian, Farhang Khademi Nadooshan.*

British Library Cataloguing in Publication Data. A catalogue record for this book is available from the British Library.

Dedicated to Mehrdad and Anahita

TABLE OF CONTENTS

Acknowledgements

First and foremost, I would like to thank Sorita d'Este, David Rankine, and Alison Jones for all their input and helpful comments on preparing this manuscript.

I would also like to thank all the authors and contributors for submitting their works to this collection, and Avalonia for publishing it.

Hymn to Anahita (Aban Nyayis)

1. Unto the good Waters, made by Mazda; unto the holy water-spring Ardvi Anâhita; unto all waters, made by Mazda; unto all plants, made by Mazda,

2. Ahura Mazda spake unto Spitama Zarathushtra, saying: 'Offer up a sacrifice, O Spitama Zarathushtra! Unto this spring of mine, Ardvi Sûra Anâhita

3. Who makes the seed of all males pure, who makes the womb of all females pure for bringing forth

4. The large river, known afar, that is as large as the whole of the waters that run along the earth

5. All the shores of the sea Vouru-Kasha are boiling over, all the middle of it is boiling over, when she runs down there

6. From this river of mine alone flow all the waters that spread all over the seven Karshvares;

7. I, Ahura Mazda, brought it down with mighty vigour, for the increase of the house, of the borough, of the town, of the country.

8. He from whom she will hear the staota yêsnya; he from whom she will hear the Ahuna vairya; he from whom she will hear the Asha-vahista; he by whom the good waters will be made pure; with the words of the holy hymns, he will enter first the Garô-nmâna of Ahura Mazda: she will give him the boons asked for.

9. For her brightness and glory, I will offer her a sacrifice worth being heard; I will offer her a sacrifice well-performed. Thus mayest thou advise us when thou art appealed to! Mayest thou be most fully worshipped.

We sacrifice unto the holy Ardvi Sûra Anâhita with libations. We sacrifice unto Ardvi Sûra Anâhita, the holy and master of holiness, with the Haoma and meat, with the baresma, with the wisdom of the tongue, with the holy spells, with the words, with the deeds, with the libations, and with the rightly-spoken words.

The Zend Avesta, Part II (SBE23), James Darmesteter,tr. [1882]

PREFACE

Mithras Reader: An Academic and Religious Journal of Greek, Roman and Persian Studies is dedicated to all the religions of the classical world. We publish academic papers from researchers and spiritual articles from practitioners of the religions of the classical world. We also welcome classical world based art work; both modern interpretations, and traditional forms. Occasional articles covering the non-religious aspects of the ancient Greco-Roman or Persian world are also considered, for example dealing with geopolitical, cultural, or relevant military history. The Journal is divided into three distinct sections. Part 1 contains the academic papers from researchers based at universities and independent scholars; Part 2 art work, sculptures and paintings inspired by the classical world; in Part 3 there are articles by modern practitioners and, rites, hymns, stories and poetry.

This is a special edition of *Mithras Reader: An Academic and Religious Journal of Greek, Roman and Persian Studies*, dedicated to the ancient Persian Goddess Anahita, to highlight the significance of her central role throughout the Persian history.

This issue starts with a general introduction to Anahita. This is followed by academic studies of her stone relief and images during the Sassanian dynasty, Achaemenid royal inscriptions to her, her role as a Pre-Christian Virgin Mother of Mithra, she as purity undefiled, a primal spiritual tradition in the way of life among the Indo-Iranian peoples, a study of a William Morris Hunt painting of Anahita, as well as a number of modern works of art depicting her and poetry. The papers and other contributions in this issue provide numerous examples of the significance of Anahita throughout Persian and Middle Eastern history.

Payam Nabarz

Editor

CONTRIBUTORS BIOGRAPHIES

In Part 1 Academic Papers

Payam Nabarz is the author of *The Mysteries of Mithras: The Pagan Belief That Shaped the Christian World* (Inner Traditions, 2005), *The Persian Mar Nameh: The Zoroastrian Book of the Snake Omens & Calendar* (Twin Serpents, 2006), and *Divine Comedy of Neophyte Corax and Goddess Morrigan* (Web of Wyrd Press, 2008). He is also editor of *Mithras Reader An academic and religious journal of Greek, Roman, and Persian Studies*, Volume 1 (2006), Volume 2 (2008), and Volume 3 (2010). His latest books are *Stellar Magic: a Practical Guide to Rites of the Moon, Planets, Stars and Constellations* (Avalonia, 2009) and *Seething Cauldron: Essays on Zoroastrianism, Sufism, Freemasonry, Wicca, Druidry, and Thelema* (Web of Wyrd Press, 2010). For further info visit: www.stellarmagic.co.uk & http://www.myspace.com/nabarz

Dr. Israel Campos Méndez is Assistant Professor in Ancient History at the University of Las Palmas of Gran Canaria (Canary Islands, Spain). His lines of research are related to the History of Religion, and in particular to the Cult of Mithra in Ancient Iran and the Roman Empire. His PhD thesis was entitled: *The God Mithra: Analysis of the processes of adjustment of his worship from the social, political and religious frame of the Ancient Iran to that of the Roman Empire.* He has written two books in Spanish about the cult of Mithra in Ancient Persia, and many others papers and articles about the Zoroastrian Religion and the Mithraic Mysteries.

Kaveh Farrokh (PhD) is at the University of British Columbia - Continuing Studies - History Lecturer, & Reader Head of Department of Traditions & Cultural History - WAALM School of Cultural Diplomacy (nominated for Nobel Peace Prize 2011). He is a Member of Stanford University's WAIS (World Association of International Studies) and Member of Iranian Studies for Hellenic-Iranian Studies.

Dr. Matteo Compareti studied oriental languages in the University of Venice and after graduation he obtained his PhD from the University of Naples, L'Orientale. He specializes in the art history of Iran and Central Asia. His latest publications are *Samaracanda Centro del Mondo – Proposte di Lettura del Ciclo Pittorico di Afrasiyab,*

Minesis, (2010), and *Iranians on the Silk Road: Merchants, Kingdoms and Religions* by Touraj Daryaee, Khodadad Rezakhani, and Matteo Compareti (Afshar Publishing, 2010). He is an independent scholar not affiliated to any institution, Italian or foreign.

Sheda Vasseghi has a Masters in Ancient History - Persia and a Masters in Business Administration. Ms. Vasseghi focuses on Iranian national identity. Her special interest encompasses Iranian philosophy as it applies to modern day social, political and religious issues. She believes history provides the answers to current problems, and that a lack of knowledge in the field leads to poor decision-making by both citizens and policymakers. Ms. Vasseghi is a regular contributor to political and historical publications on Iran's affairs, and an adjunct Professor of History at the Northern Virginia Community College. Ms. Vasseghi is also on the Board of the Azadegan Foundation and a member of www.persepolis3D.com.

D.M. Murdock is an independent scholar of comparative religion and mythology, specializing in nature worship, solar mythology and astrotheology. An alumna of Franklin & Marshall College and the American School of Classical Studies at Athens, Greece, Murdock is the author of several controversial books about the origins and relationship of religious ideas dating back thousands of years to the earliest known evidence. Her work can be found at TruthBeKnown.com and StellarHousePublishing.com.

Sam Kerr is a Fellow of the Royal Society of Medicine (London) and of several Colleges of Surgery. A Zoroastrian by birth, he migrated to Australia in 1968. He was Surgeon/Lecturer at the University of New South Wales and its College Hospitals, Sydney, Australia from 1968 to 2003. He is now Emeritus Surgeon at the University and its College Hospitals.

Rahele Koulabadi, has an MA in Archaeology, and is based at the Sistan and Baluchestan University, Iran. Email: rahele_koulabadi@yahoo.com

Dr. Seyyed Rasool Mousavi Haji was born on December 30, 1967, in Savadkouh, Iran. He received his PhD in Archaeology in 2003 from Tarbiat Modarres University of Iran. He teaches at the Mazandaran University and has published four books and several articles about the archaeology of the Sassanian and Islamic periods. His main fieldwork include: Archaeological survey in the Sistan plain in 2007 and 2008, archaeological survey in Zahedane Kohne (capital of Sistan during 5 to 9 A. H.) in 2002 and excavation to estimate the size of the Zahedane Kohne in 2007. Email: Seyyed_rasool@yahoo.com

Morteza Ataie has an M.A. in Archaeology, and is based at the University of Sistan and Baluchestan, Iran. Email: Morteza_ataie@yahoo.com

Seyed Mehdi Mousavi Kouhpar is an Assistant Professor in the Department of Archaeology at Tarbiat Modares University. Email: m_mousavi@modares.ac.ir

Seyed Sadrudin Mosavi Jashni is an Assistant Professor in the Research Institute of Imam Khomeini and the Islamic Revolution.

Farhang Khademi Nadooshan is an Associate Professor in the Dept of Archaeology, Tarbiat Modares University, Tehran, Iran.

Hassan Nia is an academic member of the Islamic Azad University Savad Koh unit, Iran.

Mehdi Sabzali is a Post graduate student in the Dept of Archaeology, Tarbiat Modares University, Tehran, Iran.

Dr. Masato Tōjō was born in Niigata City, Japan in 1957 and earned his PhD in Information Technology from the Dept. of Information Technology (now Information Science), Graduate School of Engineering, University of Tokyo in 1985. He is a Japanese committee member of ISO/IEC JTC1 SC18 WG9 from 1992 to 1996. Chairman of Mithraeum Japan (Founded in 1997). His published books include: *Qewl - Holy Book of Mithra* (MIIBOAT Books, 2006), *Mithraic Theology* (Kokushokankōkai, 1996), *Dictionary of Gods of the World* (Gakken, 2004), *Esoteric Astrology of Mithraism* (MIIBOAT Books, 1998), *Let's Read the Secret Doctrine* (Shuppanshinsha, 2001) and *Encyclopedia of Tarot* (Kokushokankōkai, 1994). Official website - http://homepage2.nifty.com/Mithra/index.html

Behzad Mahmoudi is a Post Graduate student at the Islamic Azad University, Central Tehran Branch, Iran. Email: archeaologist_ir@yahoo.com

Amir Mansouri is a Post Graduate student at the Islamic Azad University, Central Tehran Branch, Iran.

Dr Kamyar Abdi is an Iranian archaeologist. He received his M.A. from the Department of Near Eastern Languages and Cultures, University of Chicago, and his PhD in Archaeology/Anthropology from the University of Michigan.

Dr Gholamreza Karamian is an Associate Professor at the Department of Archaeology, Islamic Azad University, Central Tehran branch.

Saman Farzin M.A is based at Iranology Department of History, University of Shiraz, Iran. Email: saman_farzin2006@yahoo.com

Maryam Zour M.A. is based at Archaeology University of Sistan and Baluchistan Zahidan-Iran.

Babak Aryanpour M.A. is based at Iranology, University of Shiraz, Iran.

Reza MehrAfarin is an Associate Professor, University of Sistan & Baluchestan.

In Part 2 Arts.

Akashanath is a Ceremonial Magician with a background in both Thelema and the Golden Dawn systems. He is also a Sanyasin of the Adinath Sampradaya and a practitioner of English Rune Magick.

Shapour Suren-Pahlav co-founded *The Circle of Ancient Iranian Studies* (CAIS) in 1998, as an independent non-profit educational programme, with no affiliation to any political or religious group, dedicated to the research, protection and preservation of the pre-Islamic Iranian civilization.

Ana C. Jones was born in Brazil and trained as a teacher and electrical engineer, in 1989 she moved to England with husband and their three children. Her interest in Traditional Astrology led her to complete C. Warnock's Renaissance Astrological magical course, plus two others of the same calibre. At the moment she is studying Alchemy from Adam McLean courses, Hermetic Magic with the OMS as well as Mithraism. She practices Traditional British Witchcraft and Stregoneria. She finds inspiration among her studies and practices to express herself through her drawings, paintings and sculptures.

In Part 3 Religious Articles, Poetry, Stories.

Katherine Sutherland is a poet and author, her collection *Underworld*, a reworking of the Persephone myth, was recently published (Web of Wyrd Press, 2010). She has papers published in the following anthologies: *Both Sides of Heaven: Essays on Angels, Fallen Angels and Demons* (Avalonia, 2009), *From a Drop of Water* (Avalonia, 2009), *Hekate: Her Sacred Fires* (Avalonia, 2010).

Figure 1: Anahita statue in snow, photo by Payam Nabarz.

Introduction to Anahita the Lady of Persia

by Payam Nabarz

Mighty Anahita with splendour will shine,
Incarnated as a youthful divine.
Full of charm her beauty she will display,
Her hip with charming belt she will array.
Straight-figured, she is as noble bride,
Freeborn, herself in puckered dress will hide.
Her cloak is all decorated with gold,
With precious dress Anahita we shall behold.

(Original poem based on Kashani's Persian folk songs, from an Avestan invocation to Anahita)

Abstract

The name Anahita is still used for girls in Iran, and in recent decades, the use of this name has been gaining in popularity. Therefore the link to Anahita from circa 3000 years ago is still alive today in common culture, and is not just limited to the domain of history books. In this article, which is a basic general introduction to Anahita, I review some of the sources which mention her from ancient Persia to modern day Iran in a chronological order to demonstrate a sense of the continuation of her influence. The review aims to set the scene for more detailed academic papers and articles by various other authors in this anthology, *Anahita: Persian Goddess & Zoroastrian Yazata*.

Anahita's full title is *Aredvi Sura Anahita*, which means *'Moist'*, *'Mighty'* and *'Immaculate'* (pure); the significance of her epithet of *'pure'* is discussed in Sam Kerr's paper. Anahita is an Indo-Iranian Mother Goddess, and her cult is similar to other Indo-European deities and Near Eastern goddesses, some of whom are discussed in the papers by Kaveh Farrokh, Matteo Compareti and D.M. Murdock. Anahita in India could be linked with the Hindu goddess Saraswati, while in the Near East she has been linked to the goddess Ishtar. She is the mythical world river that emerges from mount Hara into the great sea and is the source of all the waters; she is closely associated with the investiture of kings and is a goddess of sovereignty. The historian Herodotus also refers to a Persian *'Aphrodite'*, though he names her Mithra. It is within the Zoroastrian body of texts that much of her lore is preserved. Therefore, an examination of how Anahita is placed in the schema of Zoroastrianism is necessary.

Zoroaster is thought to have lived in north eastern Iran sometime during the sixth or fifth century BCE, although some scholars believe it could have been as early as 1400 BCE. Zoroaster is said to have had a miraculous birth: his mother, Dughdova, was a virgin who conceived him after being visited by a shaft of light. Zoroaster's teachings led to the world's first monotheistic religion, in which Ahura Mazda, the *'Wise Lord'* of the sky, was the ultimate creator. In this religious reform, many gods and goddesses of the Persian pantheon were stripped of their sovereignty as well as their powers and their attributes were bestowed upon the one god; Ahura Mazda.[1]

The *Avesta* is the Zoroastrian holy book. It is a collection of holy texts, which include the *Gathas*, the word of the prophet Zoroaster himself, and the *Yashts*, the ancient liturgical poems and hymns that scholars believe predated Zoroaster and were modified to reflect the reformation. It also contains rituals, precepts for daily life and rites of passage for birth, marriage, and death. Because of the *Avesta*, the Zoroastrians were the first *'people of the book'*; *Avesta* probably means *'authoritative utterance'*[2] and is sometimes separated into the *Old Avesta* (mid to late second millennium BCE), and the *Young Avesta* (early to mid-first millennium BCE).[3]

The *Gathas* are seen as the original teachings of the Prophet Zoroaster; other texts in the *Avesta* belong to the Zoroastrian body of texts, some of which predate Zoroaster and some of which are later than Zoroaster himself. In some cases, like that of Zurvanism, it is seen as an offshoot and a heresy. In the *Gathas*, the concept of angels and demons are as abstract figures and ideas, while in earlier texts and later texts they are substantive figures and beings.

---

[1] Payam Nabarz, *The Mysteries of Mithras: The Pagan Belief That Shaped the Christian World*, 2005.
[2] Peter Clark, *Zoroastrianism: An Introduction to an Ancient Faith*, 1998:X.
[3] Jenny Rose, *Zoroastrianism: An Introduction*, 2011:243.

Some of the *Yashts* are hymns to ancient Persian deities, who, in Zoroastrianism are demoted to the ranks of archangels or angels, with Ahura Mazda at the top of the hierarchy. In the Zoroastrian religion, Ahura Mazda has seven immortal aspects being the Amshaspends or Spenta Mainyu (Ameshas Spenta), each of which rules over a particular realm. These holy heptads are: Vohu Mano (good thought, the realm of animals), Asha Vahishta (righteousness, the realm of fire), Spenta Armaiti (devotion, the realm of earth), Khshathra Vairya (dominion, the realm of air, sun and heavens), Haurvatat (wholeness, the realm of water), Ameretat (immortality, the realm of plants), and Spenta Mainyu, who is identified with Ahura Mazda (the realm of humanity). There are also seven Yazatas, the protective spirits: Anahita (water/fertility), Atar (fire), Homa (the healing plant), Sraosha (obedience/hearer of prayers), Rashnu (judgment), Mithra (truth), Tishtrya (the Dog Star/source of rain).[4] These can be seen in the following diagram. This figure shows the seven Ameshas Spentas and the seven Yazatas. Yazata means worthy of worship.

Zoroastrianism is monotheistic, with a strong sense of dualism, whereby Ahura Mazda's Ameshas Spenta and Yazatas, the forces of Light and Truth (*Asha*), are faced with the forces of Darkness of the Angra Mainyu, or Ahriman, who is called the Great Lie (*Druj*). He and his demons are said to create drought, harsh weather, sickness, disease, poverty, and all forms of suffering. The holy heptads the Amshaspends are faced by the unholy heptads, their polar opposites and antithesis.

Within the context of Zoroastrianism, Anahita is a Yazata, however in the Zoroastrian Hymn (*Yasht*) to her we see a glimpse of her eminent pre-Zoroastrian role as even Ahura Mazda pays her homage and asks for her help:

---

[4] Arthur Cotterell, *The Ultimate Encyclopedia of Mythology*, 2003.

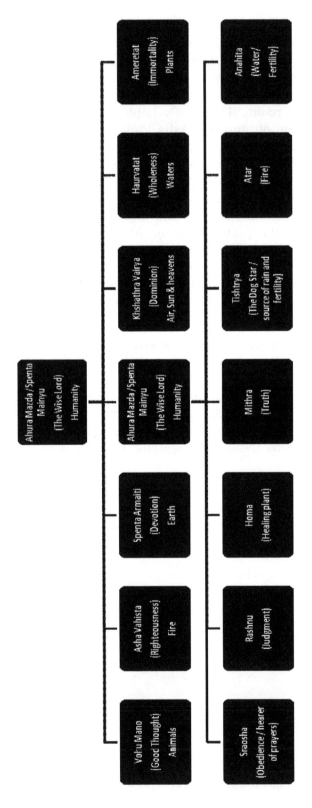

'17. "To her did the Maker Ahura Mazda offer up a sacrifice to the Airyana Vaejah, by the good river Daitya; with the Homa and meat, with the baresma, with the wisdom of the tongue, with the holy spells, with the words, with the deeds, with the libations, and with the rightly-spoken words.

18. "He begged of her a boon, saying: 'Grant me this, O good, most beneficent Ardvi Sura Anahita! that I may bring the son of Pourushaspa, the holy Zarathushtra, to think after my law, to speak after my law, to do after my law!'

19. "Ardvi Sura Anahita granted him that boon, as he was offering libations, giving gifts, sacrificing, and begging that she would grant him that boon.

'For her brightness and glory, I will offer her a sacrifice. . . .⁵

This is strange; in considering the reasons why Ahura Mazda the creator God, would make offerings to one of his lesser angels, the above passage points to the notion that despite the reformation of the Persian pantheon, Anahita kept her central role. To speculate on this, perhaps to win her followers over, concessions had to be made by the priests of the new religion, to bring her followers into the fold.

There are some key Zoroastrian texts referring to Anahita: the *Aban Yasht 5*, *Yasna 65*, and *Aban Nyayis*. From the Zoroastrian text *Aban Yasht* - the hymn to angel-goddess Anahita we inherited a vivid description of her:

'Angel-Goddess of all the waters upon the earth and the source of the cosmic ocean; you who drive a chariot pulled by four horses: wind, rain, cloud, and sleet; your symbol is the eight-rayed star. You are the source of life, purifying the seed of all males and the wombs of all females, also cleansing the milk in the breasts of all mothers. Your connection with life means warriors in battle prayed to you for survival and victory.

A maid, fair of body, most strong, tall-formed, high-girded, pure... wearing a mantle fully embroidered with gold; ever holding the baresma [sacred plant] in your hand... you wear square golden earrings on your ears ... a golden necklace around your beautiful neck... Upon your head... a golden crown, with a hundred stars, with eight rays ... with fillets streaming down.⁶

The Persian Magi reciting the hymn to her had perhaps had their prayers answered in the form of visions. From the material we have,

---

⁵ From verses 17–19 of the *Aban Yasht 5*.

the visions might have appeared as the following: sitting on a beach or near a river; as midnight approaches and time slows, the sea parts, and a large silver throne appears; on either side of it sits a lion with eyes of blue flame. On the throne sits a Lady in silver and gold garments, proud and tall, an awe-inspiring warrior-woman, as terrifying as she is beautiful. Tall and statuesque she sits, her noble origins are evident in her appearance, her haughty authority made clear and commanding through a pair of flashing eyes. A dove flies above her and a peacock walks before her. A crown of shining gold rings her royal temples; bejeweled with eight sunrays and one hundred stars, it holds her lustrous hair back from her beautiful face. Her marble-like white arms reflect moonlight and glisten with moisture. She is clothed with a garment made of thirty beaver skins, and it shines with the full sheen of silver and gold. The planet Venus shines brightly in the sky above her head.[7]

However, it is not just the Magi, Ahura Mazda or the *'good'* people that make offerings to Anahita, but the Daevas (demons) and the *'bad'* people also make her offerings; she is worshipped by both sides - and this is a sticky point for the prophet Zoroaster and he asks her:

'94. "Then Zarathushtra asked Ardvi Sura Anahita: 'O Ardvi Sura Anahita! What becomes of those libations which the wicked worshippers of the Daevas bring unto thee after the sun has set?'

95. "Ardvi Sura Anahita answered: 'O pure, holy Spitama Zarathushtra! howling, clapping, hopping, and shouting, six hundred and a thousand Daevas, who ought not to receive that sacrifice, receive those libations that men bring unto me after [the sun has set].[8]

Indeed in the *Aban Yasht* warriors from opposing armies make offerings to her, but she only grants the *'good'* warriors their prayers. This is attested to in Greek sources too, Xerxes at dawn prayed for victory over the Greeks by pouring libations into the Hellespont and flung a golden cup, a golden bowl, and a short sword into the sea.[9]

In addition to her warrior aspect, she is also a Mother Goddess:

'Who makes the seed of all males pure, who makes the womb of all females pure for bringing forth, who makes all females bring forth in

---

[6] From verses 126–128 of the *Aban Yasht 5*.

[7] This description of Anahita is based on her description in Tony Allan, Charles Phillips, and Michael Kerrigan, Myth and Mankind series: *Wise Lord of the Sky: Persian Myth*, 1999:32.

[8] From verses 94–95 of the *Aban Yasht 5*.

[9] Jenny Rose, *Zoroastrianism: An Introduction*, 2011:53.

safety, who puts milk into the breasts of all females in the right measure and the right quality;'[10]

Furthermore, she is associated with a number of different animals, and her totemic animals do vary as she changes in different parts of the Middle East and comes under the influence of different local customs, and is exposed to varied cultures, which span millennia. She is sometimes shown riding a lion when bestowing sovereignty to kings, e.g. there is a magnificent seal from the post-Achaemenid dynasties in Turkey that shows the king facing Anahita while she is standing on a lion surrounded by sun rays.[11] In addition, the *De Natura Animalium* by Aelian refers to one of her shrines as containing tame lions which would greet and wag their tails at visitors. On Sassanian ewers we see her with the doves and peacocks which the paper by Rahele Koulabadi's discusses in detail. This is further supported by the recent discovery, by Behzad Mahmoudi and published here, of a Sassanian stucco showing Anahita flanked by two winged lions and holding a dove. In the *Aban Yasht*, she rides in a chariot driven by four horses: the wind, the rain, the cloud, and the sleet. Indeed, this later vision of her is theme of the famous pre-Raphaelite sculpture *The Horses of Anahita* and painting *Anahita the Flight of Night* by William Morris Hunt, (1824–1879) which is explored in the paper by Sheda Vasseghi in this anthology.

The sources referring to Anahita are not limited to Zoroastrian texts, there are also inscriptions left by kings. For example, circa 400 BCE the Achaemenian king Artaxerxes II Mnemon (404-359 BCE) inscribes in Ecbatana in his palace:

'Artaxerxes, the great king, the king of kings, the king of all nations, the king of this world, the son of king Darius [II Nothus], Darius the son of king Artaxerxes [I Makrocheir], Artaxerxes the son of king Xerxes, Xerxes the son of king Darius, Darius the son of Hystaspes, the Achaemenid, says: this hall [apadana] I built, by the grace of Ahuramazda, Anahita, and Mithra. May Ahuramazda, Anahita, and Mithra protect me against evil, and may they never destroy nor damage what I have built.'[12]

---

[10] From verse 2 of the *Aban Yasht 5*.
[11] http://www.kavehfarrokh.com/iranica/achaemenid-era/eastern-anatolia-heir-to-a-irano-greek-legacy/
[12] See: http://www.livius.org/aa-ac/achaemenians/A2Ha.html

Figure 2: 'The Horses of Anahita' by William Morris Hunt.[13]

Figure 3: Some of the column and wall remains of Temple of Anahita at Kangavar, (photograph by Jamshid Varza, www.vohuman.org, reproduced with his kind permission.)

[13] http://en.wikipedia.org/wiki/William_Morris_Hunt

Artaxerxes II, like other Achaemenian kings, was initiated by priests at a sanctuary of Anahita in Pasargadai during his coronation. He built the temple of Anahita at Kangavar near Kermanshah, as well as many others. The Kangavar was a magnificent temple, four-fifths of a mile in circumference, built using cedar or cypress trees. All the columns and floor-tiles were covered with gold and silver. It was perhaps one of the most breathtaking buildings ever built in the Middle East.

Anahita's role as the goddess of water, rain, abundance, blessing, fertility, marriage, love, motherhood, birth, and victory became well established. This goddess was the manifestation of women's perfection. Ancient kings were crowned by their queens in Anahita's temple in order to gain her protection and support. Anahita's blessing would bring fertility and abundance to the country.[14]

The pages of history turn, and eventually the Achaemenian Empire falls to *'Alexander the Accursed'*, but Anahita is carried into the new Greek influenced empire.

Circa 200 BCE sees the dedication of a Seleucid temple in western Iran to "*Anahita, as the Immaculate Virgin Mother of the Lord Mithra*".[15] The blend of Greek and Persian cultures manifests itself in the Seleucid dynasty.

The Parthian Empire (circa 247 BCE-226 CE) replaces the Seleucid and the Parthians expand the Anahita temple at Kangavar.

Mark Anthony marches into Armenia (circa 37 BCE - 34 BCE), and in one of the latter campaigns reached the Anahita temple at Erez:

'The temple of Erez was the wealthiest and the noblest in Armenia, according to Plutarch. During the expedition of Mark Antony in Armenia, the statue was broken to pieces by the Roman soldiers. Pliny the Elder gives us the following story about it: The Emperor Augustus, being invited to dinner by one of his generals, asked him if it were true that the wreckers of Anahit's statue had been punished by the wrathful goddess. 'No, answered the general, on the contrary, I have today the good fortune of treating you with one part of the hip of that

---

[14] Official entry on Anahita by the Embassy of the Islamic Republic of Iran in Ottawa, Canada on their web site:
http://www.salamiran.org/Women/General/Women_And_Mythical_Deities.html
[15] First Iranian Goddess of productivity and values by Manouchehr Saadat Noury - Persian Journal, Jul 21, 2005.
http://www.iranian.ws/iran_news/publish/printer_8378.shtml

gold statue.' The Armenians erected a new golden statue of Anahit in Erez, which was worshipped before the time of St. Gregory the Illuminator.'[16]

The Sassanian Empire is formed circa 226 CE. The Temple of Anahita in Bishapur was built during the Sassanian era (241-635 CE). The temple is believed to have been built by some of the estimated seventy thousand Roman soldiers and engineers who were captured by the Persian King Shapur I (241-272 CE), who also captured three Roman emperors: Gordian III, Phillip, and Valerian. The design of the temple is noteworthy: water from the river Shapur is channeled into an underground canal to the temple and flows under and all around the temple, giving the impression of an island. The fire altar would have been in the middle of the temple, with the water flowing underground all around it. One might interpret this as a union of water – Anahita - with fire - Mithra.[17] This fits well with Greek accounts of Persian reverence for fire and water. Indeed Porphyry (circa 232-305 CE) in his work *Cave of the Nymphs* (water spirits) states that the Persian worship in cave-like spaces: *'Thus also the Persians, mystically signifying the descent of the soul into the sublunary regions, and its regression from it, initiate the mystic (or him who is admitted to the arcane sacred rites) in a place which they denominate a cavern. For, as Eubulus says, Zoroaster was the first who consecrated in the neighbouring mountains of Persia, a spontaneously produced cave, florid, and having fountains, in honour of Mithra, the maker and father of all things; a cave, according to Zoroaster, bearing a resemblance of the world, which was fabricated by Mithra... ...so to the world they dedicated caves and dens; as likewise to Nymphs, on account of the water which trickles, or is diffused in caverns, over which the Naiades, as we shall shortly observe, preside.'*[18] The line on water trickling reminds one of the Zoroastrian shrine of Pir e Sabz, or Chek Chek (*'drip drip,'* the sound of water dripping), in the mountains of Yazd, Iran.

---

[16] Vahan M. Kurkjian, *A History of Armenia*, 2008.
[17] For the Temple of Anahita at Bishapur, see
http://www.vohuman.org/SlideShow/Anahita%20Bishapur/AnahitaBishapur00.htm
[18] Thomas Taylor (trans.) *On the Cave of the Nymphs in the Thirteenth Book of the Odyssey from the Greek of Porphyry*, 1823.

Figure 4: Bronze head of the goddess Anahita, Hellenistic Greek, 1st century BCE found at the ancient city of Satala, modern Sadak, north-eastern Turkey, now in The British Museum.

Figure 5: The Temple of Anahita in Bishapur, Iran, on the site of the ancient city built by Shapur I, Sassanian Emperor (241–272 CE) in celebration of his victory over three Roman Emperors - Gordian III, Phillip, and Valerian. (Photograph by Jamshid Varza, www.vohuman.org, reproduced with his kind permission.) Top general view, bottom left Stairs from main floor, middle and right water canal access.

Eventually the Sassanian Empire falls to the Arab Islamic invasion in 651 CE. Yet, even now Muslim pilgrims make their way to the 1100 year-old shrine of Bibi Shahr Banoo, the Islamic female saint, near the old town of Rey (South of Tehran). The town of Rey is thought to be 5000 years old, and the site of this shrine with its waterfall is believed by some to have once been an Anahita shrine. It is also close to the Cheshmeh Ali Hill (the spring of Ali Hill), which is dated to 5000 years ago. Perhaps this is an echo of Mithra-Anahita shrines being located close to each other and then becoming linked to later Islamic saints, a process seen frequently in Christianised Europe too; for example, sites sacred to the Celtic goddess Brighid became sites dedicated to Saint Brigit.

Furthermore, according to Susan Gaviri: *Anahita in Iranian Mythology* (1993):

'*...it must not be forgotten that many of the famous fire temples in Iran were, in the beginning, Anahita temples. Examples of these fire temples are seen in some parts of Iran, especially in Yazad, where we find that after the Muslim victory these were converted to Mosques.*'[19]

Modern day Zoroastrian pilgrims in Iran continue to visit the Pre-Islamic Zoroastrian shrine of Pir-e Sabz, or Chek Chek, in the mountains of Yazd. This is still a functional temple and the holiest site for present-day Zoroastrians living in Iran, who takes their annual pilgrimage to Pir-e Sabz Banu, '*the old woman in the mountain*', also called Pir-e Sabz, '*the green saint*', at the beginning of summer. *Pir* means '*elder*', and it can also mean '*fire*'. The title of Pir also connotes a Sufi master. *Sabz* means green.[20]

Pilgrims also continue to visit Pir-e Banu Pars (*Elder Lady of Persia*) and Pir-e Naraki located near Yazd. The Pir Banoo temple is in an area that has a number of valleys; the name of the place is Hapt Ador, which means Seven Fires.[21] Banu means '*Lady*' and Pars means '*Persia*'; it is this epithet of Anahita I have used for the title of this paper. Both Pir-c Sabz and Pir-e Banu Pars have legends of Sassanian princesses associated with them. The Pir-e Banu Pars site related to the youngest daughter of the last Sassanian king Yazdegird III (632-51CE) and queen Hastbadan, local legend tells us:

---

[19] *Anahita in Iranian Mythology*, 1993:7. This book is in Persian—translation here by Payam Nabarz.
[20] For the temple at Pir-e-Sabz, see
http://www.vohuman.org/SlideShow/Pir-e-Sabz/Pir-e-Sabz-1.htm
[21] For the temples of Pir e Banoo Pars and Pir e Naraki, see
http://www.sacredsites.com/middle_east/iran/zoroastrian.htm &
http://www.heritageinstitute.com/zoroastrianism/worship/setinaraki.htm

'As the young princess fled before the Arabs, she was beset by thirst and paused briefly at a farm and requested from the farmer for a glass of milk. He began to oblige by milking his cow. When he had finished and placed down the pale of milk, the cow stirred and kicked the pale slipping the milk into the ground. Now with the Arabs closing in on her and no time to wait, she fled into the folds of the mountain. With no water in sight and the pursuers now in plain sight, she lifted her arms in prayed pleading to be saved from the clutches of the enemy. As with the others, the mountain responded by opening its side and without a moment to loose, she disappeared into its embrace. The princess Banu-Pars is known by several names such as Sherbanu and Khataribanu. Years passed and a blind man happened to rest at the very spot where the princess had disappeared into the mountain. In his sleep a vision of a beautiful maiden came to him telling him what had transpired at that very spot and he knew he must built a shrine at that place and while still asleep resolved to do so. When he awoke, his sight returned to him.*

Today, the shrine, popular with Zoroastrians and non-Zoroastrians alike, is also called Mazreh-e Mehr Yazad, meaning the 'Farm of Angel Mithra' and Pir-e Banu Pars. It has another name as well: Pir-e Meherbanu, the *'ancient holy place of the lady Mehr'*.[22]

The local legend associate with Pir-e Sabz is:

'The grotto-shrine at Pir-e Sabz is dedicated to the royal princess Nikbanu (also spelt Nikbanoo, meaning Good Lady). The princess was the daughter of the last Sassanian king Yazdegird III and queen Hastbadan. According to legend, after the fleeing royal party had split up in an effort to avoid capture by the invading Arab horde, princess Nikbanu fled to Pir-e Sabz. The Arabs caught up with her and now trapped, she prayed devoutly and a cleft in the mountain parted taking the princess into its womb. The rock face closed before the eyes of the bewildered Arabs, but not before a piece of her garment was trapped in the cleft of closed rock face. The piece of cloth petrified as a piece of coloured rock and was visible until recently. The waters that now emerge from the rocks and drip along the 'cheeks' of the cave walls are the princess' tears of grief. The course of the trickling water is lined with wisps of par-e siavoshoun or maidenhair fern, symbolic of the princess' hair. The spring and waters are known as ab-e Hayat meaning the water of life. The allusion here is also to the archangel Armaiti, guardian of the earth, and the angel Anahita, guardian of the waters. The waters gather in a small pool and support a patch of greenery - greenery, sabz, that gives its name to the site - that includes

---

[22] www.heritageinstitute.com/zoroastrianism/worship/banunarestaneh.htm

an old plane tree as well as an old drooping willow. Legend has it that the plane tree grew out of the cane Nikbanu used to help her ascend the cliff-face. The tree is said to catch fire and miraculously renew itself every thousand years. The willow is stooped with age and its branches droop down and across the pool before spreading across the terrace.[23]

Local legends also describe a similar fate for Queen Hastbadan which forms the basis of another sacred site the Seti Pir: *'this site located at Maryamabad, a northeast suburb of Yazd city, is dedicated to the last Zoroastrian queen of Iran, Shahbanoo Hastbadan, mother of the princess Banu Pars and Hayat Banu, and wife of Yazdegird III, the last Sassanid king. According to legend, this is where the pursuing Arabs caught up with her. With no escape possible, the exhausted queen laid down on a rock at the pir, prayed, and together with her two attendants was taken into the rock. The other legend is that to save their honour, the queen and her two attendants jumped into the deep well at the pir.*[24]

A further and similar local legend is also associated with the Pir-e Naraki site, of Nazbanu who too was being chased by the Arab army:

'According to legend, Nazbanu's (some call her Zarbanu) escape route led her to Taft from where she began to seek refuge in the nearby mountains, climbing the slopes of Dar-e Zanjir or Kuh-e La-Anjir. Arriving exhausted at the Pir-e Naraki site, she prayed and asked for divine intervention, when as with the others, a portal opened in the mountain side to welcome her into its womb. When the portal closed, at the place where she entered the mountain, a spring started to gush water.[25]

In Iran praying to Anahita continued at her shrines near Yazd despite rise of Islam, and in other parts of Iran under the guise of praying to female Islamic saints. This was the state of play for about 1500 years, until the twentieth century!

In the early 1900s one of many branches of twentieth century occult and spiritual revival in the West was the Mazdaznan a religious movement based on Zoroastrian and Christian thinking. The founder called himself Otoman Zar-Adusht Ha'nish (1856–1936). His work is much ignored, unlike that of contempories of his such as Gurdjieff, Rudolf Steiner and Aleister Crowley. One of his works is of particular interest here, in 1913 he published *Ainyahita In Pearls* a 196 page book, consisting of 23 chapters which are: *'I Mazda and Ainyahita, II*

---

[23] Ibid
[24] Ibid
[25] Ibid

Ainyahita in the Presence of Mazda, III Ainyahita and Her Relation, IV Ainyahita and Her Good Thought, V Ainyahita on the Battlefield, VI Ainyahita and her Fravashis, VII Ainyahita and the Lord of Hosts, VIII Ainyahita at the Shrine of Mana, IX Ainyahita and the Ancient of Days, X Ainyahita and the Serpent, XI Ainyahita and the Resurrection, XII Ainyahita and the Shadow, XIII Ainyahita and the Rock of Ancestry, XIV Ainyahita and her Elementals, XV Ainyahita and Earth's Redemption, XVI Ainyahita and the Voice, XVII Ainyahita in her Prayers, XVIII Ainyahita and the Spirit of the Earth, XIX Ainyahita and the Spirit of Adjustment, XX Ainyahita and Mithra, XXI Ainyahita and the Spirit of Ancestry, XXII Ainyahita and the Lord's Anointed, XXIII Ainyahita and the Lord of Lords.'

This book is product of its time, and like many other contemporary occult and spiritualist works the text has been given a pseudo-history: *'The discoveries of valuable ancient manuscript in the Desert of Gobi and later finds in the Plateau of Tibet led to the addition to the Pearls published in the Mazdaznan in 1907, 1908 and 1909. These fragmentary writings have aroused so much favor among men of learning that it encouraged the continuation of this oft time great task of clothing a rhetorical thought in more simple language, abbreviating lengthy discourses and presenting them in a more concise form. Ainyahita constitutes the subject matter of friendly discussion in as great a measure as the Rubaiyat. To familiarise one's self with Ainyahita one must read her and study her. To the Avestan she proved a subject of worship, to the Greeks one of laud.'*[26] What Otoman Zar-Adusht Ha'nish started is a modern worship of Anahita in the West and he wrote a *Liber Anahita* to achieve this. However, he views her as an actual person who lived *'9000 years ago'*.

The Central Bank of Armenia in 1997, issued a commemorative gold coin with an image of Anahita on it. The bank literature states that: *'This commemorative coin issued by the Central Bank of Armenia is devoted to Goddess Anahit. Anahit has been considered the Mother Goddess of Armenians, the sacred embodiment and patron for the crops, fruitfulness and fertility. In 34 BCE, the Romans have plundered the country town Yeriza of the Yekeghiats Province in the Higher Hayk, where the huge golden statue to Anahit was situated. They smashed the statue to pieces and shared among the soldiers as pillage. On the turn of the 19th century, a head part of a bronze statue referring to Anahit was found in Satagh (Yerznka region), which is presently kept in British Museum.'*[27]

---

[26] *Ainyahita In Pearls*, Otoman Zar-Adusht Hanish, 1913.
[27] http://www.cba.am/CBA_SITE/currency/aanahit.html?__locale=en

The importance of Anahita in Armenia, which was once part of Persia, can further be seen in the images of her appearing on their current stamps and bank notes.

Figure 6: Commemorative gold coin with image of Anahita, 1997.

Figure 7: A 5000 Dram bank note in Armenia with image of Anahita.

Figure 8: A stamp in Armenia with image of Anahita.

The higher social status of women in Iranian society compared to its Arab neighbours has been suggested by some to be due to its long respect for Lady Anahita. Indeed, the first Muslim woman to win a Nobel Peace Prize (2003) was from Iran.

Time passes ... history take place ... Yet Anahita is still remembered as we can see from this firsthand account:

'Tomorrow (21.8.03), I (Jalil Nozari) will take part in a ceremony to commemorate a very poor, old woman, a relative of mine, who died recently. Her name was Kaneez. The name in modern Farsi has negative connotations, meaning a "female servant." But, in Pahlavi, the language spoken in central Iran before the coming of Islam, it meant "a maiden," a virgin, unmarried girl. Indeed, it has both meanings of the English "maid." Anahita, too, means virgin, literally not defiled. But this is not the end of story. When I was a child, there was a place in Ramhormoz, my hometown, which now is under a city road. In it, there was a small, single-room building with a small drain pipe hanging from it. Women in their ninth month and close to delivery time stood under this pipe and someone poured water through it. There was the belief that getting wet under the drain would assure a safe delivery of the baby. The building was devoted to Khezer (the green one).[28] *Yet, the cult is very old and clearly one of Anahita's. The role of water and safe child delivery are both parts of the Anahita cult. My deceased aunt, our Kaneez, was a servant of this building. The building was demolished years ago to build a road, and Kaneez is no more. I wonder how will we reconstruct those eras, so close to us in time yet so far from our present conditions. It is also of interest that there exist remains of a castle, or better to say a fort, in Ramhormoz, that is called "Mother and Daughter." It belongs to the Sassanides era. "Daughter," signifying virginity, directs the mind toward Anahita. There are other shrines named after sacred women, mostly located beside springs of water. These all make the grounds for believing that Ramhormoz was one of the oldest places for Anahita worshippers.'*[29]

---

[28] There is a folk tradition about Saint Khezer or Khidar (the green one): if one washes (pours water) on one's front door at dawn for forty days, he will appear. Khider is described as being a friend of the Sufis, and is said to stand at the boundary of the sea and the land. He is also said to have drunk from the fountain of immortality.

[29] Personal communication from Jalil Nozari, August 20, 2003.

*Figure 9: Goddess Anahita Sculpture by Jenny Richards (2009); among
water lilies, photo by Payam Nabarz.*

In 2004 another seeker meditating by the sea makes an
observation on the relationships between Mehr and Aban (modern
Persian names for Mithra and Anahita). The Autumn Equinox marks
the beginning of the Persian month of Mehr, and the start of the
festival of Mehregan. The month of the sun god Mithra is followed by
the month of the sea goddess Anahita (according to ancient sources
both the partner and mother of Mithra). The month of the sun thus
leads into the month of the sea. The sun sets into the ocean. The
sunset over the ocean is one of the most beautiful sights there is; as
the sun unites with the ocean, its light is reflected upon the water.

Mehr, coming together with Aban, gives rise to a third word:
mehraban, which translates as *'kindness'*, or *'one who is kind'*. Thus,
this metaphorical child of light that comes out of the marriage
between Sun and Sea is *kindness*. The child of light is the Inner
Light, which is in everyone. The Sun (light of God) and the Sea (Divine
ocean), united within each person, creates perhaps the most
important spiritual quality - that of human kindness.

In 2009 a new proposal is made by *Basak Company* and *Ayandeh
Saz Fund* to build a giant statue of Anahita as part of a leisure
complex in the Iranian holiday island resort of Kish, the statue will be
one of the largest in the world. The project is called the *'Lady of the
Persian Gulf'*:

'*Anahita statue (Area: 15000 sq meters). One of the specifications which distinguish this complex from others is the large statue of Anahita. In ancient Iran, water had always been an element of value; so much so that this value has been embodied at the heart of the unique myth, Anahita. This lady of the waters is a symbol of cleanliness and beauty which guards waters and it has been written that it is as large as all the waters which flow on the earth. This statue has been designed to be integrated with the entrance to the hotel, seemingly seated on a large cliff, on the basis of this historical and Iranian myth and also beautiful waters surrounding the island. It is the second tallest statue in the world in terms of height and is the only statue which been designed for such a purpose. A combination of architecture and sculpting as well as a modern and natural element is a new approach which has been manifested in this complex. The height of this statue is 96 meters in 26 stories each being designed for special application. The stature of this hotel is to such an extent that it will be seen from remote areas and also from the surrounding waters.* [30]

Figure 10: Anahita, the Lady of the Persian Gulf

---

[30] http://www.basak-inc.com/product/45 &
http://www.skyscrapercity.com/showthread.php?t=887640

Figure 11: Anahita, the Lady of the Persian Gulf

Figure 12: Anahita, the Lady of the Persian Gulf

This project will be a good reminder of the continuing importance of Anahita in Persian culture, and that *She* is still remembered.

This brings us to 2012 and this anthology which is the single largest study of Anahita in 1000 years. In this article a basic introduction to Anahita was given, setting the scene for the more detailed academic papers and articles by the other authors in this anthology.

Figure 13: Anahita, the Lady of the Persian Gulf, images produced here by kind permission of Basak Company.

Further reading:

Allan, T. & Phillips, C. & Kerrigan, M. (1999) *Wise Lord of the Sky: Persian Myth.* Myth and Mankind series. Time Life Books

Boyce, M. (1990) *Textual sources for the study of Zoroastrianism.* University of Chicago Press

Aban Yasht online translation at
http://www.avesta.org/ka/yt5sbe.htm

De Jong, A. (1997) *Traditions of the Magi. Zoroastrianism in Greek and Latin Literature.* Leiden

Frye, Richard N. (1993) *The Heritage of Persia.* Mazda

Gavri, Susan (1993) *Anahita in Iranian Mythology, (Anahita dar usturah ha-yi Irani).* Tehran, Intisharat-i Jamal al Haqq, (year 1372)

Gershevitch, Ilya (trans.) (2008) *The Avestan Hymn to Mithra.* Cambridge University Press

Nabarz, Payam (2005) *The Mysteries of Mithras: The Pagan Belief That Shaped the Christian World.* Inner Traditions

Noury, M.S. (2005) *First Iranian Goddess of productivity and values.* In *Persian Journal,* July 21st 2005.

Rose, Jenny (2011) *Zoroastrianism: An Introduction.* I.B. Tauris

Taylor, Thomas (trans.) (1823) *On the Cave of the Nymphs* in the *Thirteenth Book of the Odyssey from the Greek of Porphyry*

Part 1
Academic Papers

Narseh relief at Naqsh-i Rustam, Investiture of King Narseh (in the middle) by Goddess Anahita (on the right),
late 3rd or early 4th Century CE.
Photo by Rahele Koulabadi.

ANAHITA AND MITHRA IN THE ACHAEMENID ROYAL INSCRIPTIONS

by Dr. Israel Campos Méndez

It is increasingly difficult to argue, as it has been sustained by Iranian historiography, the monotheistic character of Zoroastrianism practiced by the Achaemenid kings, since there is a lot of direct and indirect evidence that suggests the presence and the maintenance of the worship of a considerable number of Iranian traditional deities. Darius I first used the Achaemenid royal inscriptions, usually written in cuneiform and Persian, Elamite and Aramaic, as his official propaganda, and they were the main vehicle to venerate Ahura-Mazda as the principal God, and the One that provides the kings his protection and acknowledgement. However, at the end of 5th century BCE, with the arrival of Artaxerxes II (405-359 BCE), later succeeded by Artaxerxes III (359-338 BCE), an interesting change occurs: although these kings also maintained an important propaganda work through the royal inscriptions, the novelty is that Ahura-Mazda is no longer the only deity invoked by name; he appears accompanied by two other gods, Mithra and Anahita, forming a divine triad who acted together as the main gods among the Persians.

The importance of Mithra in Iranian religiosity is well known.[31] The goddess Anahita[32] is related to the path of the goddess-mothers'

---

[31] Campos, I. *El dios Mitra en la Persia Antigua.* 2006; Ries, J. "Le Culte de Mithra en Iran", *ANRW* II. 18.4, 1985:2728-2775; Frye, R. "Mithra in Iranian History", in Hinnells, J. *Mithraic Studies I*, 1975:62-69.

[32] About the origins of Anahita, different theories have been provided. While the goddess appears at the text of the Avesta a little blurred and clearly in the background, previous evidence suggests an important role before the Zoroastrian reform. Her origin could come from the regions of Armenia and western Iran (which were called Anahit). She plays the role of guarantor of fertility, in line with the cult of the Great Goddess of the Middle East. In this sense, the connections with Ishtar and Nanai are accepted. Her cult could be also associated with the planet Venus (Anahiti in Iranian), which also would have conferred her authority on love and health. Boyce has suggested the hypothesis on the origin of Anahita and its connection with the planet Venus.

characteristics of the Middle East. The importance of this goddess in this period should be taken into detailed consideration, because Anahita is firmly present in the *Avesta*. This Goddess received popular support, especially in the western region of Iran. This could explain her role within the Zoroastrian religion, adopting new forms of worship, such as an anthropomorphic representation, and its connection to royalty. An edict of Artaxerxes II quoted by Berosus (Clement of Alexandria, FRG 680 F11) ordered the erection of a statue in honour of this goddess:

'Then, however, after several years, began to worship statues in human form ... Artaxerxes, the son of Darius, the son of Oco, introduced this practice. He was the first who raised an image of Aphrodite Anaite in Babylon and retained their worship by Susiana, Ecbatana, Persian, Bactrian, and Damascus and Sardis.'

The royal inscriptions of these kings found in Hamadan (A2Ha, A2Hb), in Susa (A2Sa, A2Sd) and Persepolis (A3Pa) repeat the traditional formula of invoking the protection of Ahura-Mazda for the Achaemenid monarchy, but with the novelty that the last sentences also introduced the two new gods to confirm that authority. The most significant example is the commemoration of the restoration of the Audience Hall (Apadana) at Susa Palace (A2Sa):

'Artaxerxes, the great king, the king of kings, the king of all nations, the king of this world, the son of king Darius [II Nothus], Darius the son of king Artaxerxes [I Makrocheir], Artaxerxes the son of king Xerxes, Xerxes the son of king Darius, Darius the son of Hystaspes, the Achaemenid, says: My ancestor Darius [I the Great] made this audience hall [apadana], but during the reign of my grandfather Artaxerxes, it was burnt down; but, by the grace of Ahuramazda, Anahita, and Mithra, I reconstructed this audience hall.

May Ahuramazda, Anahita, and Mithra protect me against all evil, and may they never destroy nor damage what I have built.'

Or to remember the construction of part of that same palace (A2Sd):

'I am Artaxerxes, the great king, the kings' king, king of all nations, king of this world, the son of king Darius, the Achaemenid. King Artaxerxes says: By the grace of Ahuramazda, I built this palace, which I have built in my lifetime as a pleasant retreat [paradise]. May

---

Boyce, M. "On Mithra's Part in Zoroastrism", BSOAS 33 1970:22-38. For an overall view on Anahita, see De Jong, A., *Traditions of the Magi. Zoroastrianism in Greek and Latin Literature*. 1997:103-106.

Ahuramazda, Anahita, and Mithra protect me and my building against evil.'

The ascent to the throne of Artaxerxes II is accompanied by an armed confrontation with his brother Cyrus the Younger, ('War of the two brothers', 404-401 BCE),[33] which greatly convulsed the whole empire and even led to the involvement of foreign forces, as is the issue of the ten thousand Greek mercenaries, among whom was Xenophon. Greek authors endorsed the efforts of both contenders by launching propaganda campaigns in order to consolidate the legitimacy of their respective positions:

"[2] Accordingly, Cyrus relied quite as much upon the people of the interior as upon those of his own province and command, when he began the war. He also wrote to the Lacedaemonians, inviting them to aid him and send him men, and promising that he would give to those who came, if they were footmen, horses; if they were horsemen, chariots and pairs; if they had farms, he would give them villages; if they had villages, cities; and the pay of the soldiers should not be counted, but measured out. [3] Moreover, along with much high-sounding talk about himself, he said he carried a sturdier heart than his brother, was more of a philosopher, better versed in the wisdom of the Magi, and could drink and carry more wine than he. His brother, he said, was too effeminate and cowardly either to sit his horse in a hunt or his throne in a time of peril. The Lacedaemonians, accordingly, sent a dispatch-roll to Clearchus ordering him to give Cyrus every assistance." (Plutarch, Art. VI.2-3)

In this context, I think that Artaxerxes had to direct his attention not only to the war front, but also to obtain loyalty from the people who made up the Empire. The mithraphoric names that have been identified both in the classical sources, inscriptions and coins[34] (Mitriya, Mithrapates, Mithradates, Umithra, etc.), are related to members of the upper classes, linked in many cases with the Persian aristocracy that occupied significant positions in the imperial administration. Hence, it can be considered that devotion to this deity

---

[33] Briant, P., *From Cyrus to Alexander. A History of the Persian Empire.* 2002: 615-30.

[34] The presence of these Mithraic Theophorus has been considered by different authors as a strong testimony of the continuity of the cult of this deity, although it cannot serve to clarify the extent of depth of that devotion. In this sense, Frye, R. "Mithra in Iranian history" in Hinnells, R. (ed.), *Mithraic Studies I.* 1975:62-69. The further study on this issue is that of R. Schmitt, "Die mit Theophoren Eigennamen Altiranisch * Mitra." Acta Iranica. Vol IV., 1978:395-455. In this issue we have also devoted our attention on I.

would enjoy a particular acceptance among certain influential Iranian nobility. In the same way, looking for the composition dates of the Avestan hymn dedicated to Mithra (*Mihr Yasht*), many scholars[35] have made different proposals about the last years of the fifth century BCE, the dates corresponding to these two kings. Something very similar happened in relation to the worship of Anahita.[36] The Achaemenids' devotion to this goddess evidently survived their conversion to Zoroastrianism, and they appear to have used royal influence to have her adopted by the Zoroastrian pantheon.

Taking all these elements into consideration, I propose that the incorporation of Mithra and Anahita into the royal inscriptions of Artaxerxes II, may be the written expression of a new royal commitment (as Darius had done in his reign) to widen the ideological and religious bases that supported his own monarchy. The difficulties experienced by the implementation of Ahura Mazda[37] as supreme deity were evidenced in the *Daiva* inscription which has been studied from different perspectives by several scholars.[38] The official recognition of these two traditional Iranian gods was made in the dual spheres of politics and religious thought. In the field of religious practices we can see that from this moment Mithra and Anahita played a role in the Avestan literature. This challenges the interpretations which have tried to explain the Zoroastrian reform of the religion, practiced by the Achaemenids, as a rigid monotheism.

With regard to these royal inscriptions it is important to understand the context of many interesting variations. Firstly, although we have already said that the names of Mithra and Anahita are mentioned together with Ahura-Mazda, this triad is explicitly named only in three inscriptions of Artaxerxes II (A2Sa, A2Ha and

---

Campos, (2006) and Campos, I."The god Mithra in the personal names during the Persian Achaemenid dynasty" Aula Orientalis, 24.2, 2006:165-176.

[35] I. Gershevitch, *The Avestan Hymn to Mithra*, 1959:23-25 (reimp. 1967); H. Lommel, *Die Yast's des Avesta*, 1927:62-63; R. Frye, *The Heritage of Persia*, 1975:150-1.

[36] Atousa, A. "The evidences for the prominence of the goddess Anahita during the reign of Artaxerxes II (358-405 BCE)" *Pazhuhesh-Nameh Farhang-o-Adab*, (Fall 2007-Winter 2008), 3(5), 2008:139-148.

[37] Kellens points "la prééminence rituelle d'Ahura Mazda semble avoir subsisté jusqu'à la fin du règne d'Artaxerxès Ier, non sans susciter quelques conflits". Cfr. J. Kellens, *Le panthéon de l'Avesta ancien*, 1994: 126.

[38] R.G. Kent, *Old Persian. Grammar. Texts. Lexicon*, 1953:150-1. G. Cameron, "The 'Daiva' Inscription of Xerxes: in Elamite", *Die Welt des Orients*, 2, 1959:470-6; R. Schmitt, *Corpus Inscriptionum Iranicorum. Part. I. Inscriptions of Ancient Iran. Vol. I. Old Persian Inscriptions. T. II. The Old Persian Inscriptions of Naqsh-I Rustam and Persepolis*, 2000. Lecoq, P., *Les inscriptions de la Perse achéménide*, 1997:256-8.

A2Sd); while in the preserved ones from his successor Artaxerxes III (A3Pa) Anahita's name disappears, and there is even instances of inscriptions in which only Ahura-Mazda reappears (A2Hc and A2Sc) or, more significantly, only Mithra (A2Hb). These variations are not determined by place of occurrence of registrations, so I can assume that the process of incorporation should be neither uniform nor definitive. On the contrary, it could have been the result of successive concessions and responses to the pressure exerted by the monarch, as the final expression of a dispute that was being resolved elsewhere.

The ellipses of Anahita in several inscriptions did not necessarily mean that the kings's recognition had been let down very soon. Taking into consideration the above quoted information provided by Berosus about an edict of Artaxerxes II erecting a statue of Aphrodite Anaitis, it is possible to confirm that there was a definite intention to present Anahita as a monarchy divinity. Basirov argues that particular devotion to the goddess Anahita could be due to the influence exercised by the Queen Mother Parysatis, who had been promoting the syncretic cult of Anahita-Ishtar within the royal family.[39] Strabo (XI.14.16; XII.3.37) described many centuries later the existence of places of worship of Anahita promoted in Asia Minor by the Persians.

"The Persians raised a mound of earth in the form of a hill over a rock in the plain, (where this occurred,) and fortified it. They erected there a temple to Anaitis [Anahit] and the gods Omanus and Anadatus, Persian deities who have a common altar. They also instituted an annual festival, (in memory of the event,) the Sacaea, which the occupiers of Zela, for this is the name of the place, celebrate to this day. It is a small city chiefly appropriated to the sacred attendants. Pompey added to it a considerable tract of territory, the inhabitants of which he collected within the walls. It was one of the cities which he settled after the overthrow of Mithridates." (Strabo, Geo. XI.8.4)

The presence of Mithra alone into an inscription is a sign of special preference for this god as compared with the other two. However, it is difficult to separate these testimonies from what is happening in the process of redefinition of the Zoroastrian religious message. Hence, I argue that the only inscription preserved of Artaxerxes III, which refers exclusively to Ahura-Mazda and Mithra, could have a direct connection with the finding in the Avestan hymns of the dvanda Mithra-Ahura.

---

[39] Basirov, O., "Evolution of the Zoroastrian Iconography and Temple Cults" ANES, 38, 2001:173-4.

In fact, what these inscriptions reflect is how the religious daily life in the Achaemenid Empire was often conditioned or influenced by political circumstances. The adoption of Zoroastrianism by the-founder of the empire Darius I, has been considered as an act of political propaganda in order to give legitimacy to his dark ascension to the throne and that offers an innovative project that brings unity to the Persian people after the parenthesis of the reign of Bardiya. I consider that a similar example, but in lesser scale, is provided by the incorporation of both Mithra and Anahita to the level of deities who openly support the monarchy, expressed through the inscriptions studied. This is also a deliberate political act, which, while not excluding the legitimate religious sentiment that could have brought monarchs to these gods, we cannot escape from the context of instability and the subsequent need of additional political and popular support.

Further reading:

Basirov, O. (2001) *Evolution of the Zoroastrian Iconography and Temple Cults.* In *ANES,* 38:173-4

Bianchi, U. (1978) *Mithra and Iranian Monotheism.* In Duchesne, J. (ed.), *Études Mithriaques. Acta Iranica* vol. IV. Téhéran, 1978:21.

Boyce, M. (1970) *On Mithras Part in Zoroastrism.* In *BSOAS* 33:22-38

Boyce, M. (1981) *Varuna the Baga.* In *Acta Iranica* 21:59-73

Briant, P. (2002) *From Cyrus to Alexander. A History of the Persian Empire.* Winona Lake

Cameron, G. (1959) *The 'Daiva' Inscription of Xerxes,* in *Elamite, Die Welt des Orients,* 2:470-6. Göttingen

Campos, I. *El dios Mitra. Los orígenes de su culto anterior al mitraismo romano.* (en prensa).

Campos, I. (2000) *El dios iranio Mithra y la Monarquía Persa Aqueménida, Vegueta* 5:85-97

Campos, I. (2002) *El culto al dios Mithra en la Persia Antigua.* Las Palmas de G.C.

Dandamaev, M. & Lukonin, V. (1990) *Cultura y Economía del Irán Antiguo.* Sabadell

De Jong, A. (1997) *Traditions of the Magi. Zoroastrianism in Greek and Latin Literature.* Leiden

Frye, R. (1975) *Mithra in Iranian History,* in Hinnells, R.(ed) *Mithraic Studies* I:62-69. Manchester

Frye, R. (1963) *The Heritage of Persia.* Cleveland Gershevitch, I. (1975) *Die Sonne das Beste,* in Hinnells, J. *Mithraic Studies.* I:80-1. Manchester

Gershevitch, I. (1959) *The Avestan Hymn to Mithra,* Cambridge

Gnoli, G. (1980) *Zoroaster's Time and Land.* Naples

Kellens, J. (1994) *Le panthéon de l'Avesta ancien.* Wiesbaden

Kent, R.G. (1953) *Old Persian Grammar. Texts. Lexicon.* New Haven

Lecoq, P. (1997) *Les inscriptions de la Perse achéménide,* Paris

Lommel, H. (1927) *Die Yäst's des Avesta* Göttingen

Schmitt, R. (2000) *Corpus Inscriptionum Iranicorum. Part. I. Inscriptions of Ancient Iran Vol. I. Old Persian Inscriptions. T. II. The Old Persian Inscriptions of Naqsh-I Rustam and Persepolis,* London

Schmitt, R. (1978) *Die Theophoren Eigennamen mit Altiranisch *Mitra.* In *Acta Iranica.* Vol. IV:395-455

Sims-Williams, N., & Mithra the Baga, & Bernard, P. & Grenet, P. (dirs.) (1991) *Histoire et Cultes de l'Asie Centrale Préislamique.* Paris

Exploring the Possibility of Relationships between the Iranian Goddess Anahita and the Dame du Lac of the Arthurian Legends

by Kaveh Farrokh (PhD)

Abstract

This paper endeavours to explore the possibilities of links between the Iranian goddess Anahita and the Dame du Lac (Lady of the Lake) figure of the Arthurian legends of ancient Britannia. The paradigm of the discussion is set through an overview of Celtic-Iranian links in legends, linguistics and culture, as well as the larger frame of Iranian influences upon Europe since pre-Classical times. The arrival of Iranian–speaking (Alano-Sarmatian) Ia-zges warriors into ancient Britannia is outlined, followed by an introduction to Iranian and Arthurian parallels in Goddess and Sword/Power Motifs, which are explored especially with respect to (a) Arthur's mythical Excalibur sword and the Iranian veneration of the sacred sword and (b) the Dame du Lac (Lady of the Lake) figure of the Arthurian legends and her parallels with Anahita. The paper concludes with the enigma of the late Aubrey Vincent Beardsley's portrayal of the Arthurian motifs and its close parallels with the Taghe Bostan panel, especially with respect to the similar depictions of the Dame du Lac and Anahita.

The Goddess Anahita: a brief overview

The Iranian goddess Anahita (Ardvi Sura, the Waters) was greatly revered in ancient Iran as noted by Classical Greek writers. She is clearly described by *Yasht V* as being a beautiful, glorious, tall and strong woman,[40,41] mistress of all waters of the earth and the source of the cosmic ocean,[42] the source of fertility for humans, animals and plants,[43] and the purifier of the seed of all men and the wombs of all women.[44] Anahita has also been proposed as being the female counterpart of Mithra (Mitra, Mithras),[45,46] the Iranian god of war who came to be worshipped by Roman soldiers.[47] The primary importance of Anahita to the warrior king can be seen in the inscriptions of Darius the Great who in addition to his worship of the supreme lord Ahura-Mazda, also invokes the names of both Mithra and Anahita.[48] As noted by Nigosian, in the Zoroastrian faith "...*no distinction is made between the genders...both occupy the same place of honour...on the same level in...power*"[49]. Like Mithra, Anahita was seen as one who would come to the aid of her worshippers in times of distress. Warriors would offer sacrifice to Anahita in search of beneficence and pray to her (as they did to Mithra) to receive life and victory. Mithra's additional role of *'Lord of the Pastures'* provides him an additional link to Anahita who is the mistress of the waters.[50] Anahita additionally drives a chariot pulled by four horses[51] just as Mithra drives a chariot drawn by four horses.[52] Like Mithra who fights against evil,[53] Anahita is seen as "...*efficacious against the Daevas* [demons]...".[54] This delineates a clear linkage between the sovereign or/warrior-king and the goddess Anahita in Iranian mythology.

Anahita played an especially important role in Iranian kingship. She was to play an increasingly important role in the Achaemenid triad of Ahura Mazda-Mithra-Anahita, as noted by Darius the Great's aforementioned proclamation. Colpe notes that Anahita legitimized the sovereign by carrying out the investiture, a process which was to

---

[40] Hinnells, 1988:28; For details consult *Yasht V*, 26-28 and analysis by Sarkhosh-Curtis, 1993:13.
[41] Dhalla, 1914:138. One school of thought noted the parallels between the description given of Anahita in *Yasht (V)* and that of the portrayal provided by Artaxerxs' Mnemon.
[42] Sarkhosh-Curtis, 1993:12.
[43] *Yasht, V, 2, 34, 120, 130).*
[44] Hinnells, 1988:27.
[45] Taraporewala, 1980:52.
[46] For a thorough analysis of Mithraism, consult Yamauchi, 1990:498-521.
[47] Consult detailed discussion of this topic in Hinnells, 1985:74-91.
[48] Taraporewala, 1980:65.
[49] Nigosian, 1993:81.
[50] Taraporewala, 1980:151-152.
[51] Hinnells, 1988:27.
[52] Haug, 1878:205.
[53] Nigosian, 1993:18.
[54] *Yasna, 65, 1.*

be further developed by the Sassanian dynasty (224-651 CE).[55] This is vividly demonstrated in Sassanian rock reliefs at Naghshe Rustam where Anahita stands beside king Narseh (Narses) (Figure 1) and at Taghe Bostan where Anahita is present, along with Ahura-Mazda, in the bestowing of the *'Farr'* (Divine Glory) upon Khosrow II (Figure 2). As noted further below in this paper, the Iranian theme of the goddess bestowing kingly glory or power upon a sovereign or warrior-king resonates with the legends of King Arthur in Celtic Britain.

Figure 14 - Anahita partaking in the bestowing of the "Farr" (Divine Glory) of kingship to king Narseh (Narses) (photo courtesy of Mani Momeni, 2010).

---

[55] Colpe, 1983:.

Figure 2 - Taghe Bostan investiture of Khosrow II: Anahita (raised hand at left), Khosrow II (centre with broadsword) and Ahura-Mazda (right) as depicted at the inner sanctum at Tagh e Bostan, Kermanshah in Iran (photo: Kaveh Farrokh, 2001).

Figure 3 - Aubrey Vincent Beardsley's depiction of Arthur (centre) learning of the sacred Excalibur sword from the lady at the lake (left) with Merlin standing at Arthur's right.

There is also a little-noticed *'western'* connection in the Nagsh e Rustam depiction of Anahita (Figure 3). The goddess's hairstyle is virtually identical to that of the ancient Greek goddess Kore (Figure 3). This is a notable relationship requiring further study, especially as the figures are centuries apart; the Anahita depiction was made in the mid-late 3rd century CE with that of Kore originating as far back as 600 BCE. This supports Spatari's thesis that the Iranian plateau and the Mediterranean had been linked (through Anatolia) for millennia since pre-Achaemenid times.[56] An even more curious find linking Kore with the Iranian goddess figure was found in the Republic of Georgia in the late 1990s (Figure 4).[57] The figure is believed to be that of Goddess Anahita and crafted possibly in the late Achaemenid or Parthian era. The *'Georgian Anahita'* bears a strong resemblance to a Parthian-era statue of Anahita discovered in Iran (Figure 4). The Geogian figurine's *'Kore'* hair-style parallels with the Anahita depiction at Naghshe Rustam (Figure 3). The figurine makes it clear that the Anahita fertility goddess was well known in the Caucasus where the northern Iranian Scythians and their Sarmatian successors were prominent well up to the 3rd century CE. The North Iranians shared a common Iranian culture and Avestan-based language with the Medes and Persians of Iran,[58] which helps explain their close ties with the Iranian cultural arena and its pantheon (i.e. Anahita). Littleton and Malcor (2000) have argued that these northern Iranians influenced Arthurian mythology, especially with respect to the north Iranian goddess Satana and her influences on the Arthurian Dame du Lac (Lady of the Lake) figure. They do not however explore the possibility of the Goddess Anahita and her links to the Dame du Lac. This paper will discuss the parallels between the Dame du Lac and the goddess Anahita, noting also the parallels of the latter with her north Iranian counterpart, Satana.

---

[56] Spatari, 2003:87-127, 180, 186-187.

[57] A report of this was submitted to Dr. David Khoupenia of the Georgian Academy of Sciences and the author of this article in 2000. A three-page report (one in English and the other in Georgian) of another one of the artifacts (a Persian winged-lion of the Safavid era circa 1622) was submitted by Professor Tsisania Abuladze to the Institute of Manuscripts of the Georgian Academy of Sciences, Tbilisi, Republic of Georgia.

[58] Sulimirski, 1970:22; Mallory, 1989:51-53. As noted by Cotterell "*:...the close relations of the Scythians (Saka) with the Persians is perhaps most illustrative...in the ... fact that the Scythians and Persians spoke closely related languages and understood each other without translators*" (2004:61); also corroborated by Danadamaev & Lukonon (1989:50, 223) and Freiman (1948:239).

Figure 4 - Parallels in hairstyles of Kore and Anahita. LEFT: Greek Goddess Kore as depicted in approximately 600 BCE (Iranian Embassy delegation photo taken in Athens Greece, 1962 in Acropolis Museum, Athens Greece with consent of Greek authorities in 1962). RI

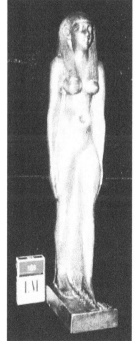

Figure 5 - Fertility goddess figure possibly late Achaemenid or Parthian-era with "Kore" hairstyle discovered in the Republic of Georgia in the late 1990s – note cigarette box next to statue to provide dimensional perspective (photo courtesy of Farrokh & Khoup

Figure 6 - A Parthian-era statue of Anahita discovered in Iran (photo courtesy of Fereydoun Farrokh's ambassadorial mission to former East Germany in 1973-1977 – photograph taken by the Iranian Embassy Staff in 1974 in the Staatliche Museen, Preussicher Kuturbes

A Brief Overview of Celtic and Iranian links in legend, linguistics, and culture

Before discussing the introduction of Iranian mythology into Celtic Britannia in the 5th century with the arrival of the Iranian-speaking Sarmatian contingent, mention must be made of Celtic-Iranian connections dating back to much earlier, even pre-Classical times. References to ancient Celtic-Iranian relations first came from Irish writers who connected their ancestry with the Iranian-speaking Scythians (Saka).[59] The great Gaelic-Irish text, *Lebor Gabala Erenn* (LGE), even claims that the Scots are of Scythian origin[60] and makes

---

[59] Rankin, 1996:26.
[60] LGE, 2.52:14.

reference to a certain bard, poet and record keeper known as Fenius Farsaid, who is identified as a prince of Scythia.[61] Farsaid's father *"...Baath Mac Magoc Iathfed, it is from him came the Gael and the men of Scythia...".*[62]

Much has been written of the relationship of the Celtic and Italic languages and how these diverged from a single branch of the Centum (western) branch of the Indo-European languages.[63] Notable linguistic parallels exist however, between the Celtic and Iranian language families; Iranian is of the Satem (eastern) branch of Indo-European languages. Wagner was perhaps the first linguist to specially attribute an eastern origin to Celtic languages towards Eastern Europe[64] which would have been Iranian or proto-Iranian speaking by at least the second-third millennium BCE.[65] He also discovered that despite its classification as a Centum or Western Indo-European language, Celtic has a number of striking parallels with the Iranian Scythian language,[66] which is essentially the same as Avestan[67] with close linguistic ties to the Old Persian of the Achaemenids.[68,69] One example is the phoneme /k/ which often becomes /s/ in Celtic, a feature seen only in Satem (not Centum) languages such as the Iranian group.[70] Another example of linguistic parallels is the Irish word for Hen *'cearc'* which is almost exactly the same in Iranian languages (i.e. Ossetian (kark), Kurdish (kerk), Mazandarani (karak), etc.).[71] The Iranian term *Airya/Arya* (Avestan=nobleman) or *Eire* (Middle Persian) has a close cognate in the word in *Aire* (freeman) in Irish.[72] The Iranian term for land of the Aryans or *Eire-An* (in Middle Persian), *Ir-An* (new Persian) or *Ir-On* (Ossetian) has a near equivalent in *Eire* which is the modern Irish term for Ireland or other Gaelic terms such as *Erin, Erinn* or Old Irish *Erenn.*

---

[61] Ibid, 2.52:141.
[62] Ibid, 2.44.
[63] See discussion by Mallory, 1989:9-23.
[64] Wagner, 1971:29.
[65] Mallory, 1989:48-56.
[66] Wagner, 1971:29.
[67] Sulimirski, 1970:22.
[68] Cotterell, 2004:61.
[69] Interestingly similar linguistic parallels have also seen cited between Celtic and Thracian, which has often been classified as occupying a linguistic position between the Centum and Satem branch of Indo-European (Wagner, 1971:212).
[70] Wagner, 1971:29.
[71] Ibid, 1971:212, 225.
[72] Rankin, 1996:31.

Despite sources such as the *Lebor Gabala Erenn*, linguistic and cultural parallels between the Celts and the Iranians, Western and British writers in particular have not explored these links in depth at the academic level, with Rankin going so far as to suggest that such links may have been "*...invented...*".[73] This academic paradigm may explain why the notion of a Celtic or indigenous origin for the legend of King Arthur has often led to a de-emphasis of the study of possible Iranian origins for that legend.[74] One of the possible links that have not been explored is the possible influences of the goddess cult of Anahita upon the Arthurian legends.

Iranian influences upon Europe: An Overview

The Iranian plateau has had cultural contacts with the Caucasus from at least the 18th century BCE.[75] Iranian artistic and architectural styles are now believed to have been transmitted into Europe through a north Iranian people known as the Scythians as early as Achaemenid times.[76] The Trans-Caucasus and eastern Anatolia were under Achaemenid political domination from approximately 550-331 BCE. By the 550s BCE the Scythians or the Saka had been classified into three categories: the *Saka Tigrakhauda* (pointed-hat Saka),[77] *Saka Haumavarga* (the Hauma-bearing Saka),[78] and the *Saka Paradraya* (Saka beyond the sea) (Head, 1992:5). The Tigrakhauda and Haumavarga were located in modern Central Asia with the Paradraya located approximately in the area corresponding

---

[73] Rankin, 1996:26.

[74] As noted by Littleton & Malcor "*With the popularity of the Celtic origin hypothesis (i.e. of Arthurian Heroes) advanced by Loomis, much of this scholarship (i.e. of Iranian origin) has been ignored*" (2000:130).

[75] Miron and Orthman (1995:30, 32) cite the finds in the Trialeti region of a silver bowl displaying two friezes with Near Eastern themes (i.e. Hittite style portrayals of the Tree of life and golden stag figurines). Farmanfarmaian (2009:pp.3) has recently noted that the history of Bronze Age technologies, arts and architecture require major revision given the recent discoveries of the Jiroft civilization in Iran, especially the role these played both within the Iranian plateau and in the transmission of culture northwards into the Caucasus. Specific artistic influence upon the Caucasus region from the Iranian plateau was fully manifest by the middle part of the second millennium BCE, and well into 1000 BCE (Tsetskhladze, 1999:478-82).

[76] Tsetskhladze, 2001:472.

[77] The reference to the pointed-hat refers to the tall pointed leather caps worn by these peoples. The first depiction of such headgear can be seen in the mummies of Urumchi in northwest China and later in the depictions of such peoples at the Achaemenid city-palace of Persepolis.

to the modern Ukraine, extending westwards towards the eastern regions of modern day Bulgaria and Romania. It is the Paradraya, who are known as the Scythians or the Skifii in the west, who by the 8th century BCE, had settled in much of the Ukraine, southern Russia and other parts of Eastern Europe. The eastern regions of the Saka Paradraya reached into the borders of modern Georgia or what is now the Iranian-speaking Ossetian region located in modern Georgia and southern Russia.

Achaemenid artistic and architectural styles continued to flourish even after the destruction of the Achaemenid Empire by Alexander in 333-323 BCE. This impact of post-Achaemenid Iranian styles was seen in the adjacent Bosphoran Kingdom of modern Southern Russia and Ukraine.[79] The Scythians were then completely superseded by another Iranian people known as the Sarmatians by 100 BCE,[80] who then dominated the Bosphoran kingdom.[81] Sarmatian artistic and heraldic influences migrated westwards into Rumania[82] and from there to the Celts of Central and Western Europe.[83] Examples of eastern-inspired Bosphoran arts influences upon the Celts include Achaemenid style bird-god motifs and other Medo-Persepolis style influences seen in such locales as Vettersfeloe or the later Sutton Hoo treasures in England. Similar finds have been reported in the Baltic-Scandinavian regions as late as the 7th century CE, an example being a fragment of a helmet plate displaying post-Achaemenid warriors dancing in Sassanian costume. It was the Caucasus, notably the Georgian region which played a crucial role in linking the Iranian plateau to Eastern Europe. This dynamic allowed for the continued exchange of arts, architecture and technology even after the fall of the Bosphorus Kingdom to Hun-Turkic invaders in the 4th century CE.

Migrating Iranian tribes such as the Sarmatians, Alans, and Roxolans left a distinct Iranian cultural imprint upon Europe. Groups of Alans settled in France and Visigothic Spain where much of their martial and cultural legacy was passed onto the populations and

---

[78] Hauma was an ancient potion or drink used in the mystical rituals of ancient Iranic peoples. It is also a sacred drink in the ancient Zoroastrian religion.

[79] The Bosphoran artistic and architectural style that flourished in the Ukraine at the time of the city-palace of Persepolis applied the fine, detailed, polished Hellenic style upon the Near Eastern motifs stemming from the Iranian plateau.

[80] Brzezinski & Mielczarek, 2002:7-8.

[81] Sulimirski, 1970:92-94.

[82] Ibid, 1970:154, 168-171.

[83] Jacobstahl, 1944:156; Boardman, Brown, & Powell, 1971:183.

aristocracies of those nations.[84] By the time the Alans had joined the Vandals (Siling and Asding) and Sueves in the early 400s CE, Iranian style equipment was becoming commonplace among Europe's *'barbarian'* and Germanic warriors.[85] The Alans soon merged their Iranian culture with the natives of Europe. Nickel, Pyhrr and Tarassuk note that the *"...blending of the Iranian horseman culture and the Germanic system of mutual loyalty...resulted (in) the social phenomenon known as chivalry".*[86] Groups of Northern Iranians also merged with the incoming Slavic population as they had with the Germanic Ostrogoths. Sulimirski has identified a relatively large number of European geographical sites and cities with names of Iranian origin[87] with Ghirschman having outlined the Partho-Sassanian artistic and architectural influence on Europe and its transmission through migrating northern Iranian peoples.[88] The names of three major European peoples such as the Serbs, Sorbs and Croats are now recognised as being of North Iranian origin.[89] Iranian tribes who settled in ancient Poland exerted a profound cultural influence (i.e. heraldry[90]).[91] Like the western Europeans influenced by a Greek and Roman military tradition, the Poles were influenced by a Northern Iranian martial legacy which was to have much in common with Parthian and Sassanian Iran. The northern Iranian tribes are also believed to have left a powerful imprint on Celtic Britain's Arthurian legends. One notable heritage of this legacy are the depictions of the dragon standard made in the illustrations of

---

[84] The specific details of the movements of Iranian peoples into Europe has been described by Kriwaczek (2002:79-80, 81-82, 10, 131, 201)

[85] Boss provides a detailed description of this process (1993:7-8, 33-34) and provides reconstructions of Germanic warriors wearing Iranian costume and equipment (Plate B) and a Sassanian warrior in service with the Roman armies of General Justinian in Europe (Plate 3, item B). See also detailed article by Boss in *Ancient Warrior Magazine*, 1994/1995:18-25.

[86] Quote from Nickel, Pyhrr, & Tarassuk (1982:13); see also discussion by Nickel (1975:150-152).

[87] Sulimirski, 1970:164-203; consult map on p.175 which outlines chronology of arrivals and settlement patterns of Iranian peoples in Europe.

[88] Ghirshman, 1962:283-315.

[89] Sulimiirski, 1970:166, 189, 190-192.

[90] Ibid, 1970:167, 203.

[91] The sense of pride in their Alan origins, led much of the *Szlachta* Polish nobility to adopt Northern Iranian or 'Tatar' costumes. As noted by Brzezinski and Mielczarek, many of the 17th century Polish nobility called themselves Sarmatians (Brzezinski and Mielczarek, 2002:39-41). Although it is not possible to outline all the possible reasons for their pride in a Sarmatian past, Brzezinski and Mielczarek have recently suggested that this may be due to them being *"...jealous of Western Europeans who could claim descent from the Romans, the Poles copied what they imagined was the armour of their Sarmatian ancestors".*

Geoffrey of Monmouth's *Historia Regum Britanniae* or Sir Thomas Mallory's *Le Morte d"Arthur,* or the *Psalter of St. Galen* (Figure 5). The dragon standards in these depictions are identical to the *Simurgh* and *dog-god* motifs and banners found in Partho-Sassanian Persia and among Northern Iranian peoples.

ET SYRIAM SOBAL· ET CONVERTIT

Figure 7 - The 9th century Psalter of St. Galen. Note virtual identical appearance of dragon-fish windsock to the Persepolis, Partho-Sassanian and North Iranian dragon-motifs over a thousand years previous to the St. Galen Psalter. Despite differences in armour

Iranian arrival to Britannia and the Arthurian Legends

Traditional scholarship has often focused on the Celtic or wider Indo-European bases for the origins of the Arthurian legends. Recent studies by Littleton and Malcor (2000) however, have discovered distinct Iranian themes inherent in the Arthurian legend. These were introduced by northern Iranians who settled in Britain in the 2nd century CE. Emperor Marcus Aurelius (121-180 CE) had defeated the Ia-zyges Alans (of the larger Sarmatian family of north Iranian peoples) in Pannonia (Hungary) and exiled 5000 of their cavalry to Britain in 175 CE. They were settled in Chester, Ribchester and Hadrian's Wall, initially under the command of Roman general

Artorius Bastus.[92] Although Artorius was to later leave Britain, his Iranian troops remained there; the latter and the person of Artorius are now believed to have given rise to the Celtic legend of King Arthur. The characters and motifs of the King Arthur legend have direct parallels in Iranian mythology as discussed below. In addition, researchers have noted an *'Arthurian'* connection among the Yamato-Takeru (The Brave of Yamato) legends of Japan. As noted by Littleton and Scott, *"The tales of Yamato-Takeru's...magical sword...bear a remarkable resemblance to King Arthur...these two heroes (Yamato-Takeru and King Arthur)...and [North Iranian] Batraz...all derive from the same ancient source..."*[93]

Iranian and Arthurian parallels in Goddess and Sword/Power Motifs

Northern Iranian legends of the exploits of King Batraz and the Narts are virtually identical to the legend of King Arthur and the Knights of the Round Table.[94] Batraz is the legendary north Iranian leader of a super-human race known as the Narts. Satana is the wise mother and goddess of the Narts. The primary enemy of the Narts is identified as the Turks; and this is consistent with the fact that Hun-Turkic peoples launched massive attacks against Northern Iranian peoples in Central Asia and Europe[95] as well as mounting invasions of Sassanian Iran in 484, 588, and 619 CE.[96] Iran`s post-Islamic *Shahname* epic by the poet Firdowsi (940-1020 CE) vividly recalls the battles of ancient Iran against the Hun-Turkic invaders.

The Narts also have mythical enemies known as the *Vaigs*, who devour human flesh and even dare attack heaven itself; this is not unlike Zoroastrian theology which emphasizes the battles of the *Daevas* or demons against the angels of good[97] or the exploits the mythical blacksmith Kaveh who led the ancient Iranians against the evil hordes of the tyrannical serpent-shouldered king Zahak.

The Narts would repose, rejoice, celebrate, feast and drink in the great hall of *Nykhas* much as the Parthian and Sassanian knights of Iran would feast and celebrate in great banquets presaging those that

---

[92] For a detailed analysis of the movements and arrivals of Iranian peoples to Britain, consult Turner's 2-volume work (1993) and Shadrake & Shadrake (1994/1995) in the references.
[93] Littleton, 1995:260.
[94] Littleton & Malcor, 2000:176.
[95] Newark, 1994:65.
[96] Farrokh, 2007:216-217, 244-247, 255-256.
[97] Nigosian, 1993:80-89.

would appear in medieval Europe.[98] The array of Nart heroes includes figures such as Uryzmag, Atsamaz, Hamytz and Soslan.

There are also parallels between the Arthurian legends and Partho-Sassanian Persia. The convening of knights at the round table for example was seen among the Savaran knights of Sassanian Persia.[99] Northern Iranian legends and exploits have also been commemorated in the *Shahname*. Many '*Arthurian*' themes are to be found in the *Shahname* such as the tales of the exploits of *Guiw* (British: Gawain) and *Kay-Kavoos* (British: Kay).

The name for King Arthur's fortress, *Camelot*, may have eastern roots as well. The etymology of Camelot may be derived from either the old French term *camelot* (lit: '*eastern fabric*')[100] or from the Latin term *camelus* (lit. '*camel*').[101] The French term is plausible as Sassanian fabrics were popular in Europe and continued to be so after the Arab conquests of Sassanian Persia.[102] If proven, this would suggest an indirect Sassanian connection to Arthur's Camelot fortress. The Latin term Camelus is also a possible connection as the skeleton of a camel was discovered at an early 2nd century CE gravesite of a North Iranian Sarmatian woman.[103] Camels were of course well-known by north Iranian steppe peoples, as well as in Iran. Littleton and Malcor have suggested that there may be a connection between the Sarmatian arrivals to Britain and the eventual entrance of the term '*camelus*' into Camelot.[104]

There is also a striking parallel in the love affair between Guinevere (queen of Arthur) and the knight Lancelot, and the legendary romance between Shireen (Queen of Khosrow II) and Farhad (from the Sassanian era in Iran). The Guinevere-Lancelot love story also has parallels with the romance between the (north) Iranian goddess *Satana* and the Alan Batraz.[105] Satana means '*the mother of a hundred sons*'; the term derives from the Iranian '*Sat/Sata*' (one

---

[98] Farrokh, 2007:157-158; Chardin (1983:268, 290) notes of the influence of Achaemenid-Sassanian Persia on Georgia with respect to Persian style mansions, welcoming ceremonies for guests of the court, royal and wedding banquets, posture and stance, and bejeweled drinking vessels.
[99] Farrokh, 2007:245.
[100] Simpson & Weiner, 1989, 2:603-805, 807.
[101] Littleton & Malcor, 2000:176.
[102] Ghirschman, 1962:302, 309-315.
[103] Sulimirski, 1970:147.
[104] Littleton & Malcor note that may be "*remotely possible*" (2000:175-176) as they propose that this may have been mediated through the legends of St. Hugo.
[105] Littleton & Malcor, 2000:153.

hundred), northwest Caucasian *'na'* (mother) and attributive suffix *'a/ya'*.[106]

(a) Excalibur and the Iranian veneration of the sacred sword.
One of the key symbols of the Arthurian legend is Arthur's sacred broadsword known as *Excalibur*. This is the sacred sword that was thrust into stone to be pulled only by a young Arthur who would wield this as king. The theme of the Excalibur thrust into the stone has direct parallels with Iranian sword mythology which has been practiced as far back as 2500 years or more at the time of the Scythians.[107] The legendary Batraz also pulls a sacred sword from a tree as a young man; from that time forward Batraz's power, like Arthur, is eternally associated with the sacred sword.

The practice of sword worship and thrusting it into the earth or stones at gravesites is an ancient Iranian custom, one that was practiced by the Sarmatians who arrived in Britannia.[108] The sacred sword plays a central role at the time of Batraz's death, just as it does in the Arthurian legend. In the north Iranian legend, Batraz asks his fellow warrior, Sainag-Alder, to cast the sacred sword into the ocean just as the dying King Arthur asks Percival to throw the Excalibur sword into the lake. Both Sainag-Alder and Percival hesitate at first, but in the end they do throw the sword into the waters. A goddess figure then rises from the water in both the Iranian and Arthurian legends, to catch the sword.

The arts of the Sassanian dynasty highlight the role of the broadsword as a symbol of power, royalty and association with higher deities. Examples include the depiction of Shapur II (c. 309-379 CE) enthroned and wielding broadsword at Bishapur (Figure 6), metalwork discovered in the village of Strelka, Russia depicting Khosrow I Anoushirvan (c. 531-579 CE) enthroned and wielding broadsword (Figure 7), the investiture of Ardashir II (c. 379-383 CE) who is bestowed the *'Farr'* (divine glory) by Ahura-Mazda and the god Mithra who seems to be *'knighting'* the king at Tagh e Bostan (Figure 8). Also at Taghe Bostan (right above the structure housing the statue of the armoured knight, king Khosrow II *'Parviz'* and his steed Sabdiz), is a panel in which the sacred and regal role of the broadsword is affirmed (Figure 2).[109] As seen in Figure 2, Khosrow II

---

[106] Littleton & Malcor, 2000:176.
[107] Izady, 1992:152.
[108] Brzezinski & Mielczarek, 2002:41, Plate B.
[109] See also reconstruction of Khosrow II and the sword at Taghe Bostan in Farrokh, 2005, Plate F.

(c. 590-628 CE) stands with his broadsword in the middle, flanked to the left by the Goddess Anahita (who is raising her right hand) and by the supreme god Ahura-Mazda standing to the right. The panel shows a clear association between a broadsword-wielding warrior-king and the goddess Anahita.

Figure 8 - A depiction of Shapur II enthroned and wielding broadsword at Bishapur (photo Farrokh, 2001).

Figure 9 - Sassanian metalwork discovered in the village of Strelka, Perm region, (6th Century CE) depicting Khosrow I Anoushirvan seated on throne wielding broadsword (photo courtesy of Hermitage museum of St. Petersburg, granted to Farrokh, 2005).

Figure 10- The Investiture of Ardashir II (right) who is bestowed the 'Farr' (divine glory) by Ahura-Mazda (centre) and the sun-rayed Mithra wielding a ceremonial sword (left) at Tagh e Bostan Kermanshah Iran (photo Farrokh, 2001).

The symbolic importance of the broadsword in the Sassanian royal court is evidenced by the presence of an official *Shapsheraz* or *'he who brandishes the sword'*, much like the royal courts of later medieval Europe. What is especially noteworthy is that the broadsword continued to be depicted in symbolic fashion even as this weapon became militarily obsolete by the late 6th and early 7th centuries CE.[110] The Sassanian army had begun to phase out the broadsword (Figure 9) from its order of battle from the time of Khosrow I Anoushirvan or perhaps even earlier during the reign of Kavad/ Kaveh I (c. 488-496, 499-531 CE) in favor of the Central Asian sword (Figure 10) and lappet suspension system (Figure 11).[111] Even as the armies of Khosrow II deployed the sword-lappet suspension system, the broadsword continued to be represented in a ceremonial fashion.[112]

---

[110] Farrokh, 2005:12-13.
[111] Farrokh, 2007:224, 229-232.
[112] Farrokh, 2005:12-13.

The ancient rite of sword worship has survived the millennia and is practiced in the Iranian cultural arena. The Dimili Kurds of Turkey continue to practice sword worship,[113] while the Qaderi Kurds of Iran continue to practice dagger and sword ceremonies.[114] The Persian *Pahlavans* were known for thrusting their *Qameh* (Iranian dagger) into the earth before the onset of duels.

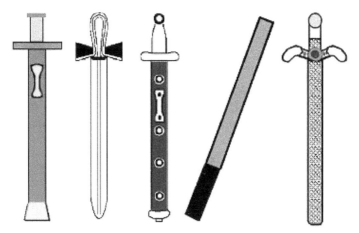

Figure 11 - Sassanian scabbard-slide broadswords. From left to right Shapur I at Nagsh-e-Rustam 3rd century CE; Bishapur 3rd century and other sites 4-6th centuries CE; Sassanian based partly on metalwork finds depicting Khosrow I in Tcherdyne (Perm); Mithra or Shapsh

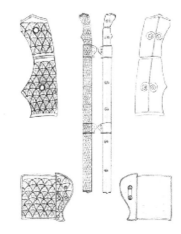

Figure 12- Late Sassanian sword (Farrokh 2004; reprinted Hughes 2010, p.51). Entire sword from front and back; sword handle at front and back; sword mount at front and back.

---

[113] Izady, 1992:152.
[114] Singer & Woodhead, 1988:164-171.

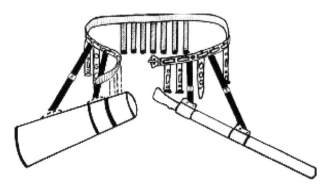

Figure 13 - Late Sassanian belt found at Nahavand (Farrokh 2004; reprinted Hughes 2010:52). This belt system utilizes the Turco-Avar lappet suspension system for swords and quivers.

(b) The Dame du Lac and Anahita. A prominent female figure in the Arthurian legends is the Lady of the Lake or Dame du Lac. The notion of a possible linkage between the Arthurian legend's Dame du Lac and the Iranian goddess Anahita was first proposed by Gallais, who also saw a common Celto-Iranian connection at the more ancient Indo-European level.[115] Coyajee had noted earlier of the Arthurian legends emphasis on lakes and their relationship with the Iranian *Xwarnah* (divine glory, halo).[116] Anahita, as the mistress of all waters, the source of the cosmic ocean,[117] fertility,[118] and purification[119] is strikingly similar to the Dame du Lac whose abode is a place of "*eternal spring... eternal joy... eternal youth... eternal health*".[120] The Dame du Lac is also parallel to the legends of the North Iranian goddess Satana, who like Anahita is associated with the life-giving force of water.[121] Satana and the Dame du Lac share another distinction by wearing white garments.[122] As noted previously the Alans were present in Gaul (roughly modern France) and other parts of Europe where their legends, especially that of the mistress of the lake became introduced to the local folklore.

---

[115] Gallais, 1978:248-249.
[116] Coyajee, 1939:12.
[117] Sarkhosh-Curtis, 1993:12.
[118] *Yasht, V, 2, 34, 120, 130.*
[119] Hinnells, 1988:27.
[120] Littleton & Malcor, 2000:165.
[121] Colarusso specifically notes of the linkage between Satana and water and how she is "*...credited with the discovery of water's life force*" (1989:5).
[122] Littleton & Malcor, 2000:156.

In one of her many manifestations the Dame du Lac rises out of the water with a sword in hand. This is also found in the mythology of Satana where the world beyond is viewed as being under the sea. It is in this realm where heroes are raised and which is the domain of Satana's mother's origins. Perhaps even more significant than the sword-water theme is the primary significance of the goddess as the agent of change. The change in this case is the bestowing of power upon a sovereign or warrior-king. As noted previously, it is Anahita who plays a crucial role in the bestowing of the Farr (Divine Glory) upon Kings Narseh (Narses) at Naghshe Rustam (Figure 1) and Khosrow II at Taghe Bostan (Figure 2) respectively. So too does the Dame du Lac bestow the *'Farr'* upon King Arthur by granting him the sacred sword of Excalibur. Note that the broadsword is prominent in the Farr ceremony of Khosrow II.

The association between the goddess and the sword in pre-Islamic Iran however, was not merely symbolic. Iranian women did carry weapons into battle, wore armour and fought on horseback during Sassanian times[123] as attested to by Roman sources. One such example is provided by the Roman historian Zonaras who in reference to the campaigns of Shapur I (c. 242-272 CE) against Roman forces recorded that "*...in the Persian army...there are said to have been found women also, dressed and armed like men...*".[124] Northern Iranian (Scythian, Sarmatian, Alan, etc.) women are also known to have fought like men using swords and archery equipment[125] a fact attested to as far back as the ancient Greeks.[126] There are reports that Alan tribes invading ancient Gaul also had female warriors on horseback.[127] The post-Islamic *Shahname* epic also makes reference to ancient Iran's warrior women.[128]

The northern Iranian goddess Satana is known for having either instructed warriors on the use of arms or lecturing them on their use.[129] The notion of women encouraging their men to fight by making specific reference to weapons is a long-standing Iranian tradition. An example of this phenomenon is seen in relatively

---

[123] Farrokh, 2005, Plates A, C.

[124] *Zonaras, XII*, 23, 595, 597-596, 599.

[125] Sulimirski, 1970:34; Cernenko, 1989, Plate F; Brzezinski & Mielczarek, 2002, Plate A.

[126] Consult Wolfram, 1988:28.

[127] White, 1921:335.

[128] In one of the passages describing as epic duel between female warrior Gordafarid with the warrior Sohrab, Firdowsi writes in the Shahname "*...as she [Gordafarid] was turning in her saddle, drew a sharp blade from her waist, Struck at his lance, and parted it in two*".

[129] Littleton & Malcor, 2000:159.

modern times with the impending arrival of Russian troops to bombard the Iranian parliament (Majlis) in 1911. Price notes that Iranian women stormed the Majlis with guns, exhorting their men to fight for democracy or face being gunned down on the spot.[130]

Littleton and Malcor (2000) now seriously question the Celtic-origin hypothesis of the Dame du Lac, especially with respect to her warrior facet, by noting that "...*the warrior aspects of the Dame du Lac do not link her to the Celtic Morrigan...*".[131] Interestingly the Dame du Lac was to be increasingly edited out of the Arthurian legends by zealous Christian monks during the Middle Ages.[132]

Art history inquiry: The Taghe Bostan panel and the '*Arthurian motifs*' of Aubrey Vincent Beardsley.

Interestingly, a visual reconstruction of the Arthurian figures of the lady of the Lake, Arthur and the wizard Merlin (Figure 2) by the late artist Aubrey Vincent Beardsley (1872-1898) bears strong resemblances to the Taghe Bostan depictions of Anahita, Khosrow II and Ahuramazda (Figure 2). Like Khosrow II at Taghe Bostan, Beardsley's King Arthur stands in the middle with the Celtic druid-wizard Merlin standing to the right just as Ahuramazda stands to the right at Taghe Bostan. In contrast to the sword-clasping Khosrow II at Taghe Bostan, Arthur holds a spear. Unlike Ahuramazda at Taghe Bostan, Merlin holds his hands together. Merlin's headgear also appears '*eastern*' in that almost resembles a turban, whereas Ahuramazda wears a ceremonial cap at the Taghe Bostan depiction. The most striking parallel is that seen between Beardsley's Dame du Lac and Taghe Bostan's Anahita. Both stand to the left of the sovereign and both raise their right hand towards that sovereign.

It is not clear whether the parallels in Beardsley's depictions are the result of being influenced by the Taghe Bostan panel, which is highly unlikely as there are no records of him having travelled to the

---

[130] Price. 2005:153; Shuster provides a valuable insight into the crucial role of the Iranian women in the promotion of democracy in Iran by noting that "...*the Persian women played the crowning act of the noble and patriotic part...the Persian women since 1907 had become almost at a bound the most progressive...in the world. That this statement upsets the ideas of centuries makes no difference. It is the fact...the women did much to keep the spirit of liberty alive...overnight became teachers, newspaper writers, founders of women's clubs, and speakers of political subjects...*" (1912:183-189).
[131] Littleton & Malcor, 2000:162.
[132] Exceptions cited by Littleton & Malcor (2000:178) are the religious scribes Ulrich von Zatzikhoven and Chretien de Troyes.

Kermanshah region in Iran during his lifetime[133]. Beardsley's portrayals often focused on Western historical and mythological themes which raises the question of whether he had consulted ancient British or even Celtic sources in his portrayal of the Arthurian themes (Figure 2). If this had been the case, what mythological themes guided him to place the Dame du Lac, Arthur and Merlin to the left-centre-right respectively? This also raises the question as to why the Sassanian artists chose to place Anahita, Khosrow II and Ahuramazda to the left-centre-right respectively?

References

Abaev, V.I. (1960) *The pre-Christian Religion of the Alans.* Moscow: Oriental Literature

Boardman, J., Brown, M.A., & Powell, TGE (eds.) (1971) *The European Community in Later Pre-History.* London: Routledge & Kegan Paul

Boss, R. (1993) *Justinian's Wars: Belisarius, Narses and the Reconquest of the West.* Stockport: Montvert Publications.

Boss, R. (1994/1995). *The Sarmatians and Early German Mounted Warfare.* In *Ancient Warrior* Volume 1:18-25

Calloway, Stephen (1998) *Aubrey Beardsley.* New York: Harry N. Abrams

Cernenko, E.V. (1989) *The Scythians 700-300 BC.* London: Osprey Publishing

Chardin, J. (1983) *Voyage de Paris à Ispahan I: De Paris à Tiflis.* Paris: Maspero

Collarusso, J. (1989) *The Women of the Myths: The Satanya Cycle.* In *Annual for the Study of Caucasia,* 3:3-11

Colpe, C. (1983) D*evelopment of religious thought.* In E., Yarshater (Ed.), *Cambridge History of Iran: Vol.3(2) The Seleucid, Parthian and Sassanian Periods.* Cambridge: Cambridge University Press

Cotterell, A. (2004) *The Chariot: The Astounding Rise and Fall of the World's First War Machine.* London: Pimlico.

Coyajee, J.C. (1939) *Iranian and Indian Analogues of the Legend of the Holy Grail.* Bombay: Taraporewala

Dandamaev, M.A., & Lukonin, V.G. (1989) *The Culture and Social Institutions of Ancient Iran.* New York: Cambridge University Press

Davis-Kimball, J. (1997) *Warrior Women of the Eurasian Steppes.* In *Archaeology,* January/February:44-51

Dhalla, M.N. (1914) *Zoroastrian Theology: From the Earliest Times to the Present Day.* Oxford: Oxford University Press

Farrokh, K. (2005) *Elite Sassanian Cavalry.* Oxford: Osprey Publishing

Freiman, A.A. (1948) *Plenennyi Vrag Dariya – Skif Skunha.* In *Izvestiya Akademii Nauk Otdelenie Literatury i Jazyka,* 7(3):235-240

---

[133] Consult biography of Beardsley by Calloway (1998) in the references section.

Gallais, P. (1972) *Perceval et l'initiation; essays sur le dernier roman de Chretien de Troyes; ses correspondences "orientales" et sa signification anthropologique*. Paris: Editions du Sirac

Ghirshman, R. (1962) *Iran: Parthians and Sassanians*. London: Thames & Hudson

Haug, M. (1878, reprinted 2004 by Kessinger Publishing) *Essays on the Sacred Language, Writings and Religion of the Parsees*. Boston: Houghton, Osgood & Company.

Hinnells, J.R. (1988) *Persian Mythology*. London: Hamlyn Publishing.

Hughes, I. (2010). *Belisarius: Rome's Last General*. Barnsley: Pen & Sword Books Limited

Izady, M. (1992) *The Kurds: A Concise Handbook*. Taylor & Francis.

Jacobstahl, P. (1944) *Early Celtic Art*. Oxford: Oxford University Press

Khorasani, M.M. (2006) *Arms and Armour from Iran: The Bronze Age to the End of the Qajar Period*. Germany: Verlag

Kriwaczek, P. (2002) *In Search of Zarathushtra: The First Prophet and the ideas that Changed the World*. London: Weidenfeld & Nicolson

Littleton, C.S. & Malcor, L.A. (2000) *From Scythia to Camelot*. London: Garland Publishing

Littleton, C.S. (1995). *Yamato-Takeru: An "Arthurian" hero in Japanese tradition*. In *Asian Folklore Studies* Vol. 54/2:259-274

Mallory, J.P. (1989) *In Search of the Indo-Europeans: Language, Archaeology and Myth*. London: Thames & Hudson Ltd

Mariusz, R. & Mielczarek, R. (2002) *The Sarmatians: 600 BC-450 AD*. Osprey Publishing.

Miron, A., & Orthmann, W. (eds.) (1995) *Unterwegs zum goldenen Vlies: Archäologische Funde aus Georgien*. Saarbrücken: Museum für Vor- und Frühgeschichte Saarbrücken.

Newark, T. (1994) *The Barbarians: Warriors & Wars of the Dark Ages*. London: Blandford Press

Nickel, H. (1975) *The dawn of Chivalry*, in *From the Lands of the Scythians: Ancient Treasures from the Museums of the U.S.S.R., 3000 B.C – 100 B.C*. The Metropolitan Museum of Art Bulletin:150-152

Nickel, H., Pyhrr, S.W., & Tarassuk, L. (1982) *The art of Chivalry: European Arms and Armour from the Metropolitan Museum*. New York: The Metropolitan Museum of Art

Nigosian, S.A. (1993) *The Zoroastrian Faith: Traditions and Modern Research*. Montreal: McGill-Queen's University Press

Price, M. (2005) *Iran's Diverse Peoples: A Reference Sourcebook*. Santa Barbara, California: ABC-CLIO

Puhvel, J. (1987) *Comparative Mythology*. Baltimore & London: Johns Hopkins University Press

Rankin, D. (1996) *Celts and the Classical World*. London & New York: Routledge

Sarkhosh-Curtis, V. (1993) *Persian Myths*. British Museum Press & University of Texas Press

Shadrake, S. & Shadrake, T. (1994-1995) *Britannia and Arthur*. In *Ancient Warrior* Volume I:26-33

Simpson, J.A., & Weiner, E.S.C. (1989) *The Oxford English Dictionary.* Oxford: Clarendon

Spatari. N. (2003) *Calabria, L'enigma Delle Arti Asittite: Nella Calabria Ultramediterranea.* Italy: MUSABA

Shuster, M. (1912) *The Strangling of Persia.* London: Adelphi Terrace

Singer, A., & Woodhead, L. (1988) *Disappearing World.* London: Boxtree Limited

Soudavar-Farmanfarmaian, F. (2009) *Georgia and Iran: Three Millennia of Cultural Relations: An overview.* In *Journal of Persianate Studies,* 2:1-43

Sulimirski, T. (1970) *The Sarmatians,* London: Thames & Hudson

Taraporewala, I.J.S. (1980) *The Religion of Zarathushtra.* Tehran: Sazman e Faravahar

Tsetskhladze, G.E. (2001) *Georgia iii. Iranian Elements in Georgian Art and Archeology.* In EIr. X:470-480

Turner, P.F.J. (1993) *The Real King Arthur: A History of Post-Roman Britannia A.D. 410-A.D. 593 (2 Volumes).* SKS Publishing Company

Wagner, (1971) *Studies in the Origins of the Celts and of Early Celtic Civilization.* Belfast: The Queen's University

White, H.G.E. (translated 1921) *Paulinus Pellaeus, The Eucharisticus.* In *Ausonius,* Vol 2:293-351. New York: Putnam

Wolfram, H. (1988, translated by T.J. Dunlop) *History of the Goths.* Berkley, Los Angeles & London: University of California Press.

Yamauchi, E. M. (1990) *Persia and the Bible.* Michigan: Baker Book House.

THE REPRESENTATION OF ANĀHITĀ IN SASSANIAN ART: THE CASE OF TAQ-I BUSTAN ROCK RELIEFS AND FIGURATIVE CAPITALS

by Dr. Matteo Compareti

Anāhitā is the only Mazdean divinity (*yazata*) to be described in detail in the *Avesta*, in *Ābān Yasht XXX*:126-129. It is said that she is a beautiful young woman wearing precious garments, jewels (necklace and earrings) and an enigmatic golden crown embellished with stars. Other details are described in that passage: her clothes are made with beaver fur and in her hand she is holding the *baresman*, that is a bunch of sticks still used in Mazdean rituals in Iran and India.[134]

Some studies devoted to the iconography of Anāhitā in Sassanian art have considered the *Avestan* passage just observed.[135] A very convincing paper has been presented by J. Choksy who proposed identification of Anāhitā in some coins of Bahrām II (276-293). She is wearing a long robe and she is conferring a beribboned ring to the Sassanian sovereign (*shāhanshāh*) exactly as it can be observed on several Sassanian rock reliefs, especially at Taq-i Bustan.[136]

Taq-i Bustan is an enigmatic monumental complex located in the outskirts of Kermanshah, in Western Iran, where several Mazdean divinities appear together with the *shāhanshāh* who commissioned its parts. This site is not only important for its very unusual Sassanian rock reliefs, but also because in the park that is surrounding the area

---

[134] The passage has been translated by: Malandra, 1983:129-130.
[135] Shepherd, 1980; Bier, 1985; Luschey, 1990. A unique badly preserved stone ossuary (?) from Bishapur considered by R. Ghirshman and others to be Sasanian presents every side embellished with a fragmentary human figure. One of them could be Anāhitā because of the long robe and the two fishes symbolizing the aquatic element: Ghirshman, 1948:298-299; Teixidor, 1981:fig. 8. Such an attribution appears to be arbitrary.
[136] Choksy, 1989:126-133.

some figurative capitals are preserved. Those capitals present four sides: two embellished with human figures and two embellished with vegetal decorations. Their images have been published several times and many scholars understood immediately that one side was destined to a haloed divinity who is always represented in the act of giving a beribboned ring while, on the opposite side, a king seems to be ready to receive that symbolical object.[137] They all use the right hand exclusively to do so. The gesture seems to be very important and some hypotheses have been proposed to explain the meaning of the beribboned ring. A very interesting idea has been recently advanced by B. Kaim who suggests a symbolic representation of the contract between a divinity and a king or between a king and an important person of inferior rank like a prince, a viceroy or a governor.[138]

When the papers focusing on Anāhitā's iconography were written there was not yet enough evidence available to establish that the divinities represented on the figural capitals are actually different ones and so they have been considered to be all representing Anāhitā. Unfortunately, the faces of the divinities on those capitals have been deleted by iconoclasts, possibly during the Islamic period. There is then to consider that the hips and the breast are always represented quite pronounced so giving the idea of a woman. It seems to be a typical Sassanian characteristic to also represent men with defined muscles, resembling a feminine breast.

Only one recently found figural capital preserved at Taq-i Bustan presents also the faces of the god holding the beribboned disk and the king receiving it (fig. 1). Every detail of their faces can be recognised and, especially, it is possible to observe that they both have a long beard. Most likely, the *yazatas* on the other capitals could have been represented with a beard, although it is not possible to exclude the idea that some other male gods did not have beards or moustaches. In a few words, the facial characteristics of those divinities cannot be considered univocal for their identification. The problem of muscles resembling a female breast and the absence of a beard also for male divinities has been discussed in my paper *The Representation of Zoroastrian Divinities in Late Sassanian Art and their Description according to Avestan Literature* that I presented on the

---

[137] For the all the details on the capitals and their recovery, see: Compareti, 2005/2006; Compareti, 2006.a.

[138] Kaim, 2009. Such disks can be beribboned when they are always given by a divinity to a king: Choksy, 1989: 127-129. Images of kings in the act of giving a beribboned ring can be observed on some golden emissions of Kavad I and Xusrow I: Mosig-Walburg, 1994.

occasion of the twenty-eight international ARAM conference *Zoroastrianism in the Levant* at The Oriental Institute, Oxford 5th-7th July 2010. The paper will be published in an issue of the ARAM Journal which has been dedicated to that conference. This does not mean that Anāhitā was absent from the capitals at Taq-i Bustan. In fact, other details could be useful to propose a possible identification.

Figure: 1

According to the *Ābān Yasht*, Anāhitā was wearing a *"long-sleeved, much embroidered, golden coat"*, some jewels and a crown embellished with several stars. Comparing the garments of the female divinity standing next to the king in the upper part of the bigger grotto at Taq-i Bustan (which is usually called *'Taq-i Bustan III'*, see fig. 2) with one specific figural capital of the group under study which is allegedly said to come from Bisutun (fig. 3), one would immediately observe that they are almost identical. Not only the position of the typical sleeved coat just draped over the shoulders but also the decoration on the coat itself is almost the same.

The Japanese team that studied the rock reliefs at Taq-i Bustan in detail during the 1970's also presented very accurate sketches of the decorations on the clothes worn by every single statue: the one universally considered to be Anāhitā (fig. 4) has some decorations resembling stylized eight-petalled flowers, (or stars), on her coat and also a pointed-star decoration on the right shoulder.[139] For this reason she can possibly be identified with the only *yazata* on a figural capital who is wearing a coat in the same way above her shoulders, with very visible sixteen-pointed stars (or flowers) inside roundels as the only decoration, together with another star which is slightly visible on the right shoulder (fig. 3).

The fact that the rays (or the petals) of those decorative elements are sixteen does not change the parallel with the decorations on the statue at Taq-i Bustan that much, since the base is always the number eight, and has possible symbolical connections.[140] This star is also mentioned in the *Ābān Yasht* although together with the crown and its decoration. Unfortunately, the crown in the capital is not viewable anymore, while the one that Anāhitā is wearing in the upper part of the bigger grotto at Taq-i Bustan presents very interesting elements resembling leafs under arcades. They do not seem to represent the Byzantine-style arches embellished with a kind of Saint Jacques shell (scallop shell) which can be observed on the upper rim of the capital in figure 3 although there is some resemblance. It is not clear if there is an association between that specific element and Anāhitā, although the arcaded crown of Shapur III (383-388) has been compared to the one of the goddess at Taq-i Bustan III, as indicating a special veneration (and protection) by that *shāhanshāh* for her. The god standing on the other side of the central king at Taq-i Bustan III has been identified with Ahura Mazdā and his crenellated crown has been adopted by several Sassanian sovereigns, probably for the same reasons just suggested for Anāhitā.[141]

---

[139] Fukai, Horiuchi, 1972: pls. XXI-XXIII, XXVII.
[140] Teixidor, 1981:756; Compareti, 2007.
[141] Schindel, 2004:18, tab. 1.

Figure: 2

Figure: 3

The coat, its decoration and the way it is worn at Taq-i Bustan III and in that figural capital, seems to be the only element in common between the two monuments just described as well as the written sources. There is also the observation that the garments of the goddess worn under her coat do not present any decoration, while other divinities present a typical three-dots element spread on their clothes exactly as can be observed in the upper part at Taq-i Bustan III on the garments worn by Ahura Mazdā. Written sources can be useful only in some cases and in a much reduced form. This is possibly due to the precise gesture of the figures (divine and human) represented on the capitals, as possibly responding to a precise formula originating in late Sassanian art.

It must also be acknowledged that Taq-i Bustan III also presents some difficulties. Let us focus on the attributes of the *yazatas*. Some characteristics of the goddess do not appear exactly as described in the Avesta: for example, she is not *"holding a baresman"* but a jar from which she is pouring water, which is also her element. On the other side of the centrally positioned king, Ahura Mazdā is certainly holding the beribboned ring with his right hand and with his left hand he is doing something which is not clear, as that point of the sculpture was not preserved enough (fig. 2). It is unlikely that he would have held a weapon since Mazdean divinities never appear armed on rock reliefs.[142]

In the figural capital from Bisutun attributed to Anāhitā at present in the park at Taq-i Bustan, only the beribboned device appears in her right hand, while with her left fingers she is holding something very small, maybe one part of her garment or, possibly a part of the jewel that she is wearing on her breast. Also, for the meaning of this last detail there is no precise identification, although it should be observed that every *yazata* represented on one side of the capitals at Taq-i Bustan is represented according to the same stance.

Lastly the parallel between Anāhitā and some other goddesses of both the Mesopotamian and Hellenistic traditions which some scholars have already studied should be considered. Female divinities from the Near East have been associated with Anāhitā, and in Pahlavi astrological literature she is clearly associated with Venus.[143] In Armenia (where Mazdeism had spread before Christianisation) an

---

[142] Vanden Berghe, 1988:1519; Vanden Berghe, 1993:74.

[143] Kellens, 2002-2003; Taqizadeh, 2010:132. In Isalmic iconography, the exaltation of planet Venus is in Pisces and this association between a woman and one big fish can be observed in illustrated manuscripts and many other pieces of art: Hartner, 1938. There could be a possible connection with the "ossuary" from Bishapur mentioned in note 96 of the present study.

enthroned goddess appears on some 1st-2nd century terracotta statuettes from Armavir together with children around her and an object in her hand, possibly a pomegranate (fig. 5). It is not possible to identify this goddess, but it is worth mentioning that similar statuettes of sitting Hera holding a pomegranate in the same way have been excavated at the Heraion of the Sele River and the Southern Shrine of Hera at Paestum (6th-5th century BCE). These are now kept in the Archaeological Museum of Paestum, not far from Naples. Possible other representations of Anāhitā in Armenian art present us with iconographical characteristics mixed with that of the Winged Nike-Victory.[144]

The association with those female divinities is particularly expressed in some Greek written sources where there are no clear descriptions, and on the contrary great confusion exists.[145] Greek (and Roman) authors, starting with Herodotus, always tried to make a parallel with their own divinities. First of all they would call the foreign gods with names belonging to their religious system (*interpretatio graeca*). This is not limited to Iranian gods. In fact, the same phenomenon happened with Caesar describing the habits of the Celts in *Gallia*, as well as with many other writers. The main problem is rooted in the Mazdean creed itself which, as many scholars already pointed out, was originally an aniconic religion and even the transposition of rituals and material were probably avoided for reverential reasons in very ancient times.[146]

The encounter with Greek civilization at the time of Alexander the Great's invasion definitely gave great impulse to the figurative representation of Iranian divinities that started to appear represented according to the Hellenistic attire (*interpretatio iranica*). This happened also in India (*interpretatio indica*), especially in the case of Buddhism in Gandhara, although many scholars do not agree on many aspects of the genesis of this particular aspect of ancient Indian art.

The comparison with India is particularly interesting because, there also, the very conservative priest caste did not want divinities to be represented in arts or the rituals to be recorded in the form of written texts. However, the impact of Mesopotamian art and culture on the Iranian civilizations of Persia and Central Asia should also not be underestimated. For the period that we are dealing with (7th-8th centuries), the situation is extremely complex because, for some

---

[144] Catalogue Arles, 2007: cat. 135, 154. See also: Russell, 1990:2682-2683.
[145] De Jong, 1997:268-284.
[146] Bausani, 1968:138-141.

reasons which are not completely clear, the Sogdians had already started to abandon their own religious iconography in order to accept the Indian one.[147] Hellenistic and Mesopotamian elements continued to be used as well.

Figure: 4

Figure: 5

---

[147] Grenet, 2010.

It is curious that, at the present stage of our knowledge, there is not much evidence to shed light on what happened in proper Persia. The situation in Central Asia presents some aspects which are better investigated especially because of an intense period of archaeological excavations, practically uninterrupted from Soviet times to the present day. This is particularly true for Sogdiana, the historical region corresponding to modern eastern Uzbekistan-Western Tajikistan and the Sogdian colonies of the Tarim Basin, a region corresponding to the modern Xinjiang Uighur Autonomous Province (China).

Images of local gods with many hands and heads are quite a common theme among the votive wooden tablets and paintings found at Dandan Oilik (Khotan), datable to 7th-8th century. The image of a three-headed ithyphallic god holding bow and arrows with two of his four hands appears in a votive scene recently found at Dandan Oilik together with a female divinity, possibly Nanā represented as the Buddhist Hārītī, and a second god, iconographically very close to Śiva, accompanied by his vehicle (*vāhana*), the bull.[148] The only goddess of the divine triad in both the wooden tablet and in the temple paintings from Dandan Oilik, to possibly be identified according to the *intepretatio iranica*, is Nanā (fig. 6). The main argument for this identification is her four arms which are supporting the symbols of the sun and the moon above her shoulders. Actually, this detail can be noted only in the wooden tablet at Dandan Oilik, while in Sogdiana proper, in the painting from Penjikent and in the ossuary from Kashka Darya, where she appears together with Tishtrya, she always has four arms and is depicted sitting on a lion.[149] As B. Marshak pointed out, the hand holding the sun is normally represented above the head of the lion. In inscribed Kushān coins Nanā appears sitting on a lion but she is always represented with only two arms (fig. 7).[150]

Images of Nanā sitting on a lion can also be seen at the 8th-9th century site of Kala-ye Kakhkaha (Ustrushana, modern north-western Tajikistan), but here her face shows clear exotic

---

[148] Mode, 1991/92. According to Mazdean literature and Sasanian art, the moon god Māh has as a proper *vāhana* the bull but such an identification would appear inappropriate in consideration of the Indian style of the painting.
[149] During the last archaeological seasons, some more painting displaying images of Nanā have been recovered at Penjikent but the reports appeared just in Russian in very rare publications: Marshak, Raspopova, 2003: fig. 107.
[150] Rosenfield, 1967:pl. VII.142.

characteristics such as almond shaped eyes.[151] The sinicization of traits represents an important consequence in Central Asian art due to the protectorate extended by the Tang Dynasty in these regions not necessarily converted to the Buddhist faith. One of the panels of the funerary bed kept the Miho Museo (Shigaraki, Japan) which, most likely, belonged to a prominent Sogdian who lived in China, displays a clear image of Nanā with four arms holding sun and moon above.[152]

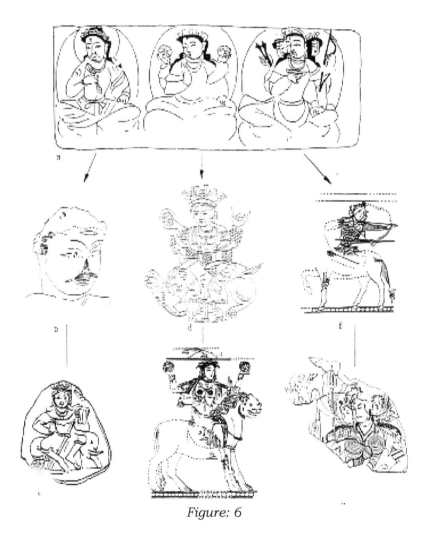

Figure: 6

---

[151] Negmatov, 1973:figs. 4-8, 12-4.
[152] Juliano, Lerner, 1997:fig. 1.b.

Another interesting image of Nanā with four arms sitting on the lion can be recognised among the Khoresmian bowls where a goddess sitting on a dragon also appears.[153] The latter was probably an important Iranian divinity since she can be recognised also in 6th century paintings from Temple II at Penjikent and in other metalwork produced in the territories of Iran and Central Asia after the arrival of the Arabs.[154] Nevertheless, it is not clear which connections existed between the goddess on the dragon and Nanā and, in any case, the goddess presents clear Indian features such as her four arms.

Figure: 7

Figure: 8

The association of the great goddess of Sogdiana with Nanā is almost certainly because of the lion, the normal *vāhana* of other western goddesses such as Ishtar or Rhea/Cybele. They were identified – iconographically speaking – with Nanā, but it is not that straightforward for Hārītī.[155] It is highly probable that the Sogdians recognised Nanā as the Iranian Anāhitā, even though her name and iconography were clearly modelled on that of Mesopotamian

[153] Azarpay, 1979; Marschak, 1986:figs. 170-172 ; Mode, 1991/92:fig. 14.b.

[154] For the painting, see : Belenitskii, Marshak, 1981:fig. 13; Azarpay, 1981:140. For the metalwork, see: Marshak, 1986:figs. 184, 187. Another female divinity appears at Penjikent but her throne is supported by so-called *Senmurv*: Belenitskii, Marshak, 1981:fig. 34. According to B. Marshak, also Druvaspa can be recognised in newly found painting at Penjikent and she can be identified for the horse held under her arm: Marshak, Raspopova, 2003:figs. 98-99. Also for Druvaspa, nothing is due to Indian iconography.

[155] Tanabe, 1995; De Jong, 1997:268-84; Potts, 2001. For some parallels between Nanā and Hārītī see: Ghose, 2006.

goddesses mixed with Indian elements.[156] At Dandan Oilik, once again, the model of the goddess with children is Indian, and there are no Sassanian specimens to be used as a good parallel. Only one rare Sogdian terracotta statuette from Afrāsyāb which shows a female standing goddess with a child beside her (fig. 8) reminds us of the Khotanese images of Hariti.[157] The iconography of Sassanian Anāhitā does not represent a good parallel for Sogdian art, although there are the two Armenian terracotta statuettes from Armavir already considered above (fig. 5) to be (cautiously) connected with the images of the goddess at Dandan Oilik and Afrāsyāb, even though there are no traces of lions in these at all.[158]

The situation described is extremely chaotic and only some new archaeological findings, or support in written sources, will allow a better comprehension of such a complicated phenomenon. At the present stage of research, one can only state that the iconography of Anāhitā respected the canons described in the Avesta only in late Sassanian art, while in Central Asia it followed other models rooted in Mesopotamian culture, with very evident Indian borrowings. Taq-i Bustan is one of the main Sassanian sites for a very appropriate comparison with the description given in the *Avesta,* even though some details, such as chronology, are still obscure, as well as the location itself and many other points.

Further reading:

Abdullaev, K. (2003) *Nana in Bactrian Art. New Data on Kushan Religious Iconography Based on the Material of Payonkurgan in Northern Bactria.* In *Silk Road Art and Archaeology*, IX:15-38

Azarpay, G. (1979) *Nine Inscribed Choresmian Bowls.* In *Artibus Asiae*, XXXI.2/3:185-203

Azarpay, G. (1981) *Sogdian Painting. The Pictorial Epic in Oriental Art.* Berkeley, Los Angeles, London

Bausani, A. (1968) *La letteratura neopersiana.* In: A. Pagliaro, A. Bausani, *La letteratura persiana*, Firenze.

A. M. Belenitskii, B. I. Marshak (1981) *The Paintings of Sogdiana,* in *Sogdian Painting. The Pictorial Epic in Oriental Art*, G. Azarpay. Berkeley, Los Angeles, London

---

[156] Azarpay, 1981:132-139; Tanabe, 1995; Grenet, Marshak, 1998.
[157] Meshkeris, 1962:fig. 4.3.
[158] The two statuettes are clearly based on more ancient Near Eastern specimens. Recently found Bactrian statuettes of a goddess sitting on a throne from Payon Kurgan (Kashka Darya Region, Uzbekistan) have been identified with images of Anāhitā: Abdullaev, 2003. See also the supposed representations of Anāhitā in Parthian art: Invernizzi, 2005:77-78.

C. Bier, (1985) *Anāhīd. iv. Anāhitā in the Arts*, in: *Encyclopaedia Iranica*, I, ed. E. Yarshater. London, Boston, Henley

Catalogue Arles (2007) *Au pied du Mont Ararat. Splendeurs de l'Arménie antique*; Arles

Choksy, J.M. (1989) *A Sāsānian Monarch, His Queen, Crown Prince, and Deities: the Coinage of Wahrām II.* In *American Journal of Numismatic*, 1:117-135

Compareti, M. (2005-6) *Remarks on Late Sassanian Art: The Figural Capitals at Tāq-e Bostān.* In *Nāme-ye Irān-e Bāstān*, Vol 5.1-2:83-98

Compareti, M. (2006) *Iconographical Notes on Some Recent Studies on Sassanian Religious Art (with an Additional Note on an Ilkhanid Monument by Rudy Favaro).* In *Annali di Ca' Foscari*, XLV.3.a:163-200

Compareti, M. (2007) *The Eight Pointed Rosette: A Possible Important Emblem in Sassanian Heraldry.* In *Parthica*, 9:206-230

De Jong, A. (1997) *Traditions of the Magi. Zoroastrianism in Greek and Latin Literature.* Leiden, New York, Köln

Fukai, S. & Horiuchi, K. (1972) *Taq-i Bustan. II. Plates.* Tokyo

Ghirshman, R. (1948) *Études iraniennes II. Un ossuaire en pierre sculptée.* In *Artibus Asiae*, 11:292-310

Ghose, M. (2006) *Nana: The «Original» Goddess on the Lion.* In *Journal of Inner Asian Art and Archaeology*, Vol 1:97-112

Grenet, F. (2010) *Iranian Gods in Hindu Garb: The Zoroastrian Pantheon of the Bactrians and Sogdians, Second-Eighth Centuries.* In *Bulletin of the Asia Institute* Vol 20:87-99

Grenet, F. & Marshak, B.I. (1998) *Le mythe de Nana dans l'art de la Sogdisane.* In *Arts Asiatiques* Vol 53:5-18

Hartner, W. (1938) *The Pseudo-Planetary Nodes of the Moon's Orbit in Hindu and Islamic Iconographies.* In *Ars Islamica*, Vol V.2: 113-154

Invernizzi, A. (2005) *Representations of Gods in Parthian Nisa.* In *Parthica*, Vol 7:71-79

Juliano, A.L. & Lerner, J.A. (1997) *Cultural Crossroads: Central Asian and Chinese Entertainers on the Miho Funerary Couch.* In *Orientations*, Vol 28.9:72-78

Kaim, B. (2009) *Investiture and Mithra: Towards a New Interpretation of So-Called Investiture Scenes in Parthian and Sassanian Art.* In *Iranica Antiqua*, Vol 44:403-415

Kellens, J. (2002-3) *Le problème avec Anāhitā.* In *Orientalia Suecana*, Vol LI-LII:317-326

Luschey, H. (1990) *Bīsotūn.ii.Archaeology.* In *Encyclopaedia Iranica*, IV, ed. E. Yarshater. London, New York

Malandra, W.W. (1983) *An Introduction to Ancient Religion. Readings from the Avesta and Achaemenid Inscriptions.* Minneapolis

Marschak, B.I. (1986) *Silberschätze des Orients. Metallkunst des 3.-13. Jahrhunderts und ihre Kontinuität.* Leipzig

Marshak, B.I. & Raspopova, V.I. (2003) *Materialy pendzhikentskoj arheologicheskoj ekspedicii. Vypusk V.* Sankt-Peterburg

Meshkeris, V.A. (1962) *Terrakoty Samarkandskogo museja.* Leningrad

Mode, M. (1991/2) *Sogdian Gods in Exile-Some Iconographic Evidence from Khotan in the Light of Recently Excavated Material from Sogdiana.*

Mosig-Walburg, K. (1994) *Die Sogenannten «Anfangsprägungen» des Kavād I. und des Xusrō I.* In *Studia Iranica,* Vol 23.1:37-57

Negmatov, N.N. (1973) *O zhivopisi dvorca afshinov ustrushany.* In *Sovietskaja Arheologija* Vol 3:183-202

Potts, D.T. (2001) *Nana in Bactria.* In *Silk Road Art and Archaeology,* Vol VII:23-35

Rosenfield, J. (1967) *The Dynastic Arts of the Kushans.* Berkeley, Los Angeles

Russell, J.R. (1990) *Pre-Christian Armenian Religion.* In *Aufstieg und Niedergang der Römischen Welt (ANRW). Geschichte und Kultur Roms im Spiegel der neueren Forschung. Teil II : Principat. Band 18 : Religion,* ed. W. Haase. Berlin, New York

Schindel, N. (2004) *Sylloge Nummorum Sassanidarum 3/1. Shapur II.- Kawad I/2 Regierung.* Wien

Shepherd, D.G. (1980) *The Iconography of Anāhitā.* In *Berytus,* Vol XXVIII:47-83

Tanabe, K. (1995) *Nana on Lion. East and West in Sogdian Art.* In *Orient,* Vol XXX-XXXI:309-334

Taqizadeh, H. (2010) *Il computo del tempo nell'Iran antico. Edizione riveduta e integrata sulla base delle indicazioni dell'Autore. Introduzione, traduzione e cura di S. Cristoforetti.* Roma

Teixidor, J. (1981) *Anaeitis.* In *Lexicon Iconographicum Mythologiae Classicae,* I.2. Zürich, München

Vanden Berghe, L. (1988) *Les scènes d'investiture sur les reliefs rupestres de l'Irān ancien: évolution et signification.* In *Orientalia Iosephi Tucci Memoriae Dicata. Vol. II,* eds. G. Gnoli, L. Lanciotti. Roma

Vanden Berghe, L. (1993) *La sculpture.* In *Splendeur des Sassanides. L'empire perse entre Rome et la Chine [224-642],* B. Overlaet (curator). Bruxelles

All the sketches and photos by M. Compareti except figure 4 (after: K. Tanabe, "The Identification of the King of Kings in the Upper Register of the Larger Grotte: Taq-i Bustan. Ardashir III Restated", in: Ērān ud Anērān. Studies Presented to Boris I. Maršak on the Occasion of His 70th Birthday, eds. M. Compareti, P. Raffetta, G. Scarcia, Venezia, 2006: 583-601, figure 3), figure 6 (after: Mode, 1991/92) and figure 8 (after: Meshkeris, 1962: fig. 4.3).

ANAHITA AND WILLIAM MORRIS HUNT

by Sheda Vasseghi

True to her nature Anahita not only captivated men of the ancient world, but also one of America's most prominent 19th century artists, William Morris Hunt (1824-1879). For Hunt, Anahita became a lifelong theme that occupied his brilliant mind until he was able to bring her immortality to America. This paper will trace how a goddess from the ancient land of Iran came to adorn a state capitol in America, and offer a possible interpretation of Hunt's imagery of her.

Shortly after Hunt's travels to the Near East in 1845,[159] his brother gave him the following English translation of a Persian poem dedicated to the ancient Iranian guardian angel of water:

THE FLIGHT OF NIGHT.
FRESCO BY WILLIAM M. HUNT.

Figure 1: Photographs courtesy of Stuart W. Lehman (N.Y. State Capitol, Curatorial/Tour services).

---

[159] Appleton, T. G. *Life and Letters of Thomas Gold Appleton*, 1885:258.

ANAHITA

Enthroned upon her car of light, the moon
Is circling down the lofty heights of Heaven.
Her well-trained coursers wedge the blindest depths
With fearful plunge, yet heed the steady hand
That guides their lonely way. So swift her course,
So bright her smile, she seems on silver wings,
O'er reaching space, to glide the airy main;
Behind, far-flowing, spreads her deep blue veil
Inwrought with stars that shimmer in its wave.
Before the car an owl, gloom-sighted, flaps
His weary way; with melancholy hoot
Dispelling spectral shades that flee
With bat-like rush, affrighted back,
Within the blackest nooks of caverned Night
Still hours of darkness wend around the car,
By raven-tresses half concealed; but one.
With fairer locks, seems lingering back for Day.
Yet all, with even-measured footsteps, mark
Her onward course, and floating in her train
Repose lies nestled on the breast of Sleep,
While soft Desires enchain the waists of Dreams,
And light-winged Fancies flit around in troops.[160]

---

[160] Knowlton, H. M. *Art-Life of William Morris Hunt*, 1899:79.

THE ASSEMBLY IN SESSION.

Figure 15: Photographs courtesy of Stuart W. Lehman (N.Y. State Capitol, Curatorial/ Tour services).

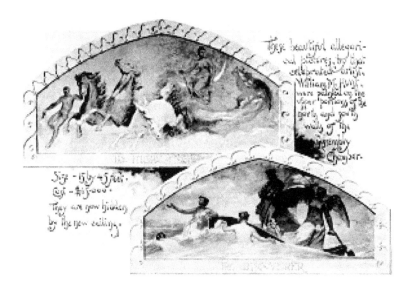

Figure 16: Photographs courtesy of Stuart W. Lehman (N.Y. State Capitol, Curatorial/ Tour services).

The theme of Anahita immediately bewitched Hunt's imagination for years until he had the opportunity to express the goddess in an artistic format. In 1878, Hunt was commissioned to paint two 45 feet long murals for the New York state capitol in Albany. The state authorities preferred that Hunt choose figures rather than scenery alone. He was keenly aware of the significance of the work and the chance to realise his lifelong dream: A mural of Columbus crossing the dark ocean looking west named *'The Discoverer'*; and a mural of his beloved Anahita entitled *'The Flight of Night'*.[161]

Prior to this historic commission, Hunt had made numerous sketches and studies of his vision for Anahita. The general idea involved the goddess seated on a rolling cloud, nude to the waist. Hunt may have been unaware that the Persians, unlike the Greeks or Romans, would have been appalled by nudity- let alone that of a sacred being! In Hunt's imagination, Anahita's right arm was extended to show power, while with a restless energy she drove her horses abreast. Her three horses were black, bay and white. The black horse was in the middle, tossing his head backwards and rearing high, while the white horse in the forefront appeared to fly. The bay coloured horse was held back by a male attendant carrying a torch. To the left of Anahita were a sleeping mother and child in a cradle-like cloud held by an angel.[162]

Hunt engrossed himself in his work and denied visits as well as turn down requests for other painting projects. He was in awe and a state of exaltation for having the chance to paint *"the great dream of his life, the Anahita."*[163] Hunt was often approached by the conservative crowd about his murals, as they were deemed wasteful of public funding. In response, Hunt reminded them that if people had not invested in similar projects, *"there would have been no Acropolis, or anything else worth having."*. He claimed the state authorities' plans to decorate the capitol building with the murals was a *"courageous thing,"* and further complained that the American rich were not active in cultural investments.[164]

Unfortunately, politics intervened and Hunt's funds for decorating the capitol were cut. Construction delays and shortage of funding forced Hunt to complete this grand project, a project later credited

---

[161] Knowlton, 1899:158-159.
[162] Knowlton, 1899:80.
[163] Knowlton, 1899:169.
[164] Knowlton, 1899:170.

with inspiring future American murals,[165] in less than seven weeks. Additionally, the completion of the capitol was assigned to incompetent builders, resulting in a defective roof which caused the fragmentation of the stone panels. In time, a large portion of Hunt's masterpieces flaked off. Ten years after his work began the remaining parts of the magnificent murals were removed.[166]

According to a few contemporary critics, the paintings were *'unsuccessful'* and *'unsuitable.'* In response, Hunt's biographer and former student, Helen Mary Knowlton, stated that the world would hardly move if every worker stopped *"to ask [the critics'] opinion before venturing upon great undertakings.".*[167] To memorialize the master artist's vision in response to the destruction and apparent public misunderstanding of the murals, Mrs. Hunt wrote a private note to close friends explaining her husband's symbolism in the images of Columbus and Anahita:

"They represent Negative and Positive, Night and Day, Feminine and Masculine, Darkness and Light, Superstition and Science, Pagan and Divine Thought, Self and Altruism....

Anahita, Persian goddess of the moon and night, represents negative or feminine force. Anahita, driven forth from her realms of fantasy and unreality, impelled by the dawn of civilization, plunges, ... into the dark and hidden caverns of superstition and barbaric thought.... The horses obey her will without the ribbons.... This suggests the power of mind over matter....the sleeping forms of a human mother and child...hints to the queen of night of other worlds than hers, where love and rest belong; and as she hurries on her course between the contending forces of day and night, light and darkness, a look of human doubt surprises the beauty of her Pagan countenance, and renders her as tragic and typical a figure as that of the Columbus, and the fitting counterpart.

Columbus represents positive or masculine force. Lonely, and led by Faith, Science, Hope, and Fortune, Columbus crosses the waters of Destiny...Columbus peers with intensity of will into the future and ignores [Faith, Science, Hope, Fortune, and Destiny]. The central figure has no theatrical posture-making character of the conqueror; but is, as it were, bowed down with the greatness of his mission, while neither

---

[165] Brockett, E. "The Influence of William Morris Hunt," Antiques & Fine Art, http://www.antiquesandfineart.com/articles/article.cfm?request=880, accessed Dec. 29, 2010: p3.

[166] Knowlton, 1899:176.

[167] Knowlton, 1899:179-180.

danger nor the chains of ignominy can divert him from this heart's desire and conviction."[168]

According to Mrs. Hunt, both paintings represented the thought period of their particular time in history. The master artist had intentionally suspended Columbus and Anahita between faith and doubt. Anahita portrays the intensity of a woman's sympathy while Columbus reflects a man's patience and serenity. By moving towards their destiny, both convey *"a fundamental and eternal truth."*[169] For Hunt, the paintings of Columbus and Anahita were complementary, abstract representations of the powerful opposing forces which control the universe.[170]

Although numerous universal lessons may be observed in these murals, an immediate and specific impression from the Anahita painting may be realised regarding women. In this matter, looking at Hunt's views and beliefs, it is easy to see how Anahita's place in Iranian philosophy seized the artist's imagination for more than thirty years. Hunt was a strong supporter of women's emancipation, and offered his female students honest criticism of their work.[171] He is further credited with being the first American master artist to enroll women in his classes.[172]

In Zoroastrianism, men and women are equal. Both are expected to lead a good life in search of the best wisdom. The tall and powerful Anahita was the warrior maiden, goddess of magic served by the magi, healer, and giver of wisdom riding a chariot with four horses representing wind, rain, cloud and sleet. The name *Anahita* means *'immaculate'* since the goddess was independent and powerful.[173] The Iranian supreme god Ahura Mazda put her in charge of watching over all creation. She withheld favours from unworthy persons, and only granted wishes to the ones with a pure body and spirit.

Pre-Islamic Iranian community provided relative freedom and power to women. They could hold and manage their own properties. They could participate in public affairs. They could work and attend feasts. Women were expected to ensure the survival of their families

---

[168] Knowlton, 1899:177-179.
[169] Knowlton, 1899:179.
[170] Knowlton, 1899:177.
[171] Brockett, p. 2.
[172] "William Morris Hunt," The Columbia Encyclopedia, 6th Ed. 2008. Encyclopedia.com. 10 Nov. 2010, http://www.encyclopedia.com.
[173] "Anahita," The Circle of Ancient Iranian Studies, http://www.cais-oas.com/CAIS/Religion/iranian/anahita.htm, accessed Jan. 10, 2011, 13 pages.

by providing heirs, or controlling family inheritance until proper heirs could be secured.

In my opinion, given that Anahita is part of Zoroastrianism, a classical school of dualism, her painting represents women's struggles in relation to the duality present in modernisation: How to balance spirituality and natural instincts with science and synthetic knowledge. Prehistoric and early human civilization placed strong emphasis on Mother Nature and women's ability to conceive and nurture. In early settlements, spirituality and dependence on powerful, unpredictable nature created a reverence for life. Women were that vital human lifeline.

As human civilization progressed, competition for limited resources and racial tensions among settlements placed the masculine physical prowess in the forefront. Warriors were needed to protect the human lifeline and material possessions. Women, the embodiment of natural instincts and providers of heirs, became part of the material possessions. As advancements in science changed how humans controlled nature and each other, society moved from equality to oppression and suppression. Women's ability to provide heirs had to be monitored and controlled, and their often misunderstood and feared inner wisdom and spirituality had to be tamed.

In this specific aspect, the Anahita mural reveals that with the dawn of civilization, women were forced into a new reality of losing their status. Their power and wisdom were forcefully subdued. Their proper role in society became a thing of the past. Women would have to struggle to regain their role against shameless and dangerous domination in the name of progress. Finally, the Anahita painting projects that in this world the struggle to recover and maintain human natural rights will never cease.

A note from the author Sheda Vasseghi:

The idea of this article began in December 2010, but was completed in January 2011 in memory of Prince Shapur Alireza Pahlavi (1966-2011). The parallel fates of the Iranian prince and the great American master artist cannot go unnoticed. Allegedly, on January 4th after years of battling depression, Prince Shapur Alireza, a Harvard post-graduate student in ancient Iranian studies, committed suicide. Similarly, in 1879, after a crippling depression, Hunt, a fellow Harvardian and admirer of the ancient Iranian goddess Anahita, apparently committed suicide – exactly 100 years prior to the Islamic Revolution that would shape the course of Prince Shapur

Alireza's destiny.   At the time of their deaths, both men lived in Boston.

Further reading:

Anahita, The Circle of Ancient Iranian Studies, http://www.cais-soas.com/CAIS/Religion/iranian/anahita.htm, accessed Jan. 10, 2011, 13 pages.

Appleton, T. G. (1885) *Life and Letters of Thomas Gold Appleton*. New York, NY: D. Appleton & Co.

Brockett, E. *The Influence of William Morris Hunt*, Antiques & Fine Art, http://www.antiquesandfineart.com/articles/article.cfm?request=880, accessed Dec. 29, 2010, 3 pages.

Knowlton, H. M. (1899) *Art-Life of William Morris Hunt*. Boston, MA: Little, Brown, and Company

William Morris Hunt. In *The Columbia Encyclopedia*, 6th Ed.   2008. Encyclopedia.com. Accessed 10 Nov. 2010

Was the Persian Goddess Anahita the Pre-Christian Virgin Mother of Mithra?

by D.M. Murdock

"The Persian counterpart of the great virginal-wanton-motherly-warrior goddess was Anahita."

The Hebrew Goddess, Patai (1978:137)

"The basic Zoroastrian belief in a virgin-born Saviour of the world must have become widely known throughout the Near East in the Achaemenid period, i.e., from the 6th century BCE onward, when almost all the eastern Mediterranean lands were under Persian rule; and it appears to have exerted some influence on Judeo-Christian thought."

Astvat-Ereta: The Avestan name of the Saošyant, the Future Saviour of Zoroastrianism, Boyce (2010)

"According to some sources, Mithra's partner and virgin mother is the angel-goddess Anahita...."

The Mysteries of Mithras: The Pagan Belief that Shaped the Christian World, Nabarz (2005:97)

Summary

This paper will provide evidence that the pre-Christian Persian, Armenian and Asian Minor goddess Anahita was considered both a virgin and a mother, at some point viewed as having given birth parthenogenically to the Perso-Armenian god Mithra.

For evidence I draw upon both ancient texts and traditions, often preceding the Common Era by centuries to millennia, as well as the opinions of credentialed modern authorities. The thesis presented here also demonstrates that certain motifs and traditions found within Christianity in reality predate that faith and possibly served as a source thereof.

- Introduction

- The Achaemenians

- Goddess of Venus and the Moon

- Cybele and Nana

- Anahita, Immaculate Virgin and Mother of the Gods

- Mithra's Mother?

- The 'Rock-Born' and 'Mountain-Born'

- The Zoroastrian Virgin-Born Saviour

- The Epic of Sasun

- History of Vartan

- Mitra, Born of the Virgin Aditi

- Macho Mithraism

- Conclusion

- Bibliography

Introduction

The ancient Persian and Near Eastern goddess Anahita, also known as Anahid, Nahid or, in Greek, Anaitis, is of significant antiquity, dating back at least to the first millennium before the common era and enjoying *'widespread popularity'* around Asia Minor for many centuries. Indeed, Anahita has been called *'the best known divinity of the Persians'* in that region, such as by Dr. Albert de Jong:

"There can be little doubt that in Asia Minor the best known divinity of the Persians was Anāhitā. She is, moreover, the only Iranian divinity whose cult gained widespread popularity in various regions of Asia Minor and who lent herself to Hellenisation and syncretistic alliances with other Graeco-Anatolian gods and goddesses...."[1]

While the Persian name *'Anahita'* may not have been applied to the concept of the goddess until 3,000 or so years ago, the divine feminine idea itself extends back much farther. For example the potential origin of the Egyptian goddess Neith some 5,000 or more years ago, as well as what are commonly accepted as *'goddess figurines'* such as the Venus of Laussel, which dates to around 25,000 years ago.

Regarding the ancient goddess concept and Anahita, Dr. Claas Jouco Bleeker states:

"On the Iranian plateaus also a mother-goddess of the well-known archaic type was venerated in prehistoric times. Female figurines have been found, apparently representing the goddess of fertility. This goddess presumably is the precursor of the great goddess Anāhitā, who is celebrated in the fifth Yasht. However, by her pronounced virginal nature Anāhitā shows a signature of her own. Her full name reads: Ardvi Sūrā Anāhitā, [which] means the moist, the strong, the undefiled. ...from this name it can be concluded that she was a river-goddess. In Western Iran she was mostly called Anāhitā.... Being [a] river-goddess, Anāhitā confers fecundity and prosperity. In the fifth Yasht, it is said in her honour that she prepares the seed in all male beings, that she makes the fruit grow in all female beings, that she alleviates childbirth..."[2]

Bleeker goes on to explain that Anahita is clearly an intrusion into fanatically monotheistic Zoroastrianism, which probably reluctantly adopted the deity in order to incorporate her widespread followers which were the result of her antiquity as a river goddess. In this regard, discussing the sacred ancient Persian prayer in honour of Anahita, the *'Hymn to the Waters'* or *Aban Yasht*, as it is called in modern Persian or Farsi, Bleeker further remarks:

"...the fifth Yasht tells [us] that Ahura Mazda rendered homage to Anāhitā and asked for her assistance in order to win Zarathushtra as champion of the new faith. This proves that Anāhitā was a too strong and autochthonous figure to be eliminated. She must have been inserted in the religion of Zarathushtra at an early age...."[3]

The *Yashts* were composed in the Avestan language, and, while they are attributed to the *'historical'* Zoroaster, who may have lived sometime between the 18th to 10th centuries BCE, the *'Younger Avestan'* hymns such as those of Anahita evidently date to the Achaemenid Empire (559–330 BCE). This particular *Yasht* contains a detailed depiction of Anahita's character by that time:

---

[1] de Jong, 1997:268-9.
[2] Bleeker 1963:98-9.
[3] Bleeker 1963:99.

"A clear and nice description of Anāhitā is to be found in the fifth Yasht. This hymn praises her as a beautiful young lady, with a handsome and tall stature, high-born and of noble appearance. Her feet are clad in shining shoes with golden laces. She wears a dress of beaver-fur and a cloak richly embroidered with golden thread. Jewels embellish her beautiful neck. Golden head-gear with a hundred stars crowns her hair. She drives a carriage with four stallions created for her by Ahura Mazda; these horses are the wind, the rain, the snow and the hail. Her relation to Ahura Mazda is double-sided. On the one hand it is said that she originated from him. On the other side Ahura Mazda worships her... In conclusion one can say that Anāhitā is the goddess of fertility, of prosperity, of the "kingly glory" and of the victory in the struggle for the truth. It can be duly stated that she explicitly was the Divine Lady."[4]

In this same regard, Dr. Payam Nabarz states:

"In Persian mythology, Anahita is the goddess of all the waters upon the earth and the source of the cosmic ocean; she drives a chariot pulled by four horses: wind, rain, cloud and sleet; her symbol is the eight-rayed star. She is regarded as the source of life... Before calling on Mithra (fiery sun), a prayer was offered to the sea goddess Anahita...."[5]

In these descriptions of Anahita, we discover many solar motifs, including the references to I items, as well as a starry crown and the quadriga chariot, with the four horses symbolizing weather, a solar creation in ancient mythology. The horses themselves are symbols of the sun, also denoting in other mythologies the four seasons, as well as the equinoxes and solstices. Another symbol of Anahita is the eight-rayed star, which is the same as a Buddhist dharma wheel, as well as representing the equinoxes, solstices and cross-quarter days. Moreover, both the goddess Ishtar and her alter ego the planet Venus were likewise represented in ancient times by the eight-rayed star or eight-spoked wheel, as we also see in Christian tradition.[6]

---

[4] Bleeker 1963:98-101. For the full text of the *Aban Yasht*, see, e.g., James Darmester's translation in *The Zend-Avesta: The Sîrôzahs, Yasts and Nyâyis*, Oxford: Clarendon Press, 1883; or, William W. Malandra's *An Introduction to Ancient Iranian Religion: Readings from the Avesta and Achaemenid Inscriptions*, Minneapolis: University of Minnesota Press, 1983.
[5] Nabarz, 2005:97.
[6] See, e.g., the "Ichthys" inscription from Ephesus, Turkey, in which the separate letters ΙΧΘΥΣ are combined to create the wheel.

The Achaemenians

Although she is doubtlessly many centuries older, Anahita gained prominence within Zoroastrianism during the fourth century BCE, when the Persian Achaemenid king Artaxerxes/Ardeshir II elevated her cult in his kingdom.[7] The intensity of Artaxerxes's reverence for Anahita is illustrated by her position and rank in the divine trinity:

"...the devotion of the dynasty to Anāhita is shown by the place Artaxerxes accords her in those of his inscriptions where her name appears directly after that of Ahuramazda and before great Mithra's."[8]

Anahita's popularity endured for centuries afterward, as her religion thrived in the Parthian (247 BCE – 224 CE) and Sassanian (224-651 CE) Empires as well.[9] Hence, there was continuous worship of this goddess for possibly 1,500 years.

Goddess of Venus and the Moon

The earliest extant mention of Anahita is from the fifth century BCE by the Greek historian Herodotus (*Hist.* 1.131), who discussed a Persian cult of a deity he compares to the Arabian goddess Alilat and the Assyrian goddess Mylitta. He then names this Persian goddess as 'Mitra', which some have deemed to be an error, while others have theorised that Mithra was bigendered.[10] Although he may have made a mistake, Herodotus' remark does show how closely Mithra was associated with Anahita centuries before the Common Era.

Herodotus and the Babylonian writer Berossus (C3rd BCE) both equate this Persian deity with Aphrodite, Greek goddess of love and procreation, while the bulk of the ancient reports identify her with the Greek virgin goddess Artemis.[11] Anahita is also identified with the Babylonian goddess Ishtar, who is likewise equated with Aphrodite.[12] Like Aphrodite and others, Ishtar is identified with the planet Venus, the very name of which in Persian is *Anāhīd*.[13]

"In Iran, the yazata Anāhitā seems to have absorbed many of the qualities of Ishtar; she is a goddess of fertility, and in Persian the

---

[7] Bleeker 1963:100.
[8] Boyce 1982:219.
[9] Hansman, 240; "ANĀHĪD," www.iranica.com/articles/anahid
[10] See, e.g., de Jong, 1997:107ff.
[11] de Jong, 1997:269.
[12] de Jong, 1997:270.
[13] See, e.g., Steingass, 2005:103.

planet Venus is called *Nāhīd*. Armenian Zoroastrians hailed Anahit as 'the mother of all chastities'…"[14]

Regarding Anahita's depiction in her Avestan hymn, Dr. Bartel Leendert Waerden states: *"It seems to me that the text of the Yasht is more easily understood if we identify Anāhitā with the planet Venus."*[15]

Anahita is identified not only with Venus but also with the moon, a common development for goddesses. The evidence for the association of Anahita with the moon includes that in both *"the Achaemenid and the Sassanian period, whenever there is a known reference to Anahita the symbol of the crescent seems also to be present."*[16]

Regarding Anahita's lunar attributes, Dr. Gülru Necipoğlu remarks:

"In the Avesta no mention is made of Anahita in the short yasht devoted to the moon, but there are certain similarities between the two deities. Anahita is the deity of water and a mother goddess, protector of mankind and responsible for the birth of human beings, the moon is the deity of the reproduction of animals, as well as responsible for the tides of the sea. The connection of the moon with the cult of the mother goddess may be even more deeply rooted in Near Eastern culture, and its manifestation in Christianity may be seen, for example, in the symbolism of the crescent in the iconography of the Immaculate Conception of the Virgin, together with her other attributes such as stars and the fountain of living water and her title Stella Maris."[17]

Thus, the moon has been associated with the Mother Goddess since antiquity, a motif also transferred to the Virgin Mary who is the Christian version of the ancient parthenogenetic goddess. Like Anahita and other goddesses, Mary was also associated with water.

Demonstrating the commonality of ancient, syncretized mythical motifs and characters, in *Mithraic Iconography and Ideology*, Dr. Leroy Campbell states:

"The association of the moon and bull was particularly Iranian. The fusion of the Moon goddess with that of the planet Venus-Aphrodite could easily have taken place in Syria and Anatolia, where the cults of Isis, Ishtar, Astarte, Cybele, Hekate and even Anahita exercised varying degrees of influence. The functions and characteristics of great

---

[14] Russell, 2004:424-5.
[15] Waerden, 1974:193.
[16] Necipoğlu, 1994:70.
[17] Necipoğlu, 1994:70.

divinities like these tended to overlap and gave rise to syncretism in identification. In the period when the mysteries of Mithra were in formation Isis was called the goddess of a thousand names, an illustration of the movements toward syncretistic monotheism.

The planet Venus, called by the ancient Sumerians [sic] Nanna and by the Babylonians Ishtar, was known to the Iranians as Anāhita and to the Greeks as Aphrodite. In the development of astrology this planet was said to have its exaltation or house in the sign of Taurus. The attribution of the Bull to Aphrodite therefore was due in large measure to planetary theology [i.e., astrotheology]. In ancient religious usage this sign marked the spring equinox, which was sooner or later regarded as the special period of Aphrodite."[18]

As Anahita is also identified with Venus, logically she too would be associated therefore with the vernal equinox, a fact that, when combined with the fact that Mithra is associated with the autumnal equinox,[19] makes these two a strongly related pair. In this regard, Anahita is the *'mother-goddess'* in *'her mountain heights'* and the *'spring-goddess of the year'*, the goddess who *"caused the yearly rise of the Euphrates at the vernal equinox when the snows melt."*[20]

Cybele and Nana

Anahita is identified also with the *'Mother of the Gods'*, a title often used to describe the popular Phrygian goddess Cybele, or vice versa, as the case may be.[21] This title *Mother of the Gods* or Μητηρ (των) θεων in Greek dates back to the Mycenaean period at least, more than 3,000 years ago.[22] Concerning Anahita and Cybele, Dr. John F. Hansman says:

"...Classical authors attest the spread of the cult of Anaitis to Armenia, Cappadocia, Pontus and especially Lydia in Asia Minor. In Lydia Anahita-Anaitis was assimilated to Artemis Ephesia and to Cybele the great mother goddess of Anatolia..."[23]

---

[18] Campbell, 1968:72.
[19] See, e.g. Boyce 1996:172.
[20] Hewitt, 1901:214.
[21] In *The Ancient Mother of the Gods: A Missing Chapter in the History of Greek Religion*, Noel Robertson evinces that the Mother of the Gods or Μητηρ (των) θεων is a very ancient goddess unto herself and that *'Cybele'* is one of her titles which, while popular with modern writers, is not as commonly found in antiquity. (Lane, 1996:239-240)
[22] Lane, 1996:240.
[23] Hansman, 1985:235.

Cybele is the virgin mother of her consort, Attis, as related by Bleeker, who says that the *"archaic myth of Pessinus actually tells this: Attis is his own father, and Kybele is the virgin-mother."*[24] Russell describes further the origin of the parthenogenetic creatrix or virgin mother, demonstrating the relationship of Cybele to Anahita:

"A pagan goddess called the Queen of Heaven received in Israel in the seventh century BCE a consecrated cake called in Hebrew Kawwān (Jeremiah 7:18, 44:19). It is she, or a goddess like her, who was later worshipped in the Hellenistic times as the Dea Syria. Patai identifies the Queen of Heaven with 'Anath, a goddess whose name is attested in ancient Israel. Her worship is well attested from Ugarit, where she is connected at once with both fertility and chastity: she is 'mother of nations' and 'the virgin'...

In Western Iran and Anatolia, the goddess came to be known as Anahita or Anaitis, evidently absorbing the traits and legends, temple estates and rites of the Great Mother goddess of Anatolia, Cybele, whose worship seems to be as old as the archaeological record: a figurine from Chatal Hüyük depicts her as potnia therōn, "Lady of the Beasts." In Armenia, numerous terra-cotta figurines depict the goddess in the form of Isis lactans."[25]

In the image he provides of the obese woman-goddess *'Cybele'* from the Turkish site of Çatal Hüyük, Russell dates the figurine to 6000 BCE.

The pre-Christian virgin-mother goddess motif can be found commonly throughout the Near East and elsewhere, as related by Bleeker:

"There have always been religious people who did not conceive of the deity as the Lord or as the heavenly Father, but as the Great Mother or the Divine Lady. Not all female gods belong to this type.... Many times they may be counted in the category of the great Mother-Goddess. However, some of them are not only mothers, but at the same time virgins. Sometimes the virginal nature is even strongly or wholly predominant....

There is no danger of confounding the goddesses in question because all of them show individual features. Nevertheless they belong to the same category, i.e. that of the Divine Lady. She is an exalted goddess...Her nature is impenetrable. This is particularly manifest when she is called the Virgin-Mother. This term indicates the mystery

---

[24] Bleeker 1963:109.
[25] Russell, 2004:434-5.

of birth which she causes to take place. The heavenly Lord creates out of nothing. The Virgin-Mother brings forth without impregnation. Both occurrences are equally mysterious: the origin of the world and of life is a secret. The people of antiquity realized that woman is inscrutable by nature and virtually inaccessible. Even when she has become mother she remains virgin in a certain sense....."[26]

In a section in *The Rainbow* entitled, 'The Virgin-Mother', Bleeker further writes:

"The prehistoric figures of women occur in two forms, i.e. as a pregnant woman and as a slim young girl, a virgin. It is likely that they are amulets, but they can also be considered as forerunners of the Great Mother-Goddess who was so popular in antiquity. Sometimes this goddess is the virgin-mother: she is mother, because she bears new life, but she does not lose her virginity. She needs no partner to give birth. She creates by her own force and proves thereby that she is a divine being."[27]

As we can see, the *'partheno-creatrix'* or virgin-mother concept is ancient, dating to several thousand years prior to the Common Era and manifesting itself in many goddesses or epithets of the Divine Lady, such as Cybele in Anatolia. In addition, Cybele's son, Attis, has been identified with Mithra,[28] which would make of Anahita the latter's mother.

Although the Great Mother Goddess Cybele is said to be a virgin when she goes by the name 'Nana',[29] the word *nanā* itself means 'mother' in Persian.[30] Naturally, we find Anahita intertwined with Nanaia or Nana, who is also a Babylonian and Elamite goddess.[31] In this regard, Russell says *"it is likely that some Zoroastrians at least worshipped Nana"*,[32] with whom Anahita is *"closely associated"*.[33]

Regarding Anahita and her connection to Nana, Russell further states:

"The great goddess of ancient Armenia was Anahit, Av. Anahita, called Oksemayr, the Golden Mother, and Tikin, the Lady.... It is

---

[26] Bleeker 1963:83-4. See also the works of Marguerite Rigoglioso, *The Cult of the Divine Birth in Ancient Greece* and *Virgin Mother Goddesses of Antiquity.*
[27] Bleeker 1975:214-5.
[28] See, e.g., Lane, 1996:109.
[29] Leeming (1998:25): *"Attis is the son of Cybele in her form as the virgin, Nana, who is impregnated by the divine force in the form of a pomegranate."*
[30] Boyce 1982:31.
[31] de Jong, 1997:273.
[32] Russell, 2004:43-4.
[33] Russell, 2004:119.

difficult to separate the cult of Anahit from that of Nanē [Nana] (who was worshipped also in Iranian lands, in Parthian times...), whose name, ultimately from Sumerian Inanna, "Lady of Heaven," in later ages must have been understood merely as a Lallwort ["nursery word"] for Mother.

Many mother-and-child terracotta figurines were found in Armenia, of the type elsewhere termed Isis lactans: they probably represent Nanē with Attis, the Anatolian dying and rising god. He was the Tammuz of the Semites, Aramaic-speaking residents of Armenia.... Zoroastrians probably called the dying and rising god Siyāvōŝ..."[34]

Like Attis, so too is the Sumero-Babylonian god Dumuzi/Tammuz the son of a virgin mother:

"In the holy marriage Inanna is the sister, the bridge, or the wife of Tammuz. She can also function as his mother. Moreover, she is represented as a virgin. She is the Virgin-Mother, i.e. the goddess, who brings forth life spontaneously, out of herself."[35]

We may thus expect to discover the same birth myth for Anahita as well, since she is identified with virgin-mother goddesses like Cybele-Nana and Inanna; hence, it would be logical to assert that Mithra was her virgin-born son.

Anahita, Immaculate Virgin and Mother of the Gods

As would be fitting for an incarnation of the virgin goddess, Anahita's very name means *'Spotless'*, *'Clean'*, *'Pure'*,[36] *'Unblemished'*,[37] *'Untainted'* and *'Immaculate'*. As Nabarz says, *"Anahita, too, means virgin, literally not defiled."*[38] Campbell calls Anahita the *"great goddess of virgin purity,"*[39] and Bleeker says, *"In the Avestan religion she is the typical virgin."*[40] Patai also states that Anahita is *"unmistakably a virgin goddess, like her Sumerian, Akkadian and Canaanite counterparts."*[41]

Regarding the virgin-mother motif and Anahita, Bleeker further remarks:

---

[34] Russell, 2004:374.
[35] Bleeker 1963:92.
[36] Boyce, 1982:29, 202.
[37] Russell, 2004:144.
[38] Nabarz, 2005:102.
[39] Campbell, 1968:78.
[40] Bleeker, 1963:100.
[41] Patai, 1978:138.

"Though the accent falls on Athene's virginity, she was also conceived of as a motherly figure.

The same can be said of Anāhitā, the Persian goddess....."[42]

Like other deities, Anahita is not only virginal but also the goddess of motherhood; indeed, she too is essentially *'Mother of the Gods'*:

"The epithet... 'Mother of the Gods' is not found in the old Armenian texts, but it suits Anahit well and may be ancient."[43]

Anahita was also the *'mother of all knowledge'*[44] or *'mother of all wisdom'*:

"During the times of the Achaemenians (558-330 BCE), Anahita was widely worshipped. She is the ancient Persian Great Mother... In Armenia, she was the Mother Goddess, known as the mother of all wisdom, the giver of life and the daughter of Ahura Mazda...."[45]

Badiozamani asserts that Mother Anahita's adoration was influential on the Mother Mary myth:

"It has been recorded that the cult of Anahita was very popular in the Parthian period, and it was exported beyond the western frontiers of Iran. Anahita, exalted as the 'Mother of the Lord', probably gave rise to the exaltation of Mary as 'the Mother of God' and the naming of many churches after her."[46]

Yet, for all her motherhood and procreation support, Anahit remains, pure, undefiled and virginal. These dichotomies come together in the epithet *'Mother of all Chastities'*,[47] a title that, once again, proves Anahita to have been perceived as *mother*.

In this regard, Dr. David Leeming adds:

"Anahita was the Mother of Waters, a traditional spouse of the solar god whom she bore, loved, and swallowed up. She was identified with the Anatolian Great Goddess Ma. Mithra was naturally coupled with her..."[48]

Certainly, as *'mother of the gods'* Anahita would also be the mother of the god Mithra, her close companion. Moreover, Alexander

---

[42] Bleeker 1975:215.
[43] Russell, 2004:144.
[44] Boyce, "ANĀHĪD," www.iranica.com/articles/anahid
[45] Turner, 2000:50.
[46] Badiozamani, 2005:97.
[47] Russell, 2004:144.
[48] Leeming 1992:198.

the Great was named a *'son of Nahid'* or Anahita,[49] making it even more difficult to believe that Mithra was not likewise thus deemed.

Concerning Anahita and Mithra, one modern writer (*Mithraism and Christianity*) asserts:

"According to Persian mythology, Mithras was born of a virgin given the title 'Mother of God'.

The Parthian princes of Armenia were all priests of Mithras, and an entire district of this land was dedicated to the Virgin Mother Anahita. Many Mithraeums, or Mithraic temples, were built in Armenia, which remained one of the last strongholds of Mithraism. The largest near-eastern Mithraeum was built in western Persia at Kangavar, dedicated to "Anahita, the Immaculate Virgin Mother of the Lord Mithras."[50]

This latter contention is very interesting, as such an inscription if real and pre-Christian would represent concrete proof that Mithra was viewed in pre-Christian times as having been born of the virgin mother Anahita.

Mithra's Mother?

To our knowledge at this time, Mithra was not openly depicted in the *Roman* cultus as having been birthed by a mortal woman or a goddess; hence, it is claimed that he was not *'born of a virgin'*. As we have seen, however, a number of writers have asserted otherwise, including modern Persian, Armenian and other scholars who, from all the evidence previously provided, are apparently reflecting an ancient tradition from Near Eastern Mithraism. In this regard, Nabarz remarks:

"Due to her popularity, another deity who retained a good deal of her importance in the new religion [of Zoroastrianism] was the water goddess Anahita, who is sometimes referred to as Mithra's virgin mother or as his partner."[51]

As another example, Badiozamani says that a *'person'* named *'Mehr'* or Mithra was *"born of a virgin named Nahid Anahita ('immaculate')"* and that *"the worship of Mithra and Anahita, the virgin mother of Mithra, was well-known in the Achaemenian period [558-330 BCE]..."*[52] Likewise, Dr. Mohammed Ali Amir-Moezzi states: *"Dans le*

[49] Russell, 2004:110.
[50] This last contention concerning an inscription at Kangavar is cited elsewhere as coming from Moghdam, 37.
[51] Nabarz, 2005:4.
[52] Badiozamani, 2005:96.

mithraïsme, ainsi que le mazdéisme populaire, (A)Nāhīd, mère de Mithra/Mehr, est vierge" — *"In Mithraism, as in popular Mazdaism, Anahid, the mother of Mithra, is a virgin."*[53]

Moreover, in the mythology of Asia Minor, Mithra is depicted as the son of Ahura Mazda or Ohrmazd,[54] representing another birth motif different from the rock-born scenario commonly found in, but not original to, later Roman Mithraism. This type of variation is precisely what we find with many myths worldwide developed over a period of thousands of years.

Regarding the different depictions of Mithra's birth, Dr. Maarten J. Vermaseren states:

"...The scarce literary evidence as well as the abundant archaeological material give us different versions of the way in which Mithras came into the world, and it is hardly possible to reconcile the two.

In the Yasht 10, the hymn of the recent Avesta, in which Mithras is specially invoked, the Persian god of light appears resplendent in a golden colour on the top of the mountain Hara bĕrĕzaiti, the present Elburz in Persia, from where he looks over the whole earth of the Aryan people.

This is not a description of a real birth, but this manifestation of the deity as the giver of light, pouring forth his largess every morning anew and, besides, the feminine name of the mountain were apt to lead to the conception of the birth of the god from a Mother-Goddess. Yet, the idea of Mithras as a son of Ahura-Mazda, the Knowing Lord, or as born naturally from a woman, though attested by some late Armenian writers, did not become traditional. Mithras' birth remained an obscure affair...."[55]

Although Vermaseren claims that these concepts are irreconcilable, if we view them within the context of other myths and with an eye to solar mythology or what is called astrotheology, we *can* reconcile these various notions. In these paragraphs we find some interesting contentions concerning Mithra's birth and ancient mythology: To wit, Mithra is the sunlight streaming over the mountains at daybreak, dawn or sunrise, and this motif along with the feminine name of the mountain naturally gives the impression that, as was the case in other mythologies, the sun god was born of a goddess.

---

[53] Amir-Moezzi, 2006:78.
[54] Boettiger, 1920:25.
[55] Gerevich, 1951:93.

In consideration of the facts that the ancient *'Mother of the Gods'* is also deemed *'mountain Mother'*[56] and that the name *'Cybele'* likewise means *'rock'* or *'mountain'*,[57] the perception of Mithra in this myth being born from a female is highly logical, especially if we factor in the motif of Anahita being the *'mother goddess'* in *"her mountain heights."*[58] In the rock-born scenario, then, we may have a depiction of the sun emanating between two mountains, as was represented in pictograms in remote antiquity.

The 'Rock-Born' and 'Mountain-Born'

Even if we ignore all the evidence of the pre-Christian parthenogenetic creatrix within Near Eastern Mithraism, we may find that the *'rock-born'* motif emphasised in imagery of the Roman period likewise represents a virgin birth, out of *matter*. The words *'matter'* or *'material'* are derived from the Latin *māteria*, sharing the root *māter*, meaning *'mother, source, origin'*. This etymological fact shows a perception in the Roman world that linked matter and mother, which also manifested itself in the *'Mountain Mama'* concept found elsewhere. Mithra's birth rock is also described as *'world-stuff'*[59] and the *'World-Rock'*,[60] whereas the earth has been perceived in many cultures as being female, such as the Greek goddess commonly known as Gaia. Thus, like Kore/Persephone, the rock-born or mountain-born Mithra is essentially generated from Mother Earth, who in other eras and cultures was perceived as *virginal*, as in *'virgin rock'*.[61]

Comparing the rock birth with that of the virgin mother, Amir-Moezzi says:

"...il y a donc analogie entre le rocher, symbole d'incorruptibilité, qui donne naissance au dieu iranien et la mère de celui-ci, Anāhīd, éternellement vierge et jeune."[62]

---

[56] Lane, 1996:239.
[57] Lane, 1996:239.
[58] Hewitt, 1901:214.
[59] Campbell, 1968:364.
[60] Campbell, 1968:380.
[61] See, e.g., Rigoglioso 2010:18ff: *"...in Hesiodic theogony, Ge/Gaia, or the Earth Goddess, was also an autogenetically produced entity. According to this same tradition (Theogony 126-32), she had parthenogenetic capacity, as well, having borne starry Uranus, the god of the heavens, without a partner."*
[62] Amir-Moezzi, 2006:79.

"...so there is analogy between the rock, a symbol of incorruptibility, giving birth to the Iranian god and the mother of that (same) one, Anahid, eternally virgin and young."

These various themes demonstrate an apparent parthenogenetic origin of Mithra in one sense or another.

The Zoroastrian Virgin-Born Saviour

The concept of a virgin-born saviour was already well known in Zoroastrian religion, centuries before the Common Era, as Zoroaster himself was *"said to have had a miraculous birth: his mother, Dughdova, was a virgin who conceived him after being visited by a shaft of light."*[63]

Moreover, the future saviour of Zoroastrianism is called the Saoshyant, Sōšyant or Saošyant, about whom Boyce says:

"...gradually it came to be believed that he would be born of the seed of Zoroaster himself, miraculously preserved at the bottom of a lake... it is held [that] a virgin will bathe in this lake and become with child, and will bear a son, the Saošyant... His virgin mother too received a name..."She who brings fulfillment to the father"....

It seems probable that the beliefs about the Saošyant's miraculous conception evolved in that region [Hāmūn lake in southeastern Iran], during the centuries which passed between the lifetime of Zoroaster (perhaps between 1400 and 1200 BCE), and the adoption of his faith in western Iran (perhaps in the late 7th century BCE)."[64]

In the same article, Boyce also states that this motif was *"widely known throughout the Near East in the Achaemenid period."*

If Zoroastrians had been expecting for centuries one or more virgin-born saviours, and Mithra has been considered by not a few to be a *'saviour'* figure,[65] logic dictates that at some point in the history of his mythological development Mithra was perceived as this virgin-born saviour, and Anahita would equally logically be the choice for his virgin mother.

---

[63] Nabarz, 2005:2. See also Turner (2000:524), regarding "Zoroaster": *"Conceived by a ray of light that entered his mother's bosom, he was born of a virgin birth."*

[64] Boyce, "Astvat-Ereta," www.iranica.com/articles/astvat-ereta-saviour

[65] See, e.g., Campbell (1968:263), who has a section titled, "Mithra Invictus, A Final Saviour." See also Duchesne-Guillemin in *The Religion of Ancient Iran*, where he refers to *"the role of Mithra as saviour or mediator in the Mysteries..."* (Bleeker 1988:367)

The Epic of Sasun

The Zoroastrian virgin-birth story was so well known that it apparently made it into third cycle of the Armenian national epic, titled *David of Sasun* (or *Sassoun*, etc.), about which Dr. Martin Schwartz says:

"Sanasar, father of the Great Mher [Mithra], and Sanasar's twin brother Baltasar, are born of a virgin [Lusik] who becomes pregnant from the water of the 'Milky Fountain of Immortality'... Combining these data with the tradition found in Elišē [Vardapet] that Mithra was born of God through a human mother..., one may suggest a transference of the miraculous birth of the Sōšyants to Mithra. In some accounts of the epic the "Milky Fountain" gushes forth from a great rock; this may be due to a conflation of the lake engenderment and the rock birth legends."[66]

This epic is estimated to be well over 1,000 years old, evidently incorporating elements much older, such as the Zoroastrian tradition of a virgin birth, the origin of which Boyce dates to possibly between 1,400 and 600 years BCE and which in and of itself proves the existence of this motif in pre- or non-Christian religion and mythology. In discussing the *"principal sacred place of the Armenian folk epic of Sasun,"* Dr. Christine Allison, et al., say that the epic's *"roots are extremely ancient"*.[67] Moreover, this conflated account appears to reconcile again the virgin-mother and rock-born motifs.

The History of Vartan

The legend of Mithra being born of a female shows up also in the works of Armenian writers towards the end of the Sassanian era in Persia, after Armenia had been significantly Christianised. In the *History of Vartan*, the Armenian historian Elišē or Elisaeus Vardapet or Vardabed (C5th CE?) recorded Armenian Christian bishops as retorting the following to Mihr-Nerseh, the *'perfidious and cruel*[68] minister of Persian king Yazdegerd II (fl. 437-458 CE), evidently in response to the official's revulsion towards Christian doctrine:

".. you said that God was born of a woman; [yet] you do not have to feel horror or contempt. Indeed Ormizd and Ahriman were born of a father and not a mother; if you think about it, you cannot accept that.

---

[66] Hinnells, 1975:418.
[67] Allison, 2009:159.
[68] Langlois, 1869:278.

There is even something more unusual: the god Mihr [Mithra] born of a woman, as if anyone could have intercourse with his own mother.[69]

Concerning this last sentence, Cumont notes that the translator Karabagy Garabed appears to have rendered the original better, when he writes:

"Votre dieu Miher est non seulement né d'une femme mais ce qui est bien autrement ridicule il est né d'un commerce incestueux avec sa propre mère."[70]

"Your god Miher is not only born of a woman but, what is far more ridiculous, he is born of an incestuous intercourse with his own mother."

In this polemic, the Christians are apparently assailing as unsustainable the belief that the Zoroastrian God and Devil were born of a male, rather than a female, as is natural. They are likewise ridiculing the belief that Mithra's consort was also his mother. This consort or female companion was Anahita, who is thus identified also as his mother, reflecting an old mythical motif that the bishops certainly did not just fabricate on the spot at that time. Indeed, as we have seen from the stories of Inanna and Tammuz or Cybele and Attis, the virgin-mother consort is likewise a widespread theme that predated the Common Era by centuries.

Vardapet also says:

"Un de vos plus anciens sages a dit que le dieu Mihr naquit d'une mére, laquelle etait de race humaine; il n'en est pas moins roi, fils de Dieu et allié vaillant des sept dieux."[71]

"One of your most ancient sages said that the god Mihr [Mithra] was born of a mother, who was of the human race; he is nonetheless king, son of God and valiant ally of the seven gods."

The fact that this information comes from an Armenian is revealing, because it appears to be more of an old *Armenian*, rather than Roman or Persian, tradition that Mithra was born of the virgin mother goddess Anahita. Concerning the Armenian preference for Anahita, Russell relates:

---

[69] Cumont 1896:5. The French translation of the original Armenian text is: "...tu as dit que Dieu était né d'une femme; tu ne dois en éprouver ni horreur, ni mépris. En effet Ormizd et Arimane naquirent d'un père et non d'une mère; si tu y réfléchis, tu ne peux accepter cela. Il est encore une chose plus singulière, le dieu Mihr naissant d'une femme, comme si quelqu'un pouvait avoir commerce avec sa propre mère."
[70] Cumont 1896:5.
[71] Langlois, 1869:194.

"*In a famous passage, Strabo asserts that the Medes and Armenians honor the same sacred rites (hiera) as the Persians; but the Armenians in particular honor those of Anaitis...*"[72]

Another Armenian writer of the fifth century CE, Eznik or Eznig of Golp, relates the tale of the evil Zoroastrian god, Ahriman, criticizing the good god Ahura Mazda/Ormuzd:

"*...if he were wise, he would go unto his mother, and the Sun [Mihr] would be born (lit. would become) as his son; and he would have intercourse with his sister, and the Moon would be born.*"[73]

Regarding the Zoroastrians of his day, Eznik remarks:

"*They say another thing, which is incredible, [namely that] at the time of the death of Ormazd, he threw his sperm into a source, and afterwards a virgin must give birth from this source. This virgin must give birth to a child who overcomes innumerable troops of Ahriman, and two other [children] who will be produced in the same way will fight the armies and exterminate them.*"[74]

These various traditions may be summarized thus, as by Nabarz, when he relates:

"*According to the Zoroastrian tradition..., Mithra the Saviour was born in 272 BCE. His birth and that of the Roman Mithras are both at the winter solstice. The Persian Mithra was born of the immaculate virgin Mother Goddess Anahita... Anahita (Anahid) was said to have conceived the Saviour from the seed of Zoroaster, which, legend says, is preserved in the waters of Lake Hamun in Sistan, Iran. This birth took place in a cave or grotto, where shepherds attended him and presented him with gifts at the winter solstice. Mithra lived for sixty-four years and then ascended to heaven in 208 BCE.*"[75]

Although it may have been believed in antiquity, the notion that Mithra had been a real person living in the third century BCE is obviously unsustainable, particularly in consideration of the fact of his being a Persian remake of the Vedic god Mitra and with his presence in the literary and archaeological record of the Achaemenian period.

---

[72] Russell, 2004:438.
[73] Zaehner, 1972:438.
[74] Langlois, 1869:381.
[75] Nabarz, 2005:19.

Mitra, Born of the Virgin Aditi

Anahita is also known as Anahid and Anahiti, which sound similar to Aditi, mother of Mithra's Vedic predecessor, Mitra. Like her Babylonian, Egyptian and Anatolian counterparts, Aditi is the *'mother of the gods'* or *Deva-Matri*.[76] Yet, she is also the inviolable or *virgin* dawn, who gives birth to the sun god.

In the Indian text the *Rig Veda* (1.49), dating to possibly 3,000 to 3,700 years ago, the dawn goddess is Ushas, about whom Dr. Carl Olson says:

"...Usas...is identified with the dawn. This virgin daughter of heaven is depicted as a young maiden who is pulled by a hundred chariots (RV 1.48). When she arrives each morning she drives away darkness (RV 6.64). She is also connected to the cosmic law (rta)...and like Aditi she is compared to a cow and called mother of cows (RV 3.58)."[77]

Thus, Ushas the dawn is both a virgin and a mother. From Dr. John Muir we discover further:

"In R.V. i. 113, 19, Ushas (the dawn) is styled "the mother of the gods, and the manifestation of Aditi"; or, as Sâyana explains, the rival of Aditi, from her appearing to call all the gods into existence when they are worshipped in the morning, as Aditi really gave them birth. Compare i. 115, I."[78]

Indologist Dr. Alain Daniélou says, *"Dawn is the visage of the Primordial-Vastness (Aditi) (Rg Veda 1.15.3; 8.90.16; 10.11.1)."*[79] Dawn is a manifestation of Aditi, who is likewise the *'mother of the gods'*, including the Adityas, deemed *'solar gods'*. As Dr. Wendy O'Flaherty states, *"The sun is one of the children of Aditi (cf. 10.72), a group of solar gods called Adityas."*[80] Mitra is one of the original Adityas, the *"son of the self-formed goddess Aditi"*,[81] as well as the *"guardian of day"*[82] and *'friendly'* aspect of the sun. Yet, Aditi is also the *'Celestial Virgin'*,[83] once again demonstrating the ancient virgin-mother myth.

---

[76] Turner, 2000:15.
[77] Olson, 2007:252.
[78] *Journal of the Royal Asiatic Society of Great Britain and Ireland*, 1.64.
[79] Daniélou, 1964:114. The French scholar also states: *"Krsna being an incarnation of Visnu, his mother, Devaki, is a manifestation of Aditi."*
[80] O'Flaherty, 1981:190.
[81] Turner, 2000:325.
[82] Turner, 2000:15.
[83] Turner, 2000:15.

Anahita has several points in common with the dawn goddess, not the least of which is that they both ride chariots drawn by horses, which is also a major attribute of a solar deity. That Anahita was likewise associated with the dawn is evident from the *Aban Yasht* (16.62), in which the goddess is invoked at dawn,[84] the Avestan word for which is *ushånghem*, like Ushas, the Vedic dawn goddess.

In this same regard, Mithra is the light –sunlight- streaming over the mountains at sunrise or dawn. He is also the sun itself, which is traditionally said to be the son of the goddess, whether the dawn, earth, moon, Venus or Virgo, etc.

Macho Mithraism

With all the evidence combined, it appears that the Persian Mithra did indeed possess the virgin-mother attribute, which seems to have been lost or deliberately severed in the all-male Roman Mithraism. As Nabarz remarks, *"Although present in the Persian worship, Anahita and other goddesses are by and large absent from the Roman form of Mithraism."*[85]

Yet, the Mithraists could not stamp out all vestiges of the highly popular goddess:

"Various female divinities were found [within Mithraism], especially in the Mithraea of Sidon... There were dedications to the Matronae and to the Goddesses of the crossroads...in the Friedburg Mithraeum...and there was a relief of Epona seated between her two horses in the First Heddernheim Mithraeum... The significance of these multiple divinities may or may not be connected with that of the Mithraic Dea triformis..."[86]

There may likewise be vestiges of Anahita in Roman Mithraism as well. In this regard, Necipoğlu describes Zoroastrian symbolism:

"On the tomb of Artaxerxes II or III, to the right of Ahura Mazda...is the bas relief of a crescent cradling a sphere.... In the case of this relief it seems that the sphere represents Mithra and the crescent Anahita."[87]

These remarks remind one of the common Mithraic imagery in which the sun and moon are represented as flanking the figure of Mithras, who himself is identified with the sun. While it is commonly

---

[84] Malandra, 1983:124.
[85] Nabarz, 2005:12.
[86] Campbell, 1968:377.
[87] Necipoğlu, 1994:68.

assumed to connote Selene or Luna, which are simply the Greek and Latin terms for the moon and the lunar goddess, the Roman Mithraic symbol of the moon could also represent Anahita. It may well be, therefore, that the moon in this imagery continued to symbolise Anahita in Roman Mithraism, as it did in the Zoroastrianism of the Sassanian Empire at least up to the 3rd century CE, but that this knowledge was a *'mystery'* or was otherwise hidden or lost in the massive destruction that followed.

Conclusion

Although it does not seem to be spelled out in any extant texts or inscriptions concerning Roman Mithraism, the tradition of Mithra being born of Anahita appears to be old, based on the relationships of the deities to whom they are compared, such as Nana and Attis or Ishtar and Tammuz. The claim that Mithra was perceived as having been born from Anahita may have been one of the ancient mysteries, rarely recorded and largely in places such as the cities in which the Anahita temples have long since been nearly completely destroyed, including in several parts of the Near East such as Iran and especially Armenia.

Indeed, this contention of Anahita as the virgin mother of Mithra seems to emanate mostly from Armenian Mithraism, as opposed to the Persian, but it is evidently influenced by Anatolian and Mediterranean religion as well. This assertion is understandable in consideration of the fact that the parthenogenetic creatrix or virgin-mother goddess concept goes back thousands of years before the Common Era throughout this very region.

In consideration of the widespread and enduring pre-Christian mythical motif of parthenogenesis, including its presence in the Vedic Mitra myth and in Zoroastrian religion along with its appearance in the Armenian national epic, as well as Mithra's *'birth'* from a female mountain and the mention of Mithra's mother many centuries later—a tradition which surely was not made up whole cloth at that time—we possess every good reason to conclude that in antiquity, in certain areas such as Armenia, Mithra was perceived to have been born of a virgin mother, the pure and undefiled goddess Anahita.

Further Reading:

"ANĀHĪD", www.iranica.com/articles/anahid

"Armenian literature", en.wikipedia.org/wiki/Armenian_literature

"Avestan Dictionary", www.avesta.org/avdict/avdict.htm

"Ichthys", en.wikipedia.org/wiki/Ichthys

Allison, Christine, et al., (eds.) (2009) *From Daēnā to Dīn: Religion, Kultur and Sprache in der iranischen Welt.* Wiesbaden: Otto Harrassowitz

Amir-Moezzi, Mohammed Ali (2006) *La religion discreete: Croyances et pratiques spirituelles dan l'islam shi'ite.* Paris: Libr. Philosophique Vrin

Badiozamani, Badi (2005) *Iran and America: Rekindling a Love Lost.* California: East-West Understanding Press

Basmajian, Gabriel, & Agop, Jack Hacikyan (2002) *The Heritage of Armenian Literature: From the Sixth to the Eighteenth Century.* Detroit: Wayne State University Press

Bleeker, Claus (1963) *The Sacred Bridge: Researches into the Nature and Structure of Religion.* Leiden: E.J. Brill

Bleeker, Claus (1975) *The Rainbow: A Collection of Studies in the Science of Religion.* Leiden: E.J. Brill

Bleeker, Claus, and Widengren, Geo (eds.) (1969) *Historia Religionum I: Religions of the Past.* Leiden: E.J. Brill

Boettiger, Louis Angelo (1920) *Armenian Legends and Festivals.* Minneapolis: University of Minnesota

Boyce, Mary. *Astvat-Ereta,* www.iranica.com/articles/astvat-ereta-saviour

Boyce, Mary (1992) A *History of Zoroastrianism, II.* Leiden/Köln: E.J. Brill

Boyce, Mary (1996) *A History of Zoroastrianism: The Early Period.* Leiden: E.J. Brill

Boyce, Mary (2001) *Zoroastrians: Their Religious Beliefs and Practices.* London: Routledge & Kegan Paul

Campbell, Leroy (1968) *Mithraic Iconography and Ideology.* Leiden: E.J. Brill

Cumont, Franz (1896) *Textes et Monuments Figurés Relatifs Aux Mystères de Mithra, II.* Brussels: H. Lamertin

Cumont, Franz (1903) *The Mysteries of Mithra.* Chicago/London: Kegan Paul, Trench, Trübner

Daniélou, Alain (1964) *Hindu Polytheism.* London: Routledge & Kegan Paul

Darmester, James (tr.) (1883) *The Zend-Avesta: The Sîrôzahs, Yasts and Nyâyis.* Oxford: Clarendon Press

de Jong, Albert (1997) *Traditions of the Magi.* Leiden: Brill

Gerevich, Laszlo (1951) *Studia Archaeologica Gerardo Van Hoorn Oblata.* Leiden: Brill

Hansman, John (1985) *The Great Gods of Elymais.* In *Acta Iranica: Papers in Honour of Professor Mary Boyce, vol. 1.* Leiden: E.J. Brill

Herodotus & de Selincourt, a (tr.) (1996) *The Histories.* New York: Penguin Books

Hewitt, James F. (1901) *History and Chronology of the Myth-Making Age.* London: James Parker and Co.

Hinnells, John R. (ed.) (1975) *Mithraic Studies: Proceedings of the First International Congress of Mithraic Studies, II.* Manchester: Manchester University Press

Jackson, S.M. & Gilmore, G.W. (eds) (1910) *The New Schaff-Herzog Encyclopedia.* New York/London: Funk and Wagnalls Company

Lane, Eugene (ed.) (1996) *Cybele, Attis and Related Cults: Essays in Memory of M. J. Vermaseren.* Leiden/New York: E.J. Brill

Langlois, Victor (1869) *Collection des Historiens Anciens et Modernes de L'Arménie, vol. 10.* Paris: Librairie de Firmin Didot Frères

Leeming, David Adams (1992) *The World of Myth: An Anthology.* New York: Oxford University Press

Leeming, David Adams (1998) *Mythology: The Voyage of the Hero.* New York: Oxford University Press

Malandra, William W. (ed., tr.) (1983) *An Introduction to Ancient Iranian Religion: Readings from the Avesta and Achaemenid Inscriptions.* Minneapolis: University of Minnesota Press

, Mohamad & Beny (1978) *Iran: A Glimpse of History.* Toronto: McClelland and Stewart

Nabarz, Payam (2005) *The Mysteries of Mithras: The Pagan Belief that Shaped the Christian World.* Rochester: Inner Traditions

Necipoğlu, Gulru (1994) *Muqarnas: An Annual on Islamic Art and Architecture.* Leiden: E.J. Brill

O'Flaherty, Wendy Doniger (1981) *The Rig Veda: An Anthology of One Hundred Eight Hymns.* New York: Penguin Books

Olson, Carl (2007) *The Many Colours of Hinduism: A Thematic-Historical Introduction.* New Brunswick: Rutgers University Press

Patai, Raphael (1978) *The Hebrew Goddess.* Detroit: Wayne State University Press

Rigoglioso, Marguerite (2009) *The Cult of Divine Birth in Ancient Greece.* New York: Palgrave Macmillan

Rigoglioso, Marguerite (2010) *Virgin Mother Goddesses of Antiquity.* New York: Palgrave Macmillan

Russell, James R. (2004) *Armenian and Iranian Studies.* Cambridge, MA: Harvard University Press

Steingass, Francis J. (2005) *A Comprehensive Persian-English Dictionary.* New Delhi: Asian Educational Services

Turner, Patricia, & Coulter, Charles Russell (2000) *Dictionary of Ancient Deities.* Oxford: Oxford University Press

Waerden, Bartel Leendert (1974) *Science Awakening II: The Birth of Astronomy.* New York: Oxford University Press

Zaehner, Robert C. (1972) *Zurvan: A Zoroastrian Dilemma.* New York: Biblo and Tannen

An-Āhītəm Purity undefiled - a primal spiritual tradition in the way of life among the Indo-Iranian peoples

by Sam Kerr

Introduction

During the period of early twilight in history when the quality of life and the very existence depended largely on strict prevention of illness rather than on finding a cure, strict emphasis on proper hygiene, good sanitation and public health was best projected to the masses by being conveyed in teachings, incorporated in a spiritual context among the Āryānic Indic and the Airyānic Avestan peoples in their primal homelands of *'Ārya avarta'* and *'Airyānā vaeja'* respectively. A phenomenally high infant mortality rate and lasting adult disability from illnesses as well as an equally high mortality rate among adults from diseases which was little understood at the time, had already laid the ground work for *'treatment'*, both herbal and surgical in instances when preventive measures had failed. Historical documented records of *'treatments'* implemented after migration of the Indo-Iranian peoples further south (and west wards and eastwards) to their New World (namely the *'Classical World'* of the time) by physicians and surgeons really occurred millennia later in Mesopotamia, Greece, Turkey ... etc. Then, as now, the subtle purpose of maintaining proper rules of sanitation governing a strict hygienic way of life in individual settlements was to keep the immune processes of the body at optimal levels for good physical wellness, as well as for the upkeep of mental health. The author does not touch on ceremonial and ritual *'purity'*, a complex subject matter in its own right.

The Av. word *'āhita*[88] means *polluted/soiled* (knowingly or unknowingly); *made foul* (negligently or inadvertently); *adulterated* (deliberately/intentionally by the addition of impurities, as in goods

---

[88] *Āhita* - See Kanga Dictionary, 1900:86.

for sale with the sole purpose of making profit) and, therefore, *'impure/defiled'*. The equivalent Vedic Sanskrit word is *'āsita'*.[89]

Grammatically, the Av. word *'an-āhita'*, then, becomes *'not polluted/not soiled'* meaning *'not impure'* and, therefore, *'pure'*. Note the double negative used by the Av. people compared to the single positive used by the Vēd. people. The author has been unable to find a double negative in the *Ŗg Vēda*. A double negative (not infrequently, to my mind) creates a different kind of emphasis, which a single positive (frequently) fails to create. Not making something impure is really not the same as having something, which is inherently pure.

Grammatically, thus, *'an-āhītəm'* indicates *'purity'*. The emphasis on the alertness at maintaining purity appears, to my mind, much greater in the latter form of speech than in the former. It is of interest to note in comparison that the Av. *'an-āhita'* (the opposite of *'āhita'*) is the Vēd. Sans. *'sita'*[90] meaning *'immaculate/chaste, white/not black'*. Its opposite *'asita'* is *'not immaculate/not chaste, not white/black'*. The Av. immaculate lady of purity, *'an-āhita'* (not impure) has thus the same meaning as the Vēd. immaculate lady of purity, *'sitā'* (pure / chaste).

Purity as chastity

Indeed, in the Epic *'Mahābhārata'* incorporating the *'Rāmāyana'*, Sitā,[91] as a person who remains chaste though her year-long captivity after being abducted by Rāvana is the very embodiment of an unblemished, immaculate lady among the peoples of Vedic origin.

---

[89] *Āsita* - See Moniér-Williams Dictionary, 1988:120.
[90] *Sita* - See Moniér-William's Dictionary, 1988:120.
[91] *Sitā* as a person – See Vyasa's The Epic 'Mahābhārata' incorporating 'The Rāmāyana'.
This quotation is from 'Srimad Vālmiki Rāmāyana' - Sanskrit *slokas* with English translation. The Yuddha Kanda (Book VI, 116.31) of Valmiki's Ramayana). *'Sita, with the shining of fresh refined gold and decked with ornaments of refined gold, plunged into the blazing fire, in the presence of all people'*.
See Tulsi Dāsa's epic poem 'Rāmaçaritamānasa' 1988:670, which slightly differs from the Mahabharata Ramayana regarding Sita's demise. Like Vālmiki, Tulsi Dāsa, philosopher, composer prefers in his epic poem 'Rāmaçaritamānasa' to create a twist in the way Sita ends her life to save her husband the stigma of public shame. He has Sita give the ultimate sacrifice by self-immolation in a pile of Fire prepared by Lakshmana, thus proving and maintaining her stance about her chastity. *'With her thoughts fixed on the Lord, Janaki entered the flames as though they were cool like sandal-paste...........! Both, her shadow form as well as the stigma of public shame were consumed in the blazing fire.........'*

Initially, even her husband Rāma had lingering doubts about her chastity but the Saint Vālmiki reassures him.

"I tell you on oath, Rāma, that Sitā is truly a chaste wife." said Vālmiki, "Lav and Kush, your two sons are from her. You sent her away to the forests merely from an unfounded fear that she may have become unchaste during her captivity. Through my meditation I profess that God will render my years of meditation fruitless if my assertion about Sita is shown untrue."

In response to Vālmiki's plea Rāma replied, *"Your words, O Sage, have left no doubt in my mind about Sita's immaculate chastity. They have reinforced my conviction as a result of the terrible ordeal she was forced to undergo earlier. It was the ill rumour that had compelled me to leave her in the forests."* It was, then, left to Lakshmana and his companions to persuade her to return to Ayōdhyā with Rāma. Little did they envisage the intuitive and resolute determination of a woman who had once been snubbed. Still, when compelled by all who approached her, she agreed to come, but only to the edge of the forest by the banks of the river Saryu where she vehemently implored upon Mother Earth *'to give her shelter by accepting her in her lap'*.

Legend has it that instantly, amidst the roar of stormy clouds and flashes of lightning, a wide opening in the earth occurred where Sitā stood, as during an earthquake. Sitā, being chaste, was instantly consumed in the wide chasm. In the *Ṛg Vēda iv.56.6*[92] Sitā is simply a divinity of the field-furrow, which bears crops for men and, after all, her life's fulfillments thus returns to her abode, the Earth. To the millions of men and women in India, however, Sitā is not an allegory; she lives in their hearts and minds as a role model of womanly love, devotion and her unstinting conjugal fidelity. The later Epics, Srimad Vālmiki's *Rāmāyana*[93] and Tulsi Dāsa's *Śrī Rāmaçaritamānasa*[94] (the Holy Lake of the acts of Rāma) however describe Sitā's demise differently.

Purity (hygiene) as a way of life.

It is a truth widely acknowledged that Zoroastrians are proud of their heritage of implementing a strict sense of cleanliness (Guj: *Chōkhkhai*) in their daily life. Zoroastrians have a holy duty to keep

---

[92] Sitā as earthly field furrow personified. See Griffiths, 1986:235.
[93] Sitā - See Srimad Valmiki's Epic, *The Ramayana.* Refer http://valmikiramayan.net/ Yuddha Kanda, VI, 116.31.
[94] Sitā - See Tulsi Dāsa's Śrī Rāmacaritamānasa (the Holy Lake of the acts of Rāma), 1991:670.

all the natural elements undefiled, whether earth, air, vegetation, water, or fire. A deeply imbibed Av. reverence to the created *'pure' elements of nature* will not allow Avestans to contaminate these Ahura Mazda bestowed natural elements. The inferences and advice in the Gāth./Av. Scriptures and the Pāh. texts are simple: *'those who do not heed them do not practice them in daily life; those who do not practice them are not holy. Thus, those who promote filthiness/defilement are not pious, since it would be akin to promoting evil -Āhitəm, which considered as having been devised by Angra Mainyu's forces of evil.'*

Should impurity/defilement *(āhitəm)* occur due to any reason - from stagnant waters, corpse on ground or in water, corpse-eating bird or dog, from disease (and some named infectious illnesses), the *Vəndidād* in several verses prescribes a strict code of hygiene to the extent that penitence for transgression of the prescribed rules of hygiene was made obligatory and even mandatory under pain of castigation and punishment: -

Ăhitim[95] - *Vən. 11.9 & 12: alludes to direct and indirect defilement and suggests chanting of four Ahunāvars in a low tone.*

- *Vən. 16.11*[96]*: alludes to the contamination from blood and bodily secretions and suggests disinfection using 'Gomez'.*

Ăhitya[97] - *Vən. 16.16: alludes to the contamination of excretory body fluids, and suggests atonements 90 times, involving the person in some form of meritorious acts.*

Ăhiticha[98] - *Vən. 5.27: Suggests that if there is a defilement of persons from a corpse 'carry the holy house fire far away and wait for 9 nights in Winter and a month in summer before returning the fire to the house'.*

- *Vən. 6.30:*[99] *Defilement of stagnant water / - Vən. 6.33: Defilement of well water/*

---

[95] *Alludes to direct and indirect defilement Ăhitim* - See Sethna, 1977:98-99, Vən.11.9 & 12.
[96] *Alludes to the contamination from menstrual secretions Ăhitim* - See Sethna, 1977:125, Vən.16.11.
[97] *Alludes to the contamination of menstrual secretions Ăhitya* - See Sethna, 1977:127, Vən.16.16.
[98] *Combating defilement of persons from a corpse -Ăhiticha* - See Sethna, 1977:46-48, 37-39, Vən.5.27; Vən.6.30, 33, 36 & 39.
[99] *Combating defilement of stagnant water, well water, dripping water from snow or sheet of ice and from flowing waters.*

- *Vən. 6.36: Defiled dripping snow or sheet of ice/ - Vən. 6.39: Defilement in flowing waters*

– *For the above defilements the prescription was removal of the impurity at least 6 steps away from the water on to dry and high ground before the water became fit for personal use.*

Ăhitayāō[100] - *Vən. 20.3 & 6.30: Thrita possessed the skilful art of extracting juices from herbal plants and Divine powers of repelling the causes of illnesses and of clearing defilements promoted by the evil forces.*

Ăhitish[101] - *Y. 10.7: '.......the Hoama worshipper beseeches all evil defilement to perish from his house'*

- *Mēhr Yt*[102] *X.50: '...the creator Ahura Mazda has bestowed a dwelling high above exalted mountains where there is neither night nor darkness, nor..............any form of evil defilement or......'*

- *Rashnā Yt.*[103] *XII.23 '.....Yazata Rashnā resides in a radiant exalted shelter where there is neither night nor darkness nor.........or any defilement....'*

The rules of hygiene include more or less the same precautionary measures in general as they are now followed by modern hospitals but in Av. times they were more stringent when a person was suspected to be inflicted by the many infectious diseases named in the *Avesta*. The use of (*'purifiers'*) - herbal decoctions, emulsions and solutions and powders for disinfection and as deodorants was recommended as also *'the recitation of the Ahunāvar four times in a low intonation'*.

While some of the advice in the code of those times may, in the present context of life, appear not to be of much relevance in modern times, it was of immense importance and certainly relevant to the saving of lives from dangerous contamination and infectious diseases during those ancient times. It is amazing how whatever was taught to me in Hygiene and Public Health during my medical studies in the early 1950s now appears rather inadequate in the modern context of life within only 60 years.

---

[100] *Thrita's Divine powers of repelling the causes of illnesses and of clearing defilements -Ăhitayāō -* See Sethna, 1977:149-150, *Van 20.3 & 6.30.*

[101] *Recitations from the Garthas, promting 'purity undelfiled' -Ăhitish -* See Sethna 1977, *Yasna 10.7, p 42.*

[102] *Yazata Mithra's abode is free of defilement -Ăhitish -* See Sethna 1976:143, *Mehr Yasht X.50.*

[103] *Yazata Rashna's abode is free of defilement -Ăhitish -* See Sethna 1976:191, *Rashna Yasht XII.23.*

Ardibēhēst Yasht 3.6[104] - *'Of the 5 types of healers, the one using purifying rites, the one who cures by the mental powers of reassurance of order and justice, the one who heals with the knife, the one who uses herbal plants, by far the most efficacious healer-of-all healers is the healer who heals by reciting the Holy Māntra.'*

While avoiding reference to ceremonial rites of purity and those during consecration I will limit my discussion and comments to aspects of purity which show reverence to Fire, the Waters and to the Cosmic heavenly bodies. One may ask, why the cosmic heavenly bodies in our Solar system and Galaxy? Because the gravitational attraction between them has governed the Eternal Law of Āshā/Ṛta and influenced the positive psyche of the Indo-Iranians without which life on Earth, as we now know, cannot exist.

Fire as it is understood in modern science is the purest form of visible physical element on earth.

It is not only pure in itself but it also helps to burn away/ consume (purify, so to say) external pollutants and extraneous impurities. *Ṛg Vēda* ii.8.5[105] mentions Ā'tri (Ātra) & Agni together. The former, in the Ved. Sense, means devourer/consumer (of impure material). In the *Avesta*, Ātar is a *Yazata*[106] and Master/Lord of the house (*nmānō-paiti*[107]- *Mēhr Yasht* 10.17) while in the *Ṛg Vēda* Agni is a *Yajata* and Master/Lord of the house (*grihapati*[108] - *'agmim grihapatim abhismavāsna'*).

Ātash Niyāyēsh, 5.8[109] refers allegorically to *'the Inner Fire'* (one's Inner Self) as the friend of the *'Outer (physical) Fire'*.

The Av./Vēd. people consider Fire (*Ātar* of the Avesta and *Agni* of the *Vēdās*) as the most sublime earthly representation of the Creator on earth. In the *Gāthās*, *Ātar* always implies the *'Inner Divine spark'*

---

[104] *Holy Mānthra* as an efficacious healer - See Kanga, *English Khordeh Avesta,* 1993:195, Ardibēhēst Yasht 3.6.

[105] *Ā'tri (Ātra) as devourer/consumer (of impure material)* - See Griffith, 1983:134, Ṛg V. ii, 8.5.

[106] *Yajata - Agni in the Vedas* is a Yajata. See Griffuth, 1983:260, Ṛg V., v, 44.11. The Av. Equivalent is Yazata - Divinity/angel. Master/Lord of the house is mentioned in several verses.

[107] *Atar in the Avesta is Nmano-paiti,* the Master/Lord of the house. See Sethna, 1976:131, *Mehr Yasht* X.18. It is mentioned in several passages in the Avesta. Also see Mirza, 1974:.

[108] *Agni in the Rg.V. is Grihapati,* the Master/Lord of the house. See Griffith's 1986:437, Ṛg V., VIII, 49.19.

[109] *One's Inner Self - Daena as the Inner Fire (found in the heart of every human being)* - See Kanga, *English Khordēh Avesta,* 1993:82, Ātash Nyāyēsh 5.8.

in the heart of every human being. It has never meant the physical Fire. It has always represented symbolically *'the inner spiritual Fire as belonging to the Supreme or as being part of the Divine Being, a spark (as it were) emanating from Him'.* The same sentiment is also reflected in the *Mundaka Upanishad 2.1.1.* – *'The inner Divine spark...* See *The 13 Principal Upanishads*, Trans by Robert E. Hume. (*'As from the blazing Fire, sparks by the thousand issue forth...'*). It is only much later in the *Younger Avesta* that the *'Spark'* metaphorically denotes the *'Son'* of Ahura Mazda.

Through their veneration of Fire, thus, the Avestans are able to generate intimate contact with Ahura Mazda symbolically deemed to be father of Ātash.

Ātash Niyāyēsh in the initial introductory passage[110] reiterates

'.....tava ātarsh puthra Ahurahē Mazdāō'

(.....unto thee, O Fire, son of Ahura Mazda).

Thus, in *Gāthā Uštavaiti (Yasna 43.4)*[111] Zarathushtra talks about Fire, one of the implications being *'inner illumination'*, the fire of enlightenment (the *'spark'* in the heart of all humans) through which the Creator bestows knowledge, courage, strength and the power to think rationally (as it were, a form of mental purity - possessing a clear, rational thinking mind without the lewdness of ignorance and impure thoughts).

'O Mazda, I shall certainly adore thee as the all-powerful giver of blessings,

- both, upon the followers of untruth as also upon the righteous -

through the power of thy Spark, the preserver of Purity.....'

In *Gāthā Spənta Mainyu (Yasna 48.5)*[112] and in *Gāthā Uštavaiti (Yasna 44.9)*[113] Zarathushtra uses the words *yāoš dā* and *yāoš dānē*

---

[110] *Fire described as '...tava Atarsh puthra Ahurahe Mazdao' in the* Ātash Nyāēsh *in its initial introductory passage and repeatedly in the Avesta.* Fire has always represented, symbolically, the 'inner spiritual Fire' as belonging to the Supreme or as being part of the Divine Being, a spark (as it were) emanating from Him. The same sentiment is also reflected in the *Mundaka Upanishād 2.1.1.* It is, much later, in the Younger Avesta that the *'Spark'* is denoted as the *'Son'* of Ahura Mazda.

[111] *'Inner illumination, spark of enlightenment'* - See Taraporewala English Edition, 1993:415, Gāthā Uštavaiti *(Yasna 43.4)*.

[112] *yāoš dā* - See Taraporewala English Edition, 1993:669, Gāthā Spənta Mainyu *(Yasna 48.5)*.

[113] *yāoš dānē* - See Taraporewala English Edition, 1993:489, Gāthā Uštavaiti *(Yasna 44.9)*.

respectively to mean just that - the maintenance of strict hygiene and *'cleanliness being the best to preserve health throughout life (that is, from birth)'*. The Vēd. equivalent is *'yóh dhā'*, which occurs several times in the *Ṛg .V.* (i, 93.7; viii, 39.4[114] ....etc). The derivation is from the Sanskrit root word *'yu'* meaning *'to incorporate, to join, to bind...'*.

To the Zoroastrians Fire stands for purity as well as holiness. It is kept burning continuously both in the Zoroastrian Temples as well as in their homes (the Hearth Fires). Orthodox Zoroastrians (on the subcontinent) still have their house fireplaces for cooking constructed in such a way that the ash from the burnt coals can be collected in a receptacle *(Guj.- Choolā Vāti)* underneath and in front of the cooking range. At the end of the day the burning embers of coal are carefully placed underneath the collected heap of ashes to be re-ignited the next morning. The emphasis is on continuity of the burning Fire, which has a deep and profound significance. It is as if when one looks at a glow in the fire one is looking at the diligent efforts and reverence of generations of ancestors who had piously laboured to keep it glowing and active. It further reinforces the practice of *'ancestor worship'* among the Indo-Iranian peoples.

The descendents of the Vēd. people, too, deeply revere Agni but there is no emphasis on maintaining continuity. Rather, they organise elective *Agni Pujā* to celebrate or commemorate an occasion or a family event. Still, their reverence to Fire remains so intense that a burning Fire is kept in the midst of the wedding ceremony as a *'witness'*, around which the couple with a knot tied between their wedding apparel walk seven times as symbolic of reverence. In fact, it was their *'Agniyāghars (Literal translation: Fire Houses)'* that the first Zoroastrian migrant refugees, who came to India after the fall of the Sassanian Empire witnessed (to their pleasant amazement) that made them name their own Fire Temples *'Agniyāries'* (except, with their Pāhlavi tongue they were unable to pronounce the *'aña'* and *'gña'* characters of the Guj. alphabet). To this day, the Zoroastrian Fire temples in India are pronounced *'Agiyāries'*.

The Sun as the cosmic Fire Supreme (Av. Hvarakhshaēta; Pah. Khorshēd)

Its Fire emits both heat and light and is considered *'pure'* by both the Vēd. as well as the Av. peoples. Sun worship was not just limited to the Āryās in their cold dark abode in the Steppes of Central Asia. In fact, there is no civilization that has not revered the Sun from

---

[114] *yoh dha* - See Griffith, 1986:59, 426, Ṛg Vēdā *(i,93.7; viii, 39.4....etc)*.

times immemorial. As Vedic and Avestan migration progressed in search of greener pastures and more amicable climes the knowledge and appreciation went with it. In the *Ṛg Vēda* I, 136.2 the Sun *(Vēd. Surya / Av. Hvara)* is called the *'eye of the universe'*[115] since it watches over to negate the natural impurities in the darkness of Space.

Note the superlative description in: -

Mēhr Yasht X.88[116]: *'anāhitəm anāhitō' referring to the radiance of the*

Fire as the 'purest of the pure' - purity undefiled.

Further, in *Mēhr Yasht X.50*[117]: 'The sun continues to remain pure,

Because Ahura Mazda has bestowed it a dwelling high above all ....where there is no illness or sorrow, defilement of evil or darkness of clouds ever able to reach such heights.'

The Moon (Av: Māonghāh; Pāh: Māh; Guj: Mōhōr).

Its reverent admiration is because of the projection of its brilliance as a soothing glow through the reflected light of the Sun, its precisely timed waxing and waning and for the fact that it has a positive influence on the moisture of vegetation and waters, the tides of the oceans. It also has a positive exhilarating influence on animal and human psyche and therefore their behaviour.

Māh Yasht VII.5[118] - *'Reverence be to the Moon, part of the Universe. It bestows bliss, brilliance and glory, promotes the tides of the seas, gives a warm soothing light, bestows mental comfort and peace, gives happiness, strength, prosperity, health and power.'*

The star, Tishtriya (Av: Tēshtar/Tir; Vēd: Pushya; Sirius/Dog Star) - Earth's 'second Sun'

It is the brightest star as seen with the naked eye from earth. It is about 70 times brighter, hotter and larger than our Sun. Being 8.7

---

[115] *Surya*, the 'eye of the Universe' - See Griffith, 1986:94, Ṛg V., I, 136.2.
[116] *Fire, the purest of the pure* - See Sethna, 1976:156, *Mēhr Yasht* X.88.
[117] *Purity of Fire* - See Sethna, 1976:142, *Mēhr Yasht* X.50.
[118] *The Full Moon has a positive and purifying influence on moisture, vegetation and waters - the tides and also on human and animal psyche.* See Sethna, 1976:78, *Māh Yasht* VII.4.

light years away, compared to our Sun, its rays take 8.7 years to reach earth while the rays of our Sun take only 8 minutes to reach the earth. It is interesting to note that modern science now knows that it is another Sun, a massive cauldron of flaming material and gases which emits direct white light of its own and not the reflected light from the Sun.

In *Tir Yasht* VIII.2.119 it is described as *'radiant, full of red hue, red, shining, beautiful, helpful, far-spreading with exalted lustre from a great distance emitting brilliant and pure health-bestowing rays.'*

The Waters [Yazata Ăvā(n) - the 'n' being nasal]

The Av. tradition promoted reverence to flowing waters by name. The personified and revered (literal translation) of the title of the River was: -

"Arēdvi Sura Anāhita Bānū (Gleaming, overflowing with water, not impure lady)."

In *Arēdvi Sura Niyāyēsh* (2.4 and 6)[120] Arēdvi Sura Anāhita is the embodiment of righteousness, the divine personification of flowing waters which pour down from Mount Hukairiya into the Sea, Vourukhasha and ultimately through thousands of channels distributes her waters to the seven Kēshvars - regions of the, then, known world.

"'May the Fravashis of the righteous......they have drawn up the waters in the form of vapour for the supply of rain water to allow the rivers to flow onwards and distribute the life-giving waters to distant places."

Impurity (Defilement): Ăhitəm

A short discussion on pervasive modern defilements would perhaps act as a corollary to the present subject matter.

Defilement of Fire

Smoking is considered by Zoroastrians an unwelcome and unhealthy activity since it carries fire to the mouth. Contamination

---

[119] *Sirius, Earth's second Sun emitting pure actinic rays of white light* - See Kanga, *English Khordeh Avesta*, 1993:218, *Tir Yasht* VIII.2.
[120] *Divine immaculate personification of purifying flowing waters* - See Kanga, *English Khordeh Avesta*, 1993:64-65, *Arēdvi Sura Niyāyēsh* (2.4 and 6).

with unclean fluids and the breath of exhalation from the oral passages and lungs further makes the indulgence unhygienic. Dedicated advocates of smoking have claimed that nowhere is it mentioned in the Zoroastrian scriptures that smoking is prohibited. The fact is that smoking was not known in the Classical world when the Gāth./Av. scriptures and the Pāh. Texts were composed. Walter Raleigh was yet to be born several centuries later (c. 1552 - 1618 CE),to sail to the New World and return with the Tobacco leaf from a place called Tobago in the West Indies. Such is the intensity with which Zoroastrians take precautions that Fire, being a primal unifying force between the Creator and humanity, is not defiled even by the bodily secretions of the normal breath of the priests as they attend to the Fire. They are obliged to wear a *'Paddan'*, a cloth mask covering the face extending from below the eyes to a considerable level underneath the jaw.

Vəndidād 11.12.121 *".......to destroy filthiness before it comes to Fire.... is, therefore, the noblest of all deeds O Mazda - by which I may, in truth, fulfill my earnest desires and prayers, achieving it through the good mind and through righteousness."*

Defilement of waters

Swimming and washing in flowing waters were considered willful attempts at fouling the water. History records that King Tiridātes of Armenia (66 CE) was invited by Emperor Nero (a Mithra worshipper who had appointed himself Sol Invictus - that is, Mithra himself) to Rome so that he could re-crown Tiridātes, King of Armenia. Armenia was at that time a loosely autonomous State under the Hellenized (and reluctantly Zoroastrian) Parthians with the Suzerain King of Kings, Vologāses I (51-78 CE) of Pārthia in Ēcbātānā, who had already crowned Tiridāte King (Satrāp) of Armenia during his appointment as Governor. The provinces of Pārs and Ēlām had been allowed to continue the practice of the religion of Zarathushtra. Tiridātes embarked on a long and devious route to Rome by land rather than sail to Rome and pollute the waters during his journey. His protracted land route crossed only the small stretch of water at Constantinople to enter Europe and then took a devious route to Rome taking three and a half months each way.

The Vēd. reverence for the River Ganges in India is as much dedicated as that of the River Arēdvi Sura Anāhita in the Avesta. To dip the entire body into the waters of the Ganges that has been

---

[121] *Preventing pollution of Fire* - See Sethna, 1977:98, *Vəndidād* 11.12.

flowing for millennia on the banks of holy city of Banares (ancient names *Varānasi/Kāshi*) and other holy cities during a pilgrimage is considered the most pious act one can undertake in life. One can draw a simile as maintaining continuity between the way the Vēd. people revered the flowing waters of the Ganges by indulging in the pious activities of their ancestors (same river; renewed waters). Likewise, when the Av. people see the glow in the Fire that has been burning for millennia they reflect on the diligent work of their ancestors to maintain the continuity of the fire and the offering of fuel to the Fire (same fire, renewed flames).

Vēdic philosophy:

'Even the purest creation can have impediments, which can mask its purity', declare the philosophical *Vēdas*. Lord Krishna (in *Bhāg. G. 18.48* [122] during his dialogue with Arjuna) advises,

"Duty, O son of Kunti, though to you may appear mundane and full of flaws must never be forsaken. All things, indeed, are clouded with defects, just as Fire is by smoke."

ABBEVIATIONS:

Gāth. - Gāthic.

Vēd. - Vēdic.

Sans. - Sanskrit.

Av. - Avestan.

Pāh. - Pāhlavi.

Guj. - Gujarāti.

Pers. - Modern Persian.

Gk. - Greek.

Vən. - Vəndidād.

Y. - Yasna.

Yt. - Yasht.

Ṛg V. - Ṛg Vēda.

---

[122] *Some impediment infiltrates all creation* - See Swami Prabhupada, Bhag. G. 1972:817, 18.48.

Bhag. G. - Bhagavad-Gita.

The author being a surgeon felt he should explain why he has ventured to establish inroads at an academic level into another field of study. There was no department of *Studies in Religions* in the three Universities in Sydney in 1968.

A Zoroastrian by birth, he had migrated to Australia in 1968. A Chair in *The Study of Religions* was established at the University of Sydney in 1977 when the first Professor, Eric J. Sharpe (an enlightened person with a wide interest in the religion of Zarathushtra and other Asian religions) was appointed the Head of the Department. The first introductory course in Comparative Religions at the University was inaugurated in 1978.

Sam Kerr is a Fellow of the Royal Society of Medicine (London) and of several Colleges of Surgery. He was Surgeon/Lecturer, the University of New South Wales and its College Hospitals, Sydney, Australia from 1968 to 2003. He is now Emeritus Surgeon at the University and its College Hospitals.

Further Reading:

Griffith, Ralph T.H. (1986) *The Hymns of the R̥gvēda*. Delhi: Motilal Banarasidass

Kanga, Kavasji Edulji (1926) *Khordēh Avesta* (Original in Gujarāti 1880/First English edition 1993 published by the Trustees of the Parsi Panchayat) Bombay: Nirnaya Sagar Press

Kanga, Kavasji Edulji (1900) *Avasthā bhāshā ni sampurna farhang* (A Dictionary of Avesta, Gujarāti and English languages). Bombay: Education Society's Steam Press

Mirza, Hormazdyar (1974) *Dastur Kayoji*. Bombay: Industrial Press

Monier-Williams, Sir (1988) *A Sanskrit-English Dictionary*. Delhi: Motilal Banarasidass

Sethna, Tehmurasp Rustamjee (1976-7) *Translations of the Avestan and Pahalvi Texts*. Karachi: 46 Parsi Colony

Swami Prabhupada (1972) *Bhagavad-Gita*. New York: Collier Books

Taraporewala, Irach J. S. (1962) *Ashō Zarathushtra nā Gāthā* (The Gāthās of Zarathushtra). Avesta Text in Gujarāti and English, Bombay: Trend Printers. This rare edition in Gujarāti was published for the benefit of the Zarathushtis of the Subcontinent. Meant to be of assistance in the pronunciation of the Gāthic words and to augment a better comparative understanding of the explanations, is complementary to the First Edition (published in the Roman script in 1951). In this respect this Edition certainly succeeds. Each verse in the Gujarāti script with the translation in Gujarati is printed on the left page of the book and the same verse in the Roman script and its translation in English on the page opposite.

Taraporewala, Irach J. S. (1993, Reprint of 1951 First Edition) *The Divine Songs of Zarathushtra*. Bombay: Hukhta Foundation

Tulsi Dāsa (1988) *Śrī Rāmaçaritamānasa* (the Holy Lake of the acts of Rāma). Delhi: Motilal Banarasidass Publishers

Vyasa (1998-2008) The Epic *'Mahābhārata'* incorporating *'The Rāmāyana'*. The cultural Heritage of India, Vol. IV, The Religions, The Ramakrishna Mission, Institute of Culture

SASSANIAN ROCK RELIEFS ATTRIBUTED TO ANAHITA

by Rahele Koulabadi, Dr. Seyed Rasool Mousavi Haji, Morteza Ataie

Abstract

Anahita, the beloved goddess among Sassanian kings, is shown in three rock reliefs of this era at Darabgird, Naqsh-i-Rustam and Taq-i-Bustan. Anahita's effigies in these reliefs are different to each other and also different to her descriptions in the Avesta (Aban Yasht). Hence, researchers have different points of views in attributing these rock reliefs to the goddess Anahita.

In this article the authors attempt to prove reasonably that the figures presented in the mentioned rock reliefs are Anahita and also a comparison is made with her descriptions in the *Aban Yasht*.

Key Words: Anahita, Aban Yasht, Darabgird, Naqsh-i-Rustam, Taq-i-Bustan

Introduction

Sassanian rock reliefs are one of the precious sources in studying the Sassanian era to help us become familiar with the social, political and religious goals of the kings. Whenever scholars confront new subjects about Sassanian history or they succeed in reading an inscription or discovering new material, they refer to these reliefs and make a comparison to them. They are the main criterions in such a way that new documents can be compared with them, so they help researchers to achieve important conclusions and discoveries (Lukonin, 2005:28).

We should seek the origin of these rock reliefs during ancient times at Sar pol-e zahab where, the Lullubian king, Annubanini, receives the diadem of kingship from Ishtar (Fig. 1) and afterward in Elamite, Achaemenid and Parthian dynasties.

In Sassanian rock reliefs, the kings, queens, courtiers and nobles and as well as deities such as Ahura Mazda, Anahita and Mithra are depicted. The presence of women in these reliefs are significant, because in contrary to Achaemenid and Parthian rock reliefs we can see pictures of women. Until now 34 rock reliefs have been discovered from Salmas, Rey, Taq-i Bustan, Barm-i Delak, Bishapur, Tang-i Qandil, Sar Mashad, Firuz Abad, Koyom, Darabgird, Naqsh-i Bahram, Naqsh-i Rajab, Naqsh-i-Rustam, and Rag- i Bibi in northern of Afghanistan (Azarnoush, 2007:81-65). In ten of these reliefs the women are depicted as queens, the goddess Anahita and courtiers: the reliefs of Bahram II at Barm-i Delak, Sar Mashad and Naqsh-i-Rustam, the reliefs of Shapur I at Naqsh-i-Rajab and Tang-i Qandil, and also a relief of Ardashir I at Naqsh-i Rajab each include pictures of queens. All of these ladies lack a crenelated crown, and some of them wear hats (kolah) with flying ribbons, and the others are depicted without hats (kolah). Royal ribbons in the head coverings are the symbolic emblems of the great status of these ladies as first class courtiers. From these reliefs in which women are depicted as courtiers, servants, minstrels and musicians, we can refer to the hunting at Taq-i Bustan. The reliefs in which Anahita are depicted include Narseh's investiture ceremony at Naqsh-i-Rustam, Piruz I's investiture ceremony at Taq-i Bustan and Anahita's profile at Darabgird.

Depicting deities and giving human personification to them is current to this period. Showing gods in human form is characteristic of Greek art in which the Olympian gods also have human effigies. The depictions of the gods and their statues are the emblems of Greek culture and dominance over various materials in Iran (Fig. 2). There was an investiture ceremony from the god on horseback before the Sassanian dynasty in Achaemenid art and a Sakas work from southern Russia confirms it (Fig. 3). Ghirshman suggests that these figures have been influenced by the West, for example Antiochus I in Commagene (Fig. 4), or in the East for example Kushans coins during the second and third centuries when Persian gods are depicted as humans (1976:133). But giving human personification to deities is seen in earlier times too, such as for example the Elamite seals discovered at Susa or rock reliefs at Kurangan (Fig. 5) and Naqsh-i Rajab.

In Sassanian rock reliefs deities like Ahura Mazda, Mithra and Anahita are depicted i.e a trinity which has been current from the Achaemenid to the Sassanian period. The face, figure, features and dressing of the Ahura Mazda and Mithra are similar to the king, and Anahita's depiction is the same as the queen. Gods are shown unarmed (Azarnoush, 1995:44) and have crenelated and uncovered crowns with the hair hugely decorated upon the head. In the *Avesta* - the holy Zoroastrian book - Ahura Mazda does not have human personification and his depictions in rock reliefs are contrary to this. There is also a clear difference between Anahita's descriptions in the Avesta and the contemporary rock reliefs at Taq-i Bustan and Naqsh-i-Rustam.

In the *Aban Yasht* in plots of 7, 13, 64, 101, 102, 123, 126- 129, Aredvi Sura Anahita is described as a young, charming, very strong maiden, well built, lovely arms as strong as a horse, high girdled, erect, noble in aspect to (her) illustrious lineage, in shoes worn to the ankle, golden latcheted and shining, wearing costly raiments, richly pleated and all golden and sometimes wearing golden armour or a garment made from three hundred beaver's skin, a girdle round her waist to form her bosom, having jewellery like golden earrings with four corners, a necklace and a crown with eight parts decorated with a hundred jewels, fair-formed, like a chariot body, golden, ribbon-decked, swelling forth with curve harmonious (Doostkhah, 1985:137-139, 152, 166-168).

We can find the origin of these contradictions in political reasons in which mythology and religion combine with politics and become a means for strengthening and legitimizing the government. The aim of the similarities between king and Ahura Mazda and queen with Anahita is in giving divinity status to them. In ancient Iranian beliefs the king was considered to be a symbol of power and people's volition and he was the only person that (after great the deity) deserved to be worshipped on the earth. He was the omnipotent ruler who had control over the people (Mashkor, 1966:1). They believed that the status of king was a divine donation from deity to king. Obedience to the king had divine blessing. God was the master of two worlds and the king was his representative on the earth (Arjomand, 1991:85-91). There are many documents and evidences about the false seeking of Sassanian kings in claiming divinity for their royalties such as the response of Ardashir Babakan to the letter of Ardavan V (216-224 CE) in which he explains his military operations against Parthians:

"The crown I have, is given from God and he enthroned me over the lands I captured. He helped me in killing rulers and kings" (Noldeke, 1979:48).

It seems that no region liked Iran especially the Sassanians who had followers with real tenets about divine status of the kings (Browne, 1956:193). On this basis, Ardashir Babakan attempted to pretend his kingdom as a divine right because he needed legality for achieving his goals. Furthermore, the titles of Sassanian kings are also emblems of their divine monarchy. Shapur I at Haji Abad inscription bears the title *"The divine Mazdayasnian, Shapur, king of kings of Iranians and Non-Iranians whose seed is from the gods."* (mazdesn bay Shapur I shahanshah eran and An-Eran) (Christensen, 1935:133). In ancient Iranian beliefs especially at the time of the Sassanians, only the person who has the Khwarrah (Divine Glory) of god can reach divine status. Khwarrah is a divine aura that if it radiates to one's heart, would gain him a higher status than his fellows. From this divine aura the person is deemed worthy of kingship and can rule over a country and bring peace and justice to his people (Pourdavood, 1979:3). Khwarrah appeared in different forms: sometimes as an eagle that gave information from the future to Ardashir and Cyrus (Xenephon, 1971:35), occasionally as a rooster that saved Ardashir Babakan from the malice and suspicion of Ardavan V's daughter (Mashkor, 1948:36). Khwarrah did not belong to anyone except the king's family, and came down to his children (Mousavi Haji, 1995:18). This divinity of reign was completed by a ring with ribbons which was the symbol of the Khwarrah of god and it was given from Ahura Mazda, and, rarely from Anahita to Sassanian kings. In fact this ring was the emblem of union and confederacy between king and god and a political idea was laid behind it. The Sassanian king got divine rights to rule by receiving this diadem of kingship which is the symbol of god's representation on the earth, and a part of divine power would be alloted to him so that he could bring about abundance, blessing and victory in war for his country (Pope, 2001:67). Receiving the diadem of kingship is also shown in seals from Susa. There are also rock reliefs with investiture scene from previous times such as the Annubanini rock relief at Sar pol-e zahab and a Parthian scene in which Ardavan V gives the diadem to the chief of Susa, *'Khwasak'* (Fig. 6). In Sassanian rock reliefs, the kings who are on horseback or on foot receive this diadem from Ahura Mazda whose face, figure, features and dress are similar to the king. The king has a crenelated crown that knotted curly hair emerging from the top and this is the symbol of his divine status. The only rock relief in which the diadem is given from Anahita to the king is located at Naqsh-i-Rustam in Fars. The goddess' face, figure, features and dress are similar to the queen.

Now with this introduction, the rock reliefs attributed to Anahita are discussed below.

Anahita's rock relief at Darabgird:

A small but very interesting bas relief of the lady is discovered at Darabgird which is situated below the more elaborate scene of the well-known victory relief of Ardashir I. (Fig. 7). This bas relief which is a part of the main relief, is depicted during Shapur I's reign. The attribution of the relief has been debated ever since and different views are given about the identity of the depicted king: whether he is Ardashir I or Shapur I. This scene resembles the well-known triumphal reliefs of Shapur I at Bishapur and Naqsh-i Rustam. Comparison and accommodation the details of the Darabgird rock relief especially the crown with other figures of Ardashir I and Shapur I demonstrate that the main character in this relief belongs to Ardashir I. Taking into account that both the relief location and the crown have a connection with Ardashir, one might speculate that it was conceived as a kind of homage by Shapur to Ardashir. As we know from literary sources and coins of Ardashir I, Shapur was appointed by his father to the kingdom while he was still alive so he wasn't crowned officially (Herrmann, 1969:87). Likewise a stone block was found in a spring-fed lake in front of the relief in which the Sassanian king depicted killing a lion (Fig. 8). The crown of the king in this block is similar to the crown of Shapur I in some of his coins (Shafia'i, 2004:91,92). The identification of the goddess Anahita is certain on the basis of her crenellated crown. Comparative material for such an isolated image as gods or ancestors of the kings can be found in the Parthian architecture on the façade of the south ivan of the temple in Hatra (Fig. 9) which is captured in 240 CE by Shapur I. Another example is on the floor mosaic of Shapur's palace at Bishapur (Fig. 10). The pictorial relationship between the main relief and the bust figure is seen in architectural structures of the late Parthian period at Dura Europos which was captured in 239 CE by Shapur I on the walls of the synagogue dedicated in 245 CE. Below the fresco panels depicting historical events are several *'dado'* panels with encircled female images wearing garlands (Fig. 11). A similar relationship can be also found in Palmyra between the large scale of the figures on the main relief and series of small bust figures encircled in medallions beneath it (Fig. 12).

In conclusion, it seems safe to propose that from a formal and typological point of view, the small bust of the goddess Anahita could have been placed below the main relief intentionally, as an integral part of the overall program (Levit- Tawil, 1992:196,199). Shapur I gained the art and culture of the western provinces of the Iranian empire (which were under control of Romans) by capturing them. The bust of Anahita is depicted 1/30 meters below the main relief in the small size in front of the spring-fed lake (Fig. 13). She is represented in a frontal view but her face is in complete profile. She has a crenellated crown which is similar to her crown on the Narseh relief at Naqsh-i Rustam (Fig. 16). The hair arrangement is rigid and knotted curls are emerging from the top of the crown. A short ringlet falls in front of the ear, and three long curls fall on the shoulders and chest. She has earrings and a necklace (Ibid:201). On the basis of her crown and the lake below the relief, Vanden Berghe suggests that the represented lady is Anahita, the goddess of fertility and water (1978:135-147). The crown, hair style and jewellery of the lady in this relief is comparable with Anahita at Naqsh-i Rustam. So we can identify her as Anahita; the battlements of her crown symbolize her warrior aspect, while the row of fluted loops which may feature stylized leaves allude to her as a fertility goddess. We can consider this relief, which is not as masterly as the first image of Anahita during the Sassanian dynasty. Some scholars such as Vanden Berghe and Dalia Levit- Tawil believe that the representation of Anahita outside the main scene implies her lesser status during Shapur I's kingdom, whereas in Ardashir I's investiture scene at Naqsh-i Rajab, the courtiers and nobles are depicted in the main scene and Ardashir I's wife appeared outside the scene in spite of her higher status (Fig. 14). Vanden Berghe believes that Shapur I did not believe in Anahita (going against his father) and he didn't allude to her at the Ka'ba-i Zardusht inscription (Ibid:135-147), whereas Shapur was in the charge of the guardian of the Anahita temple. Furthermore, Shapur built a glorious temple for Anahita in his new city, Bishapur. In the inscription of Ka'ba-i Zardusht Shapur noted the temple under the title of Nahid. So we can't consider Vanden Berghe's reasons logical. Dalia Levit- Tawil like Vanden Berghe believes that during Shapur I's reign Anahita's divine status was decreased so that there were not any pictures of her at this time (Ibid:135-147). But the disappearance of Anahita does not mandate a lesser status for her. For example, at the time of Ardashir I, there are no depictions of Anahita, but she has a high status and he offered the heads of his enemies to her temple (Tabari, 1999: 604). Likewise at the time of Ardashir I and Shapur I the king was the chief priest of temple himself, hence her role is significant during this time too. The appearance of Anahita outside the main scene is not a reason to see her as insignificant because if she is not outside it, her picture is never depicted. Vanden Berghe believes that the relief was created by followers of Anahita, not the king. This view is not acceptable because carving is a royal art (Herrmann, 1989:73) and no one except the king has the right to order depicting rock reliefs.[123]

Narseh's investiture scene from Anahita at Naqsh-i Rustam in Fars:

Among the Sassanian kings, Naresh (293-302 CE) is the only person who receives the diadem of kingship from Anahita, the goddess of fertility and protector of water instead of Ahura Mazda. This is probably the consequence of persecuting and torturing during the kingdoms of Bahram II and III in the name of Ahura Mazda by Kartir (Herrmann, 1994:119). Likewise by receiving the diadem of sovereignty from Anahita, Narseh depicted the heredity ceremony of Anahita in the Sassanian dynasty (Hinz, 2006:292). At the times of Narseh, the king himself undertook the role of chief priest of the Anahita temple (as in the times of Ardashir I and Shapur I and against Bahram II and III) - times in which it was under the control of Kartir. At the Paikuli inscription[124] which was created in commemoration of his victories, Narseh mentioned Anahita beside Ahura Mazda and all gods.[125] Narseh's crown has the symbol of Anahita[126] too (Fig. 15). These reasons are all signs of Anahita's significance at the times of Narseh. So it is not surprising that the diadem of sovereignity is given from Anahita instead of Ahura Mazda to Narseh.

Narseh's relief which is located at Naqsh-i Rustam in Fars is 5/70 meters long and 3/70 meters wide (Fig. 16). We know the king Narseh well from his crown which is carved at the centre of scene. He has a twisted mustache and long beard with the tip pulled through a ring and has bushy hair which falls around his neck. He is represented in a frontal view with the profile turning of the head to the lady who is standing opposite to him. He wears a necklace, earrings and a

---

[123] There is an exception and that is Kartir, the high priest during Bahram II's reign who was awarded much authority and left inscriptions and reliefs such as Sassanian kings as a memorial.

[124] This inscription written in both Parthian (Pahlavik) and Sasanian Middle Persian (Parsik) and is located at present Khaneqein in Iraq. In this inscription, Narseh emphasized that sovereignty over Persia given from deity and his ancestors. He also mentioned to the courtiers and supporters who helped him to reach this status (Lukonin, 2005:193).

[125] We are going to Iran Shahr in the name of the Ahura Mazda and all deities and Anahita (Ibid:191).

[126] The palmette on the crown refers to Anahita as a goddess of fertility and vegetation. This symbol seen on Narseh and Shapur III's crown (Sarkhosh Curtis, 2008:141). Stylized petal decoration of Anahita's crown also seen on her stucco bust from palace I at Kish and Taq-i Bustan rock relief.

closefitting tunic. He has a cloak over the tunic that ends joining together on the chest by two buttons and its trail is shown as a broad garment with intensive folds at the back. His wrinkled and loose trousers are intricately carved. He also wears shoes that have rippling ribbons which spill on the ground. His crown in this relief embodies fluted loops with a big globe installed upon it. This crown exactly resembles the crown in some of Narseh's coins. In front of the king, a lady is carved in a proper figure and sober shape, and (following the rules of ancient eastern depictions) her figure is shown larger than the king. Her clothes are similar to those which the king wears, a long mantle which is brought over the shoulders and which the wind has wrinkled from the waist to the bottom. It is caught at the chest with a double disk clasp and pendant ribbon ties. She also has a belt at the waist. The hemline sweeps out over the ground like boiling matter pouring on the earth reminiscent of shaking waves and the duty of the water goddess, Anahita (Ghirshman, 1976:176). She has a crenellated crown secured with broad ribbon ties that has knotted curly hair emerging from the top, of a type that is specialized to kings (Christensen, 2006:171). Her hair is piled on top of the head in a mass of curls and coiled into long tresses falling down the back and over the shoulders. A single lock curls down from the temple (Fig. 17). She has a beaded necklace and earrings. There is a child between the king and goddess, wearing royal robes like Narseh, who seems to be Narseh's grandson, Azar Narseh. Two courtiers or nobles are standing behind the king. The first person has a tall hat (kolah or headgear) in the form of a horsehead. His hand is raised towards his face as a sign of salutation. His cloth is similar to the king's cloth with a little difference. He has a torque probably made from gold. It seems that this figure represents Hurmuzd II. The figure of the second person is damaged by lapse of time and its details have disappeared completely (Mousavi Haji, 1998:132,133). The clothes are made from very light fabric which is moving in the wind and are different from Achaemenid coarse fabric (Houston, 2002:59). On the basis of reasons I shall give below, the authors of this article believe that the lady presented here is Anahita that her characteristics and duties are different from what has been mentioned in the *Avesta*. Since Sassanian art is royal and the king's willingness is important, so political goals penetrate the art and affect it. Therefore, it is not surprising that in the rock relief which is depicted under control of the king, Anahita's effigy is similar to the queen and different from her descriptions in *Avesta*. But some features like her tallness, well built shoulders, strong body, costly wrinkled dress, necklace and a belt hung around her waist all correspond to this relief.

Various interpretations have been expressed about this relief:

J. N. Curzon believes that there is no female figure in Sassanian rock reliefs. He identifies figures with braided hair, female muscles and a smooth face as eunuchs of the court! (1983:156). He refuses to identify the represented lady in this relief. R. Kerporter believes that this relief depicts Bahram V's (421-438 CE) marriage with an Indian princess (1821-1822:533,534) and C. Texier identifies him as Khusraw Parviz (590-628 CE) and his wife Shirin (1842:228). H. Rawlinson and A.D Mordtmann suggest that this relief shows the investiture scene of Bahram III (293 CE) from his mother. As mentioned before, the king's crown in this scene is exactly similar to Narseh's crown in his coins, thus the above reasons can be rejected. Alireza Shapur Shahbazi believes that the rock relief represents Narseh sharing his kingship with his queen, Shapurdokhtak II (1983:259). He gives a reason that the lady concealed her left hand inside her sleeve, so it must have been meant to represent a subordinate of the king, not the deity who is in a higher status than the king (1998:63). In rejection of this theory, first of all, the long sleeve is related to the manner of dress sewing, as the size of trousers is also long and her toes hidden. Secondly, the lady, bends the tips of her fingers to raise her trousers, therefore, the fingers are hidden in the sleeve. Finally, if this rock relief represents the reign between the king and queen, why is there no such reference in historical texts? Why there is no allusion to this matter in the Paikuli inscription that was established by Narseh in commemoration of his victories?

There are several reasons to reject Shapur Shahbazi's theory and attribute this rock relief to Anahita:

1- The lady in this scene has a crenelated crown that knotted curly hair emerging from the top. This kind of crown, as Christensen mentioned belongs to deity and in all the rock reliefs of that period (except the investiture relief of Piruz I at Tagh-i Bustan in Kermanshah in which Ahura Mazda appears in formal clothes (Fig. 25), indifferent to other rock reliefs), the supreme god Ahura Mazda wears this crown. So there is no doubt that she would be a deity.

2- Narseh, himself, in Paikuli inscription declares that he gained the sovereignty of Persia under the protection of Ahura Mazda and all the deities and Anahita the goddess. How would this be explained if the king introduces himself as 'Mazdaism Baq' in inscriptions and claims to have gained this sovereignty by Ahura Mazda and Anahita, but in his investiture scene, the symbol of kingdom is given to him from his wife?

3- In all the Sassanian rock reliefs, the king didn't get the royalty diadem from a mortal human directly.[127] The most evident characteristic of this diadem is a ribbon hanging from it which is recognised as one of the most important emblems of royalty.[128] Giving of the royal ring from a human being to Sassanian king was inconsistent with religious tenets. In ancient Iranian relief the king's status was a divine donation which is given from the deity to king and it is not possible that the royal ring (which is the symbol of the khwarrah of god and the god's representative on the earth) was given from a mortal human.

4- In all of Sassanian rock reliefs, the ladies lack a crenelated crown. Some wear a hat (kolah) and some of them depicted are without hats (kolah) and their hair decorated upon the head as a little globe. In all of these reliefs, the lady's clothes (dress and trousers) lack abundant pleats and ripples. This dress is like a boiling matter pouring on the ground and remaining, showing the shaking waves and duty of the water goddess, Anahita (Mousavi Haji, 1998:135,136).

5- Anahita's figure in this relief is similar to her picture on the reverse of Hurmozd I coins (Fig. 18) in which she appears with royal clothes and wears a crenellated crown that her knotted curly hair emerging from the top.

6- Anahita's costume and the way she lays her hand on the leg in this relief is similar to her stucco statuette from Haji Abad (Fig. 19) and her picture on the reverse of Bahram II coins (Fig. 20, 21) and also in a sculpted block from Istakhr[129] (Fig. 22).

7- On the basis of ancient eastern art the figures of gods are shown larger than the king. The presented lady in this relief also has a larger body than the king. So she would not be an ordinary human being because no one depicted larger than the king except deity. Even the body of the king is larger than the normal humans. So this goddess would be Anahita.

8- Some characteristics of Anahita in the Aban Yasht such as her tallness, wellbuilt shoulders, strong body, costly wrinkled dress, the

---

[127] In only the Salmas rock relief, Ardashir Babakan and Shapur I getting diadems from two humans but these rings lack the long and flying ribbons which is the emblem of khwarrah of god. So we can consider these diadems as victorious rings (Mousavi Haji, 1995:242).

[128] On the reverse of Parthian coins, the diadem which is given from the Greek deity to the king has fluttering ribbons.

[129] This stone block discovered from the Istakhr mosque which was the first Anahita temple (Bier,1883:307-316).

necklace and a robe belted at the waist to show her breast more beautifully, are also seen in Narseh's relief at Naqsh-i Rustam.

The similarities between the figure of Anahita in the Naqsh-i Rustam rock relief, Azar Anahita, the queen of queens at that time, in the Bishapur mosaic (Fig. 23) and also Azar Anahita in the Tang-i Qandil[130] rock relief (Fig. 24) declares that the queen of queens took her effigy from Anahita in order to give divinity to herself - and the aim of all these factors was giving legitimacy and divinity to the enthronement and the royal family.

Piruz's investiture scene from Ahura Mazda while Anahita is also depicted at Taq-i Bustan in Kermanshah:

There are two arches at the north eastern border of Kermanshah in which the small one depicts a scene during the reign of Shapur III and the larger one belongs to Piruz I. Five Sassanian rock reliefs are depicted inside the mentioned arches and also at their margins. In the small arch, Shapur II and his son Shapur III are represented along with the inscription which introduces them (Vanden Berghe, 2000:103). In the larger arch, two scenes are portrayed; the upper scene shows Piruz I's investiture scene. There are various views among scholars about the identity of the depicted king. K. Erdmann believes that the king is Piruz I (1937:79-97) while E. Herzfeld introduces him as Khusro Parwiz (1938:91-158) and Tanabe recognises him as Ardashir III. (1984:83-95). In the lower scene the mentioned king is depicted as armoured on a vigorous horse. On the side walls of this arch, two hunting scenes are depicted: the left side is deer hunting and the right is boar hunting. At the right hand of the mentioned arches the investiture scene of Ardashir II is depicted on the rock. In this scene, Ahura Mazda is shown along with Mithra (Haerinck,1999:57). At Piruz I's investiture scene from Ahura Mazda, the goddess Anahita is depicted behind the king while she is carrying a jug (Fig. 25). Furthermore, the women in hunting scenes seemed to be courtiers and nobles. The investiture scene of Piruz I from Ahura Mazda is carved in the larger arch and Anahita is also presented in the scene. The semicircular arch stands on two columns. Its opening is 7/30 meters, 6/70 meters in depth and 90 meters in height. At the margin of arch, decorative motifs such as trees are depicted. Above the column where the bases of the arch begin, the wrinkling plots are seen from each side which is also visible in formal clothes of

---

[130] In the relief of Tang-i Qandil, Azar Anahita, the wife of Shapur I, offering a flower of pomegranate to him which is the symbol of Anahita and Azar Anahita appeared as goddess Anahita (Sarfaraz, 1975:105).

Sassanian kings. There is a crescent shape over the arch which is decorated with royal plots. On each side of the crescent, two Roman-style victories bring the diadem of kingship. At the end of the arch inside it, two rock reliefs are depicted above each other. The upper scene shows the investiture scene of Piruz I from Ahura Mazda where Anahita is also presented. In this scene the king is standing in the centre and Ahura Mazda is depicted on the left and Anahita on the right. All of them are standing on the cubical platform. The frontal and lateral surface of the platform under the king's feet consists of two rows of patterns which are separated by a plot. In the upper plot, rows of heart-shaped quatrefoil flowers are depicted and in the lower plot, a row of circles and squares are repeated alternately and the spaces between them are filled with two balls. The frontal and lateral surface of the platform under the Ahura Mazda and Anahita's feet is also depicted with undulating patterns (Riyazi, 2003:199). The king lays his left hand in front of his stomach on the hilt of his sword which is perpendicular between his legs and receives the diadem of kingship from Ahura Mazda by his right hand. The crown of the king in this relief is similar to some of Piruz I's coins and is a crenelated crown which consists of two rows of beads and a moon crescent in the front. A large crescent is installed on top of the crown which is surrounded within a pair of wings, and a little globe consisting of three circumscribed circles is situated among the crescent. So there is no doubt that the depicted king at Taq-i Bustan would be Piruz I (Mousavi Haji, 2008:88).

The king wears wrinkled and loose trousers, a belt with rows of repeated circles and a long cloak with a little embossed circle that a bead joined to its centre, and rippling ribbons at the back. Ahura Mazda also has a crenellated crown like the king and his hair decorated as a globe, upon it and there are circles on it with three little embossed globes carved inside it. He wears a tunic and trousers like the king and a cloak decorated with flowers with six prongs on his shoulders. The margin of the cloak has a row of alternate circles. This cloak is fixed at the chest with a double disk clasp decorated with flowers with multiple prongs. The tunic is decorated with a three-circle compound pattern and rippling ribbons are fluttering at the back of Ahura Mazda. He has a necklace with a threebeaded pendant which is hanging from a ring attached to it, and earrings like the king and Anahita (Riazi, 2003:194-196). Ahura Mazda offers the diadem of kingship to the king with his right hand. Anahita is standing behind the king holding a water jug in her hand. Her crown in this relief relates to her function as a goddess of fertility and vegetation (Fig. 26) and consists of two rows of beads with an inset square plaque at the centre. The pattern of the upper margin consists of trefoil that has two lateral petals shaped in arcades and joined to the lower margin, and from this movement extended arcades created above the crown that a little branch of multi petals depicted among the arcades (Ibid:191). Her hair is gathered above the crown, a row of snail curls beneath the head plot frame the face, and a thick coil of hair drops from the temple to the breast. Two stacked rows of plaits flow over the shoulders (Fig. 27). Two rippling ribbons ties float at her back (Goldman, 1997:269). Her hair style in this relief is comparable with her stucco at Haji Abad (Fig. 28). She wears a full length, longsleeved tunic that has no design except its collar and cuff. She wears a loose, long-sleeved draped mantle fastened on the left shoulder (Fig. 29) and decorated with cruciate flowers surrounded in a circle that have petals of a special shape (Fig. 30). The margin of the mantle is also decorated with alternate circles. On her left shoulder a staged pattern shown but in this relief only a part of it on the right shoulder is visible. Above this pattern and exactly on the left shoulder, a patterned medallion consisting of a central circle with a flower which has twelve petals is seen (Fig. 31). This staged pattern is also visible at the left cuff (Riyazi, 2003:193,194). The mantle of the lady in this relief reminds us of the plot 129 in the *Aban Yasht* where Anahita wears a mantle made from the skin of three hundred female beavers (Doostkhah,1985:168). Furthermore, the star pattern of the medallion on Anahita's mantle reminds us of the descriptions of her crown with the star (Rajabi, 2003:380). The presented lady in this relief has earrings like the king and Ahura Mazda. She is carrying a diadem with fluttering ribbons which is similar to the one carrying by Ahura Mazda. She has also a jug in another hand while the water is pouring from it. Herzfeld believes that the jug in the hand of the mentioned woman introduces her as Anahita (2002:339).

From ancient times, the picture of a jug has been the symbol of heavenly water and divine blessing and soil fertilization (Christensen, 2006:328). Otherwise the jug is seen in a similar presentation of Anahita's stucco molding at Plotian Dargaz (Fig. 32, 33) and some Sassanian silver vessels (Fig. 34). So the presented lady in this relief is Anahita, the goddess of fertility and vegetation. Some scholars, especially classic tourists and geographers such as Istakhri (1968:167), Ebn-e Hoqal (1966:116) introduced her as Shirin, the wife of Khusro II. Although on the basis of the following reasons this attribution is not correct:

1- According to the crown, the depicted king is not Khusro Parwiz, so the presented lady can not be Shirin, the wife of Khusro II.

2- If the king is Khusro Parwiz, this lady can't be Shirin again, because she is holding the diadem of kingship which is the symbol of divinity of the king and this diadem could not be given from a mortal human to the king. In ancient Iranian beliefs, kingdom was a divine donation from the god or deity to the king.

3- Hypothetically, if the donation of the kingship diadem from a human being is possible, again it can't be logical from Shirin because she married Khusro Parwiz after he reigned (Mousavi Haji, 2008:89).

4- In Iranian art, sometimes a symbol is regarded as a means for explaining a specific goal. The jug in the hand of the lady in this relief which the water is pouring from, alludes to fertility, and the deity who is responsible for this duty is Anahita.

5- Summarizing historical events as a symbolic image is an ancient custom in the orient (Herzfeld, 2002:294). It seems that Sassanian artists created this relief in memory of rain falling after several years of drought which had begun during the second year of Piruz I reign (Mehrabadi, 2001:859). Probably Piruz I wanted to show the divine blessing i.e. kingdom and raining in this relief (Nafisi, 2005:257). Elsewhere, more than 50 stones of Anahita's temple at Kangavar carry the name of Piruz (Kambakhsh Fard, 1995:164) which is the sign of Piruz I's attachment to Anahita and reconstruction of the temple by him. The reconstruction of Takht-i Sulaiman[131] was also completed during his reign (Naumann, 2003:75).

Some scholars believe that the person who is standing at the left hand of the king is not Ahura Mazda, but he is a high priest of that time. This theory is not acceptable according to the following reasons:

1- If he is not Ahura Mazda, donation of the kingship diadem should be done by Anahita, not a high priest because in a scene that a divine person like Anahita is presented, a religious person who is not comparable with Anahita in view of status, can not donate the royal diadem to the king.

2- If he is a high priest, according to the Zoroastrian rules in Sassanian era, he should raise his hand against his face as a sign of salutation, that is not happening here (Mousavi Haji, 1995:85).

Conclusion:

In the *Aban Yasht*, Anahita is described differently from her effigy in the art works, and her identification is therefore difficult. As we know, artists created rock art by the king's command, based on his

---

[131] There is a temple for Anahita at Takht-i Sulaiman (Naumann, 2003:58).

plans and ideas. Hence, the artists give human personification to the deity to show that they are similar to the king and queen, in order to give spiritual and divine personification to them. In these reliefs the face, figure, toilet, jewellery, the royal ribbons hanging from the crown and dressing of the Ahura Mazda and Mithra are similar to the king and Anahita's depiction is the same as the queen.

On the whole we can mention to some of the characteristics of Anahita in rock arts as below:

1- Crenellated crown that has knotted curly hair emerging from the top and belongs to gods (Naqsh-i Rustam & Darabgird).

2- Ribbons hanging from the crown comparable with Anahita's descriptions in plot 128 in the Aban Yasht (Naqsh-i Rustam & Taq-i Bustan).

3- The jug which is the symbol of her as a goddess of water and fertility (Taq-i Bustan).

4- Donation of the ring with ribbons (which is the symbol of the Khwarrah of god) to the king (Naqsh-i Rustam).

5- Wearing clothes like Sassanian queens including a long dress with a mantle over it (Naqsh-i Rustam & Taq-i Bustan).

6- Wearing wavy clothes comparable with Anahita's descriptions in plot 126 in the *Aban Yasht* (Naqsh-i Rustam).

7- Using jewellery comparable with Anahita's descriptions in plot 127 in the *Aban Yasht* (Naqsh-i Rustam, Taq-i Bustan & Darabgird).

8- Hair styled like Sassanian queens i.e the hair emering from the top of the crown and falling on the shoulders and chest (Naqsh-i Rustam, Taq-i Bustan & Darabgird).

9-Stoutness and tallness comparable with Anahita's descriptions in plot 64 in the *Aban Yasht* (Naqsh-i Rustam & Taq-i Bustan).

10- The necessity of the crown on the goddess' head (Naqsh-i Rustam, Taq-i Bustan & Darabgird).

Figures:

Fig. 1: Annubanini and Ishtar, Sar pol-e zahab (Prada, 2004: Fig. 15)

Fig. 2: Parthian coin, Ardavan receiving the diadem of kingship from Tyche (Mohammad Panah, 2006:153)

Fig. 3: Southern Russia, investiture ceremony on horseback (Ghirshman: 1976: Fig. 169)

Fig. 4: Antiyakhus I and Apolo (Mithra), in Nimrud Dag (Ghirshman, 1976: Fig. 180)

Fig. 5: Kurangon, Two Deities (Humban & Kiririsha) and the Worshippers, (Prada, 2004: Fig. 41

Fig. 6: Susa, Ardavan V gives the diadem to Khwasak (Wieschofer, 1996: Plate XVIa)

Fig. 7: Darabgird, Bas Relief of Anahita (Levit- Tawil, 1992: Fig. 1)

Fig. 8: Darabgird, Shapur I Killing a Lion (Authors)

Fig. 9: Façade of Palace V Hatra (Herrmann, 1994:65)

Fig. 10: Mosaic of Shapur's Palace at Bishapur (Ghirshman, 1999: Plate X: 14)

Fig. 11: Fresco Wall, Synagogue, Dura Europos (Levit- Tawil, 1992: Fig. 5)

Fig. 12: Funerary Banquet Relief, Tomb of Malku at Palmyra (Colledge, 2006: Fig. 46)

Fig. 13: Bust of Anahita, Darabgird (Goldman, 1997: Fig. T.11)

Fig. 14: Ardashir I Rock Relief, Naqsh-i Rajab (Authors)

Fig. 15: Silver Drachm of Narseh (Mohammad Panah, 2006:165)

Fig. 16: Narseh relief at Naqsh-i Rustam (Authors)

Fig. 17: Anahita, Narseh relief at Naqsh-i Rustam (Goldman, 1997: Fig. A.11)

Fig. 18: Reverse of Hurmozd I coin (Goldman, 1997: Fig. A.8

Fig. 19: Stucco of Anahita, Haji Abad (Azarnoush, 1994: Plate XXI)

Fig. 20: Reverse of Bahram II coin (Goldman, 1997: Fig. A.9)

Fig. 21: Reverse of Bahram II coin (Goldman, 1997: Fig. A.10)

Fig. 22: Sculpted block from Istakhr (Authors)

Fig. 23: Azar Anahita, Bishapur mosaic (Ghirshman, 1999: Plate VII)

Fig. 24: Azar Anahita at Tang-i Qandil (Goldman, 1997: Fig. A.12)

Fig. 25: Piruz I's investiture ceremony, Taq-i Bustan, (Authors)

Fig. 26: Anahita's Crown, Taq-i Bustan (Riazi, 2003: Fig. 80)

Fig. 27: Anahita's Hair decoration, Taq-i Bustan (Goldman, 1997: Fig. T.12)

Fig. 28: Anahita's stucco, Haji Abad (Azarnoush, 1994: Pls XXII, XXIII)

Fig. 29: Anahita's cloth, Taq-i Bustan (Goldman, 1997: Fig. A.15)

Fig. 30: Medallion on the mantle of Anahita, Taq-i Bustan (Herzfeld, 2002: Fig. 421)

*Fig. 31: Medallion on the left shoulder of Anahita Taq-i Bustan
(Herzfeld, 2002: Fig. 421)*

*Fig. 32: Bandian Dargaz, Anahita carrying a jug (Rahbar, 1998:
Planche VII)*

*Fig. 33: Bandian Dargaz, Investiture scene while Anahita is also
presented (Rahbar, 1998: Fig. 9)*

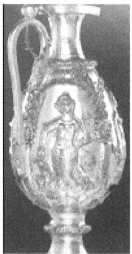

Fig. 34: Anahita, Sassanian Silver Vessel (Mohammad Panah, 2006: 198)

Further Reading:

Arjomand, Said Amir, (1991) *The Shadow of God on Earth and Hidden Imam*. Chicago: University of Chicago Press

Azarnoush, M. (1994) *The Sassanian Manor House at Hajiabad, Iran*. Monography Di Mesopotamia III, Florence: Firenze, case Editrice Letter

Azarnoush, M. (2007) *Two Mementos from a Brilliant Period in Iranshahr History*. In *Archaeognosy (Bastanpazhuhi)*, Vol. 2.4:65-81

Azarnoush, M. (1995) *Shapur II, Ardashir II, Shapur III: Another Perspective, A Suggestion for Rewriting a Part of Sasanian History*. In *Iranian Journal of Archaeology and History*, Vol. 10.1:37-45

Bier, L. (1883) *A Sculpted, Building Block from Istakhr*. In *Ami*, Plot 16:307-316

Browne, E. (1956) *A Literary History of Persia from the Earliest Times until Firdowsi Period Vol 1* (Translated into Persian by Ali Pasha Saleh). Tehran: Ebne Sina Press

Christensen, A. (1935) *L'Iran Sous Les Sassanides* (Translated into Persian by R. Yasemi). Tehran: Sedaye Moaser Press

Christensen, A. (2006) *L' Empire des Sassanides Le Peuple, L' Etat, La cour* (Translated into Persian by Mojtaba Minooy). Tehran: Comision-e Maaref Press

Colledge, M. (2006) *Parthians* (Translated into Persian by M. Rajabnia). Tehran: Hirmand Press

Curtis, V.S. (2008) *Royal and Religious Symbols on Early Sassanian Coins, Current Research*. In *Sassanian Archaeology, Art and History: Proceedings of a Conference held at Durham University, November 3rd and 4th, 2001,* Derek Kennet & Paul Luft (eds). England: Alden Press

Curzon, G.N. (1983) *Persia and Persian Question* (Translated into Persian by Gh. V. Mazandarani). Tehran: Elmi va Farhangi Press

Daems, A. (2001) *The Iconography of Pre-Islamic Women in Iran*. In *Iranica Antiqua* Vol XXXVI:1-150

Doostkhah, J. (1985) *Avesta*. Tehran: Morvarid Press

Ebn-e Hoqal (1966) *Soreho Alarz* (Translated into Persian by Jafar Shoar). Tehran: Bonyad-e Farhang-e Iran Press

Erdmann, K. (1937) *Das datum des Taq-i Bustan*. In *Ars Islamica* Vol. IV:79-97

Ghirshman, R. (1976) *Iran, Parthians and Sassanians* (Translated into Persian by B. Faravashi). Tehran: Tarjome va Nashr-e Ketab Press

Ghirshman, R. (1999) *Bichapour Vol. 2* (Translated into Persian by A. Karimi). Tehran: Iranian Cultural Heritage Organization

Goldman, B. (1997) *Women's Robing in the Sassanian Era*. In *Iranica Antiqua*, Vol. XXXII:233-300

Haerinck, E. (1999) *L'Art des Bas- Reliefs Rupestres*. In *Dossiers d' Archeologie* No. 243:54-61

Herrmann, G. (1969) *The Darabgird Relief - Ardashir or Shapur?* In *Iran* Vol. 7:63-81

Herrmann, G. (1989) *The Arts of Persia*. New Haven & London: Yale University Press

Herrmann, G. (1994) *The Iranian Revival* (Translated into Persian by Mehrdad Vahdati). Tehran: Nashr-e Daneshgahi Press

Herzfeld, E. (2002) *Iran in the Ancient East* (Translated into Persian by Homayoun Sanatizade). Shahid Bahonar University of Kerman

Herzfeld, E. (1938) *Khusrau Parwis und Taq-i Bustan*. In *Arch. Mitt. aus. Iran*, Vol. IX:91-158

Hinz, W. (2006) *Altiranische Funde Und Forschungen* (Translated into Persian by P. Rajabi). Tehran: Qoqnoos Press

Houston, M. G. (2002) *Sassanid Costume* (Translated by M. Seyedin). In *Archaeognosy (Bastanpazhuhi)* Vol. IV.9:59-63

Istakhri, (1968) *Almasalek va Almamalek* (Translated by Iraj Afshar). Tehran: Bongah-e Tarjome va Nashr-e Ketab Press

Kambakhsh Fard, S. (1995) *The Anahita Temple at Kangavar*. Tehran: Iranian Cultural Heritage Organization

Kerporter, R. (1821-1822) *Travels Georgia, Armania and Ancient Babylonia 2 Vols*. London

Levit-Tawil, D. (1992) *The Syncretistic Goddess Anahita in Light of the Small Bass Relief at Darabgird: Her Imagery on Early Sassanian Rock Reliefs and Seals*. In *Iranica Antiqua* Vol 27:189-225

Lukonin, V.G. (2005) *Persian Civilization Under the Sasanian* (Translated into Persian by E. Reza). Tehran: Elmi va Farhangi Press

Mashkor, M.J. (1966) *The Kings Status in Ancient Iran*. In *Barrasiha-ye Tarikhi (Persian Journal)* Vol. 1.1-2:1-9

Mashkor, M.J. (1948) *Karnameh Ardeshir Papakan*. Tehran: Danesh Press

Mehrabadi, M. (2001) *Complete History of Ancient Persia*. Tehran: Afrasyab Press

Mohammad Panah, B. (2006) *Ancient Land*. Tehran: Sabzan Press

Mousavi Haji, S.R. (1995) *Research in the Sassanian Reliefs*. M.A. Dissertation, Department of Archaeology, Faculty of Humanities, Tarbiat Modares University

Mousavi Haji, S.R. (1998) *The Lady Presented in Narseh's Relief: Shapurdokhtak or Anahita?* In *Journal of Humanities University of Sistan and Balouchestan* Vol 4.1:129-145

Mousavi Haji, S.R. (2008) *Another Reflection to the Rock Reliefs of Taq-i Bustan*. In *Honar-ha-ye-Ziba* (Journal of Fine Arts University of Tehran), No. 35:85-92

Nafisi, S. (2005) *History Civilization of Iran during Sassanians*. Tehran: Asatir Press

Naumann, R. (2003) *Die Ruinen Von Tacht-e Suleiman und Zendan-e Suleiman* (Translated into Persian by Faramarz Nadjd Samii). Tehran: Iranian Cultural Heritage Organization

Noldeke, Th. (1979) *Geschichte der Perser und Araber zur Zeit der Sasaniden* (Translated into Persian by Abbas Zaryab Khoyi). Tehran: Anjoman-e Asar-e Meli Iran Press

Pope, A.U. (2001) *Masterpieces of Persian art* (Translated into Persian by Parviz Natel Khanlari). Tehran: Elmi va Farhangi Press

Pourdavoud, E. (1979) *Yashts Vol. II*. Tehran University Press

Prada, I. (2004) *The Art of ancient Iran Pre-Islamic Cultures* (Translated into Persian by Y. Majidzade). Tehran University Press

Rahbar, M. (1998) *Decouverte d' un monument d' époque sassanide a Plotian, Dargaz (Nord Khorassan)*. Fouilles 1994 et 1995 in *Studia Iranica* Tome 27:213-251

Rajabi, P. (2003) *The lost Milleniums: Sasanian Vol. V.* Tehran: Toos Press

Riyazi, M. R. (2003) *Patterns and Depictions of Sasanian Clothes.* Tehran: Ganjin-e Honar Press

Sarfaraz, A.A. (1975) *Anahita, the Great Temple of Bishapur.* In *Archaeological Reports (3) on the Occasion of the 9th Annual Symposium on Iranian Archaeology.* Tehran: Iranian Centre for Archaeological Research Press

Shafia'i, F. (2004) *A Second Sassanian Relief at Darabgird.* In *Archaeognosy (Bastanpazhuhi)* Vol. 6.12:89-94

Shapur Shahbazi, A. (1983) *Studies in Sassanian Prospography Narse's Relief at Naqs-i Rustam.* In *Archaeologisch Mittei Lungen Aus Iran.* Berlin: Deutschen Archaeologischen Institut

Shapur Shahbazi, A. (1998) *Studies in Sassanian Prospography III., Barm-I Dilak: Symbolism of Offering Flowers.* In *Art and Archaeology of Ancient Persia,* Curtis, V.S. & Hillenbrand, R. & Rogers, J.M. (eds). The British Institute of Persian Studies

Tabari & Roshan, M. (trans) (1999) *Tarikh Nameh.* Soroush Press

Tanabe, K. (1984) *Royal Boar- Hunting of the Left wall, Taq-i Bustan* IV (text). Tokyo

Texier, C.H. (1842) *Description de L'Armenia, Lapese, Lameso Potamie, etc.* Paris

Vanden Berghe, L. (2000) *Archeologie de L' Iran Ancient* (Translated into Persian by E. Behnam). Tehran: Tehran University Press

Vanden Berghe, L. (1978) *La Decouverte d' une Sculpture Rupestre a Darabgird.* In *Iranica Antiqua* Vol 13:135-147

Wieschofer, J. (1996) *Ancient Persia.* London: I. B. Tauris & Co Ltd

Xenephon & Mashayekhi, R. (trans) (1971) *Cyrus Nameh 6th book.* Tehran: Bongah-e Tarjome va Nashr-e Ketab Press

Tablet 1: Sassanian Rock Reliefs Attributed to Anahita

	Darabgird	Naqsh-i Rustam	Taq-i Bustan
Place	Darabgird	Naqsh-i Rustam	Taq-i Bustan
Scene	Victory Scene	Investiture scene	Investiture scene
King	Shapur I	Narseh	Piruz I
Crown / kolah	Crenellated crown	Crenellated crown	the upper margin consists of trefoil that two lateral petals shaped to arcades and joined to the lower margin and from this movement extended arcades created above the crown that a little branch of multi petals depicted among the arcades
Clothes	-	A long sleeved tunic, a mantle brought over the shoulders caught at the chest with a double disk clasp and pendant ribbon ties, a belt at the waist	A full length, long- sleeved tunic and a long sleeved and decorated mantle over
Hair Style	Knotted curly hairs are emerging from the top of the crown. A short ringlet falls in front of the ear, three long curls fall on the shoulders and chest	a mass of curls and coiled into long tresses falling down the back and over the shoulders. A single lock curls down from the temple. Two rippling ribbons ties float at the back	Hair gathered above the crown, a row of snail curls beneath the head plot frame the face, a thick coil of hair drops from the temple to the breast. Two stacked rows of plaits flow over the shoulder. Two rippling ribbons ties float
Position	Bust	Giving the diadem of kingship to the king	The diadem of Kingship and a jug in the hands
Jewellery	Earrings, beaded necklace	Earrings, beaded necklace	Earrings

A New Look at the Sassanian Silver Ewer with Mythical Depictions

by Rahele Koulabadi, Seyed Mehdi Mousavi Kouhpar, Morteza Ataie

Abstract

The name of Anahita appeared after the name of Ahura Mazda and before the name of Mithra for the first time on Persian ancient relics, during the reign of the Achaemenid king Artaxerxes II (404-358 BCE). As a religious belief, it was seen later on the Sassanian silver ewer in a symbolic way. On the body of this ewer, Anahita is depicted under the arched frame while Mithras is carrying a bull on his shoulders beside her. This article intends to undertake a scrutiny study of motifs on this ewer from an artistic viewpoint and to address its mythical and religious aspects in order to make comparisons between our conclusion and the description of Anahita in the *Aban Yasht* and Mithras with his reliefs in the Roman world.

Key Words: Anahita, Aban Yasht, Mehr (Mithra), Mithras

Introduction

The study of the Sassanian pictorial and artistic works clearly leads to religious depictions (Sarfaraz & Avarzamani, 2004:90). Deities and mythical creatures along with their symbols which have been portrayed on many objects, such as rock reliefs, seals, coins, metal works and inscriptions are regarded as the main sources for studying Persian mythology and religion.

On the body of the mentioned ewer, there are pictures of a woman and a man who seem to be Anahita and Mithras (Fig. 1).

Aredvi-Sura-Anahita is the goddess of water, rain, abundance, vegetation, fertility, blessing, motherhood, birth, marriage, love, and victory; she is one of the assistants of Ahura Mazda. In the calendar of ancient Persia, the 10th day of each month and the 8th month of each year got their names from they deity Aban. In the 10th day of Aban in the day and month of the same name, the Abangan festival was held (Afifi, 1995:402). The fifth yasht, the *Aban Yasht*, with 30 passages and 132 subsections, is dedicated to Anahita. In plots 7, 15, 64, 78, 123 and126-129, Anahita has been described as a young, charming, very strong maiden, who is well built, with lovely arms as strong as a horse, high girdled, erect, noble in respect to (her) illustrious lineage, in shoes worn to the ankle, golden latcheted and shining, in costly garments, richly pleated and golden and sometimes with golden armour or a cloak made from three hundred beaver skins, a girdle round her waist to form her bosom, having jewellery such as golden square shaped earrings, a necklace and a crown with eight parts decorated with a hundred jewels, golden, ribbon-decked, swelling forth with harmonious curves. (Doostkhah, 1992:298, 300, 309, 311, 320-321). Furthermore, she seems to have some duties, such as: being the source of life and all the waters on the earth, the source of all fertility, purifying the seeds of all males, sanctifying the wombs of all females, purifying the milk in the mother's breasts, increase, property and the land; she is a curative, powerful goddess and the survival of the country depends on her (Ibid:297-298). The name of Anahita appeared under the reign of the Achaemenid king Artaxerxes II (404-358 BCE) beside the name of Ahura Mazda and Mithra for the first time, and, this trinity is worshipped until the Sassanian period.

Mithra (Mehr) is also one of the ancient Aryan deities, who has a high status in the Mazdaism religion. He is the god of battle, victory, power, friendship, brightness, the guardian of contracts, truth, family and country. In the calendar of ancient Persia, the 16th day of each month and the 7th month of each year got their names from Mehr. On the 16th day of Mehr in the day and the month of the same name, the Mihragan festival was held (Afifi, 1995:626). The tenth yasht, the *Mehr Yasht*, with 35 passages and 146 plots, is dedicated to Mehr. In the *Rig Veda*, Mithra is introduced as the keeper of the earth and the sky, of human beings and all five races (Aryan people) rely on him who is powerful in assistance (Jalali Naini, 1993:27, 28). The name of Mithra is seen beside Varuna and other Indian gods in a tablet which was found in Boghaz kavi dating to 1400 BCE (Amoozgar, 2006:19). His rituals spread to the west and he was worshipped there as Mithras in a different manner comparing to Persian Mehr (Mithra). There are depictions of Mithras in Roman lands with no written sources, whereas, in Persia, there are no depictions of rituals related to Mithra in existence. The Mehr Yasht is the only source enabling us to become familiar with his ceremonies (Hinnels, 1973:78).

The ewer in this study previously belonged to the Stroganoff Collection and has been lost, with only a drawing of it having been preserved (Orbeli, 1938:734).

The ewer is decorated with a beaded moulding that separates the pear-shaped body from the cylindrical neck and the body from the tall foot. On the body of the ewer underneath an arch, a woman is standing on a platform over two peacocks. She is holding a dove and a naked baby. The aforementioned picture is framed by an arch with rows of birds and is being carried on the shoulders of two naked persons. Furthermore, a naked man carrying a bull on his shoulders is depicted as being beside her.

The woman underneath the arch

The main motif seen on the ewer is that of a lady wearing a long-sleeved dotted shirt made from light fabrics with the result that her nipples, navel and public triangle are all visible. She is also wearing a blouse over a waist band. There are decorated medallions on her knees. A broad shawl of equally flimsy fabric is worn across her arms. Her hair is combed up onto her crown and tied into a large ball of curls in a topknot, with a row of waves, on either side of the head. She is heavily adorned with jewellery, including a necklace, anklets and wrist bracelets. She is presented with a nimbus around the head, which is the symbol of sacred character. Two broad ribbon ties float behind.

Apart from the royal figures depicted on the body of silver vessels associated with the Sassanian silverwork, it seems that the female figures in dancing or walking positions have the largest number of depictions on the surviving objects of this period. These motifs are usually depicted on the body of a variety of vessels including vases, ewers, plates and bowls, with vases predominating. The exterior surface of the vessels, particularly in ewers and vases, is usually divided into two, four or six segments in the form of arched frames, each showing a female figure (Mousavi Kouhpar, 2006:84). These frames consist of arches and capitals, including vine-scrolls with bunches of grapes, foliate patterns, flowers and birds. They occasionally show a shawl, carried by women holding each end of it in either hand above their heads. The women appear in different positions, standing, dancing and playing music. They are often shown while holding different things, such as musical instruments (e.g. flute, guitar, harp, panpipe, oboe, clappers), animals (e.g. bird, dog, panther, fox), plants (e.g. a single flower, a bunch of flowers), fruits (e.g. pomegranate, grapes), vessels (e.g. bucket, ewer, a bowl heaped with fruit), objects (e.g. diadem, box, a bone for a dog, torch), the hand of a small nude child or the end of a shawl. Some items seem to be depicted repeatedly, such as birds in various small sizes beside the women or in their hands (Gunter & Jett, 1992:286). A few symbols such as a dog, a panther and child are sometimes omitted on some vessels (Harper, 1971:505). In terms of clothing, the women appear in three forms: utterly dressed, stark naked and semi-nude diaphanously clad; the latter predominating over the other types. Their hair is usually topped by a small cap with a chignon above it, or they have ringlets at the ears which are held together by a diadem (Daems, 2001:59). This hair style is seen during the Hellenistic period (Fig. 2). In some cases there is a nimbus around the head.

The date and provenance of the majority of these vessels is uncertain. This makes a correct chronological classification rather difficult. Lukonin suggested that such products might belong to Shapur II period (2011:207), whereas Harper believed in a date around the 6th century CE (2002:669).

The identification and meaning of the female figures on these vessels have been extensively discussed by scholars. Some scholars strongly suggest that the females depicted in such motifs are in accordance to the females" iconic similarity with the lady who appears in the rock reliefs of Naqsh-i Rustam (Fig. 3) and Taq-i Bustan (Fig. 4), which would undoubtedly be representations of the goddess Anahita. Their main evidence is based upon similarities seen between the globe shape above the lady's crown at Naqsh-i Rustam and also the ewer held in her hand at Taq-i Bustan, with its parallel appearing on the body of silver vessels. In the same way, there would be similarities between the necklace worn by Anahita at Naqsh-i Rustam and the bucket held in her hand with its parallels amongst the female figures on the body of silver vessels (Orbli, 1938:734-5; Shepherd, 1964:84). Contrarily, other scholars believe that there is no evidence in religious or any other documents to explain the nudity of Anahita; she is royally clad (Marshak, 1998:89), while a majority of ladies on silver vessels appeared in a nude form; implying the females on silver vessels might represent characters other than Anahita (Graber, 1967: 60-5; Harper, 1971:515; Carter, 1974:201).

Orbeli compared the figures of several Sassanian vessels with two rock reliefs of Anahita at Naqsh-i Rustam and Taq-i Bustan. He also compared the figures with Anahita's characteristics and duties addressed in the Avesta. He has concluded that such representations of the female figure are personifications of Anahita in Sassanian art

(1938:734-5). Hanfmann believed that such a motif clearly shows the Persian imitation of the Mediterranean prototype of the Horae with attributes of the four seasons, but bearing Persian cultural significance (1951:1211). Shepherd claimed that the scenes in these vessels might represent the merging of the cult of Dionysus with some aspects of the worship of Anahita during the Hellenistic period, continuing through into the Sassanian period. She also mentioned that artists from the Seleucid and Parthian periods had imitated the Greeks, their way of rendering the female figure being used as a prototype. So, the figures on the vases, each according to the symbols which they hold, show different characteristics or attributes of the goddess Anahita. For instance, the bucket and the bird are her symbols as goddess of water; the vine and the flower are her symbols as the goddess of vegetation; the dog is her symbol as the guardian of the home and the flocks; the bowl of fruit is her symbol as the goddess of agriculture; and the child and pomegranate are her symbols as the goddess of fertility (1964:82, 84). G. Azarpay has interpreted scenes of the figures holding musical instruments as illustrations of the *den*, the soul's accomplishments in the material world; according to Zoroastrian texts, the *den* would be a concept personified as a *'beautiful female form'* (1967:37-48). Lukonin spoke significantly of *'toreutics of the feast cycle'* (Trever & Lukonin, 1987:81-103) stressing the connection of such silver vessels with the many Zoroastrian feasts. R. Ghirshman believed that these motifs were derived from the Gupta figures (1976:214). U. Schrato thought that these motifs are affected from Greek-Byzantine motifs (2004:89). Graber suggested that there was no evidence in what we know of Sassanian religious beliefs to make such identification with Anahita. He said these are only secular motifs (1967:60-65). Harper did not attempt to deal with the meaning of scene. Curiously, she tried to find out the derivation of each icon and finally concluded that there was a common artistic language in the mid-first millennium CE between the eastern Mediterranean countries and the near east. She also added that the near eastern artisans copied some sets of designs, in particular those of seasons from the west (1971:514, 515). Richard Ettinghausen interpreted them as secular or cultic motifs (1972:3-10). Martha Carter, in her study of the royal feast theme on Sassanian silverwork, tended to regard the female figures as bacchantes connected with different types of Sassanian festivals such as Muzdghiran, Nowrouz, Sadhak, Khuramroz, Vaharjashn, Tiraghan, Mihragan and Abhrizagan (1974:201). She also suggested that the main use of such vessels was in the court for the important celebration of Nowrouz (1978:61). The authors of this paper have different view about the interpretation of the scenes based on the existing evidence and also religious sources as below:

The evidence from previous studies: Showing females naked would have been influenced by the west and was definitely under the influence of the contemporary motifs that occurred in the eastern Mediterranean region (Levit-Tawil, 1992:217). There is, however, an imitation process from a foreign culture into assimilation and modification incorporating Iranian cultural meanings.

In Iran during the Parthian era, which was under the influence of Hellenistic culture, figures of women were seen in naked forms like a capital at Qaleh-i Yazdigird (Fig. 5) or a glazed coffin decorated with dancing females (Fig. 6). On the other hand, during Parthian and even later in the Sassanian period, the artists were trying to find parallel gods between the Persian and western lands. In fact, the artists often chose some external elements which were close to their own culture and made a new composition to express their intentions.

Dionysus is believed to be attributed with the creation of milk, honey and wine (Luker, 1987:97). As some duties of Anahita seem to be common with Dionysus, the artists would then envisage Anahita in the form of Dionysus and use some other elements in the Dionysus scenes such as musicians, grapes or one animal drinking from a jar. They however believed that their mythical function was changed (Moussavi Kouhpar and Taylor, 2008:131).

The mythology and contemporary works: In the past human life was very dependent on nature and the environment. This situation made men believe in divine aspects inherent in the natural forces and so also to worship them. They created special characters concerned with one or other natural resource or phenomena and personified them in their myth and religion in the form of a male or female deities, and depicted them in art and on other monuments.

In Iran environmental conditions also had a profound effect on the life, culture, thought and religion of the people (Mousavi Kouhpar, 2006:88). Iran is known as a dry land where water has an important role in the life of the people and was as a result regarded as one of the basic restrictions. They therefore created Anahita as a goddess of water and fertility and praised her to attract her protection. As previously mentioned, she was described in *Avesta* in a way which is different from her appearance at Naqsh-i-Rustam and Taq-i-Bustan where she was shown with royal attire (Marshak, 1998:89). This does not mean that she would not have appeared nude, as royal and political subjects are completely different from religious and symbolic concepts. This fact would not preclude the existence of such a depiction of Anahita on other objects. Furthermore, it should be considered that there is a clear difference between the clothes of Anahita at Naqsh-i-Rustam and Taq-i-Bustan. If the clothing is accepted as the only criteria for her recognition on the silver vessels, a question might be raised here regarding whether the type of clothing, as worn on those rock reliefs, should be preferred as the main criteria? In addition to that, the clothing that she and her companions wore on the rock reliefs was official dress and was also heavily affected by local culture and regional climate. These would therefore result in a conclusion that she could not appear nude in other scenes (Mousavi Kouhpar, 2006:89). On the other hand, the description of Anahita in the *Aban Yasht* and other contemporary objects attributed to Anahita seems to be extraordinarily close to female figures seen on the silver vessels as below:

1- She has been described as a life-giving goddess, the four elemental symbols of life can be recognised within the scenes, which include the human in the form of a baby (Fig. 7); the animal in the form of dove (Fig. 8), dog or beaver; the water with its symbolic signs which are the ewer and bucket (Fig. 9); and vegetation in the form of different types of fruits (Fig. 10) and flowers (Ibid:91).

2- In Plot 101 of *Aban Yasht*, her beautiful house is described with hundreds of shiny windows and thousands of well built columns upon which the house was built (Doostkhah, 1992:316). Therefore the arched frame within which the ladies are placed might be the symbol of the house described in the *Aban Yasht*. This theory might be rejected because the framing is merely an artistic device to give prominence to the figures. However, there are many ways to distinguish between the figures, implying the choice of an architectural device such as the framing must have been attributed to other contexts. It can be considered therefore that the framings might have a double function, at once separating scenes showing different aspects of the goddess and simultaneously suggesting a context of worship at a holy place (Mousavi Kouhpar, 2006:87). The temples of Anahita in Hamadan (Gutschmid, 2000:59) and also Kangavar (Fig. 11) and Takht-i Suleiman (Fig. 12) have columns too.

3- The nimbus depicted around the head of some females is the symbol of sacred character and can be seen in some images of Anahita, such as the capitals of Chehelsotoun in Isfahan (Fig. 13) and Taq-i-Bustan, a clay bullae from Takht-i Sulaiman (Fig. 14) and also on the reverse of Kanishka (Kushans king) coins (Fig. 15).

4- The flying ribbons and rich jewellery are also comparable with the images of Anahita at Darabgird (Fig. 16), Naqsh-i-Rustam and Taq-i-Bustan and her descriptions in the Aban Yasht.

5- In all Sassanian rock reliefs, the king receives the royal diadem - the symbol of khwarrah of god, and the god's representative on the earth - from Ahura Mazda, Anahita and Mithra. The most evident characteristic of this diadem is a ribbon hanging from it which is recognised as one of the most important emblems of royalty. At Naqsh-i-Rustam and Taq-i-Bustan rock reliefs, Anahita is holding this diadem which is comparable with the diadem held by the ladies in some ewers (Fig. 17).

6- In Persia from prehistoric and historical periods, many naked mother goddess statues have been discovered (Fig. 18). .These females are symbols of fertility and abundance. So it may be possible that the naked females on ewers are the goddess of fertility and plenty of its time i.e. Anahita. On the other hand, we have other depictions of Anahita during this time in which she appeared in a naked manner (Fig. 19).

7- On the silver plate which is showing Anahita held by an eagle (or perhaps Simurgh), a bunch of grape in her hand, her hair style, bare body and jewels (necklace, bracelets, anklets) are similar to some female figures on ewers (Fig. 20).

8- On a quartz bowl from the Sassanian period, a lady is depicted carrying a fish (Fig. 21). Her figure, clothes, hairstyle and jewels are exactly the same as the female figures on ewers. Fish are a symbol of Anahita as the goddess of water.

9- The hair decoration of Anahita at the Taq-i Bustan rock relief and her stuccos at Haji Abad are similar to some of the female figures on the ewers.

10- At Taq-i Bustan rock relief and wall engravings at Bandian Daragaz (Fig. 22), Anahita is carrying a jug like the females on ewers (Fig. 23).

Based upon the similarities addressed above, the lady can be identified as Anahita.

Peacock

Peacock is one of the motifs which has been occasionally depicted on the ewers beside the females (Fig. 24), in their hands (Fig. 25) or like the ewer underneath the platform on which the lady has stood. The relationship between peacock and Sarasvati might present an idea about the meaning of peacock on the ewers. In the Indian *Rig Veda*, Sarasvati was introduced as the best mother, the best river and the best deity. She has similarities with Aredvi-Sura-Anahita as listed below:

1- Sarasvati and Aredvi-Sura-Anahita ride a chariot pulled with four horses. One of the horses, Vayu, is identical in both chariots.

2- In *Rig Veda*, Sarasvati is not only a goddess but also a river in heaven like Aredvi-Sura-Anahita in *Avesta*.

3- Both of them are related to fertility and pregnancy (Gaviri, 2006:32).

4- Three functions of Sarasvati (i.e. chastity, heroic and motherhood) which are hidden in her name are comparable with Anahita's functions (i.e. innocence, strength and dampness) which are similarly hidden in her name (Duchesne Guillemin, 1996:229).

5- The peacock seems to be the common sacred animal between Sarasvati (Ions, 1983:85) and Anahita (Cotterell & Storm, 2005:263).

Dove

Birds have often appeared on the ewers in different types and sizes along with the female figures. On this particular ewer, doves have decorated the arch and are held by Anahita. It is believed that doves are related to Anahita as a patron of love (Orbeli, 1938:734).

Naked baby

In plot 87 in the *Aban Yasht*, it is emphasized that young pregnant women at the time of childbirth must supplicate to Anahita to have an easy birth (Doostkhah, 1992:313). So, the appearance of a child in the hand of the lady might be referring to Anahita as the symbol of the sacred midwife who made childbirth easy for women.

Naked figure carrying a bull on his shoulders

A bas-relief from the Roman cult of Mithras, shows that Mithras found the sacred bull grazing peacefully in a meadow. He clutches the animal round the neck but the wild and powerful beast is able to break away and drags Mithras with him at great speed. The god, however, does not relax his grasp until in the end and with a great effort he succeeds in forcing it to the ground. Mithras bore the bull away on his shoulders towards the cave. He slew the bull. From the dead body of the bull the life of plants and animals emerged. He will also strike water from a rock, which will then become an eternal spring. So the bull is the symbol of fertility and abundance.

In this ewer a naked figure is carrying a bull on his shoulders which is similar to Mithras reliefs. In the Walbrook Mithraeum in London a similar scene is depicted (Fig. 26). The symbolic significance of carrying of the bull in the Roman cult of Mithras is further supported by the following lines from the Santa Prisca Mithraeum in Rome:

"This young bull which he carried on his golden shoulders according to his ways. And after which I have received it I have borne on my shoulders the greatest things of the gods." (Meyer, 1999:207)

Conclusions

In studying Sassanian art, it is necessary to attend to religious matters. According to historical sources, Sassanian kings tried to promote Zoroastrian and all acts and deeds they did, as relevant to religion. In this situation, art, in particular played a significant role. In our ewer, there seems to be a religious message behind the scene, which on the basis of the Avesta and Mithraic art could be related to the deities Anahita and Mithras. As the cultural interactions, the motifs have greatly been influenced by the Mediterranean scenes; Anahita was influenced by Dionysus whereas Roman Mithras was depicted instead of Persian Mithra.

Figures:

Fig. 1: Silver vase showing Anahita and Mithras (Orbeli, 1938: Fig. 252)

Fig.2: Silver bowl decorated with goddess heads (Lukonin, 2011: Fig. 39)

Fig. 3: The investiture scene of Narseh, Naqsh-i Rustam (Authors)

Fig. 4: The investiture scene of Piruz I, Taq-i Bustan (Authors)

Fig.5: A naked woman, Qaleh-i Yazdigird (Hermann, 1994:78)

Fig.6: A glazed coffin decorated with female figures (Hermann, 1994:72)

Fig.7: Anahita holding a baby as a symbol of humans (Gunter & Jett, 1992:199)

Fig.8: Anahita holding a bird as the symbol of animals (Gunter & Jett, 1992:200)

Fig.9: Anahita holding a bucket as the symbol of water (Trever, 1984: Planche XXVI)

Fig.10: Anahita holding a pomegranate as the symbol of vegetation (Trever, 1984: Planche XXV)

Fig.11: The temple of Anahita at Kangavar (Authors)

Fig.12: The temple of Anahita at Takht-i Suleiman (Hermann, 1994:132)

Fig.13: The bust of Anahita, the capital of Chehelsotoun (Herzfeld, 2002: Fig. 413)

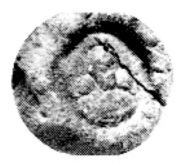

Fig.14: Clay bullae with the bust of Anahita from Takht-i Suleiman (Gobl, 2005: T. 63/23)

Fig.15: Reverse of Kanishka coin (Lukonin, 2011: Fig. 49)

Fig. 16: The bust of Anahita, Darabgird (Levit-Tawil, 1992: Fig. 1)

Fig. 17: Anahita holding a diadem with hanging ribbons (Trever, 1984: Planche XXV)

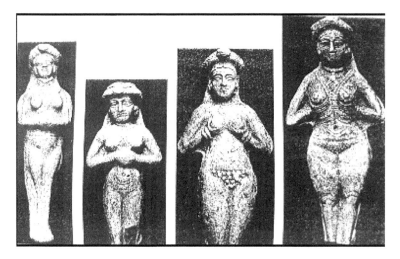

Fig. 18: Clay women figurines (Daems, 2001: Fig. 45-48)

Fig. 19: Stuccos of Anahita, Hajji Abad (Azarnoush, 1994: Pls XXII, XXIII)

Fig. 20: Anahita, Sassanian silver (Mohammad Panah, 2006:190)

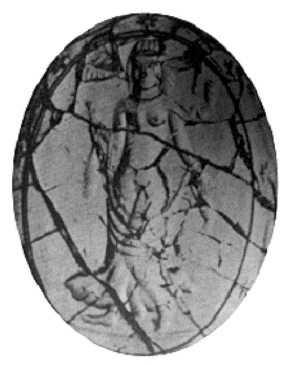

Fig. 21: A Quartz bowl, Anahita holding a fish (Shepherd, 2002: Fig. 105 a)

Fig. 22: Bandian Daragaz, Anahita carrying a jug (Rahbar, 1998: Planche VII)

Fig. 23: Anahita, Sassanian Silver Vessel (Mohammad Panah, 2006:198)

Fig. 24: Anahita standing beside a peacock (Ghirshman, 1999: Plate XXIX: 1)

Fig 25: Anahita holding a peacock (Gunter & Jett, 1992:200)

Fig. 26: Mithras carrying a bull, Walbrook Mithraeum (Eghtedari, 1975: Fig. 9)

References

Afifi, R. (1995) *Persian Mythology and Culture in Pahlavi Recorded.* Tehran: Toos Press

Amoozgar, J. (2006) *Mythological History of Iran.* Tehran: Samt Press

Azarnoush, M. (1994) *The Sassanian Manor House at Hajiabad, Iran.* Florence: Monography Di Mesopotamia III

Azarpay, G. (1976) *The Allegory of Den in Persian Art.* In *Artibus Asiae* Vol 38:37-48

Carter, M. L. (1974) *Royal Festal Themes in Sassanian Silverwork and Their Central Asian Parallels.* In *Acta Iraniqua* Vol I:171-202. Leiden: Brill

Carter, M. L. (1978) *Silver-gilt Ewer with Female Figures.* In *The Royal Hunter: Art of the Sassanian Empire,* Harper, P.O. (ed). Washington D.C: The Asia Society

Cotterell, A. & Storm, R. (2005) *The Ultimate Encyclopedia of Mythology.* Hermes House

Daems, A. (2001) *The Iconography of Pre-Islamic Women in Iran.* In *Iranica Antiqua* Vol XXXVI:1-150

Doostkhah, J. (1992) *Avesta: The Ancient Iranian Hymns and Texts Vol. 1.* Tehran: Morvarid Press

Duchesne Guillemin, J. (1996) *La Religion de l'Iran Ancient* (Translated into Persian by R. Monajem). Tehran: Fekr-e Rooz Press

Eghtedari, A. (1975) *The Signs of Worshipping Tir and Nahid, the Ancient Persian Deities.* In *Barrasiha-ye Tarikhi,* No. 5:13-64

Ettinghausen, R. (1972) *From Byzantium to Sassanian Iran and the Islamic World: Three Modes of Artistic Influence.* Leiden: E. J. Brill

Gaviri, S. (2006) *Anahita in Persian Mythology.* Tehran: Qoqnous Press

Ghirshman, R. (1976) *Iran, Parthians and Sassanians* (Translated into Persian by B. Faravashi). Tehran: Tarjome va Nashr-e Ketab Press

Ghirshman, R. (1999) *Bichapour Vol. 2* (Translated into Persian by A. Karimi). Tehran: Iranian Cultural Heritage Organization

Gobl, R. (2005) *Die Tonbullen vom Tacht-e Suleiman: Ein Beitrag zur Spatsasanidischen Sphragistik* (Translated into Persian by F. Nadjd Samii). Tehran, Iranian Cultural Heritage Organization

Graber, O. (1967) *Sassanian Silver: Late Antique and Early Mediaeval Arts of Luxury from Iran.* The University of Michigan Museum of Art

Gunter, A.C. & Jett, P. (1992) *Ancient Iranian Metalwork in the Arthur M. Sackler Gallery and the Freer Gallery of Art.* Washington D.C.: Smithsonian Institute

Gutschmid, A. (2000) *Geschichte Irans und Seiner Nachbarlander von Alexander dem Grossen bis zum Untergang der Arsaciden* (Translated into Persian by K. Jahandari). Tehran: Qoqnous Press

Hanfmann, G. (1951) *The Season Sarcophagus in Dumbarton Oaks Vol 1.* Cambridge: Cambridge University Press

Harper, P.O. (1971) *Source of Certain Female Representations in Sassanian Art.* In *Accademia Nazionale dei Lincei, Problemi Attuali di Sienza e di Cultura, (la Persia nel medioeve)*

Harper, P.O. (2002) *Sassanian Silver.* In: *The Cambridge History of Iran III, Part I: The Seleucid, Parthian and Sassanian Periods,* Yarshater, E. (ed.) (Translated into Persian by H. Anooshe). Tehran: Amirkabir Press

Herrmann, G. (1994) *The Iranian Revival* (Translated into Persian by Mehrdad Vahdati). Tehran: Nashr-e Daneshgahi Press

Herzfeld, E. (2002) *Iran in the Ancient East* (Translated into Persian by Homayoun Sanatizade). Shahid Bahonar University of Kerman

Hinnels, J. (1973) *Persian Mythology.* London: The Hamilton Publishing Group

Ions, V. (1983) *Indian Mythology.* London: Hamlyn

Jalali Naini, S. M. R. (1993) *The Selected Hymns of Rigveda.* Tehran: Noqre Press

Levit-Tawil D. (1992) *The Syncretistic Goddess Anahita in Light of the Small Bass Relief at Darabgird: Her Imagery on Early Sassanian Rock Reliefs and Seals.* In *Iranica Antiqua,* Vol 27:189-225

Luker, M. (1987) *Dictionary of Gods and Goddesses, Devils and Demons.* London: Routledge

Lukonin, V. G. (2011) *Persia II: from the Seleucids to the Sassanids* (Translated into Persian by M. Golzari & M. Vazirpour). Tehran: Ketabdar Press

Marshak, B. LK. (1998) *The Decoration of Some Late Sassanian Silver Vessels and its Subject Matter.* In *The Art and Archaeology of Ancient Persia: New Light on the Parthian and Sassanian Empires,* Curtis, V.S. et al (eds),.

London & New York: I.B. Tauris Publishers in Association with the British Institute of Persian Studies

Meyer, Marvin, ed. (1999) *The Ancient Mysteries: A Sourcebook of Sacred Texts*. Philadelphia: University of Pennsylvania Press

Mohammad Panah, B. (2006) *Ancient Land*. Tehran: Sabzan Press

Mousavi Kouhpar, S. M. (2006) *An Overview of the Depiction of Female Figures on Sassanian Silver work*. In *Humanities*, Vol 13.3:83-93

Mousavi Kouhpar, S. M. & Taylor, T. (2008) *A Metamorphosis in Sassanian Silverwork: the Triumph of Dionysos?* In *Current Research in Sassanian Archaeology, Art and History: Proceedings of a Conference held at Durham University, November 3rd and 4th, 2001*, Kennet, D. & Luft, P. (eds). England: Alden Press

Orbeli, J. (1938) *Sassanian and Early Islamic Metalwork*. In *A Survey of Persian Art from prehistoric Time to the Present* I, Pope, A.U. (ed). London: Oxford University Press

Rahbar, M. (1998) *Decouverte d' un monument d' époque sassanide a Bandian, Dargaz (Nord Khorassan), Fouilles 1994 et 1995*. In *Studia Iranica*, Tome 27:213-251

Sarfaraz, A. A. & Avarzamani, F. (2004) *Iranian Coins from the Early Beginning to Zand Dynasty*. Tehran, Samt Press

Schrato, U. (2004) *Sassanian Art*. In *Encyclopedia of World Art*, (translated into Persian by Y. Azhand). Vol. XII:702-730

Shepherd, D. (1964) *Sassanian Art in Cleveland*. In *Bulletin of the Cleveland Museum of Art* Vol 51:66-92

Shepherd, D. (2002) *Sassanian Art*. In *The Cambridge History of Iran III, Part I: The Seleucid, Parthian and Sassanian Periods*, Yarshater, E. (ed.). (Translated into Persian by H. Anooshe). Tehran: Amirkabir Press

Trever, K.V., & Lukonin, V.G. (1987) *Sasanidskoe serebro Sobranie Gosudarstvennogo Ermitazha, Xudozhestvennaja kul 'tura Irana III-VIII vekov*. Moskow: Iskusstvo

Trever, C. (1967) *A Propos des Temples de la Deesse Anahita en Iran Sassanide*. In *Iranica Antiqua*: Vol 7:121-134

POLITICS OF HOT AND MINERAL SPRINGS AND ANAHITA: A SHORT STUDY IN PARTHIAN AND SASSANIAN PERIOD

by Seyed Sadrudin Mosavi Jashni, Farhang Khademi Nadooshan, Hassan Nia, Masoud Sabzali

Abstract

In the aftermath of Alexander's invasion of Iran, the worship of Anahita alongside other deities developed in Iran. It seems that Anahita was worshipped because of her association with the natural element of water. Her temples were erected beside natural springs and caves, as well as at other locations.

Anahita, the goddess of water (rivers and springs), was worshipped throughout the Iranian territory. She was an important goddess in the Achaemenian period and her name appears in several inscriptions. She was the patron of the Iranian empire till the advent of the Sassanian period.

There are several types of springs and lakes in Iran, some of which have hydrotherapeutic or medicinal applications, attributed to their mineral ingredients. For this reason, Iranians built a number of temples to this goddess alongside these lakes and rivers. The construction of Anahita's temple reached its apogee at the time of the Parthian period. The main focus of this paper is to discuss the reasoning behind the construction of temples to Anahita, which are both political and religious in nature.

Keywords: Iran, Parthian, Anahita, goddess, spring, Sassanian, Achaemenian.

Introduction

Anahita is the Old Persian form of the name of an Iranian goddess and appears in its complete and earlier form as Aredvi Sura Anahita (*Arədvī Sūrā Anāhitā*). This is the Avestan language name of an Armeno-Aryan cosmological figure venerated as the divinity of 'the Waters' (*Aban*) and hence associated with fertility, healing and wisdom. An entire *Yast* or *Yasht* (Pour-Davood, 1964) has been devoted to Anahita in the *Avesta*, the holy book of Zoroastrianism, in which Anahita's name appears for the first time during the reign of Artaxerxes II (404-359 BCE). The *Avesta* defines Anahita as an antonym of Ahita (pollution or polluted). This Goddess, whose emergence is a matter of controversy among scholars, later played an important role in the Zorastrian religion. During the Seleucid period, some of the attributes of Greek goddesses were most probably added to those of Anahita.

There are some differences in the level of worship of Anahita during the Parthian and Sassanian periods. Due to the environmental conditions and values of water, she was worshipped almost across the entire country. There was a large temple of Anahita in Ecbatana, one of the Parthian capitals; however, it is not clear what the Parthians worshipped before occupying Medes.

The temples of Anahita were normally constructed on the side of forts, bridges, holy places, city gates, valleys, and springs. She had special temples in Istakhr, Takhte-Suliman and Kangavar (S. Kambakhsh, 2008).

Possibly in the Parthian period or even in earlier periods Anahita temples were constructed near natural sanctuaries such as lakes or mountain springs. One temple was built on a hill overarching a spring near the city of Ray. According to Seems Magian Change (C. Colpe, 1993:830) the construction of Anahita temple was based on an understanding of the chemistry of springs and other natural forces.

The Anahid was the divine patron of the Sassanian dynasty. Her cult flourished during their rule, as it was so during the two earlier empires. She was worshipped throughout the empire. There are many rock reliefs from Nahid in Sassanian period like Naghhshe-Rostam and more than a hundred metallic objects.

Hot and mineral springs in Iran

There are several springs in Iran which are still used for hydrotherapy. The hot springs, which occur in many locations worldwide, are classified into the following groups: sulphur, bicarbonate, chloride and iron rich water. Some of these springs, which contain radioactive elements in their water, are rich in radon gas. Each of these springs have a special property for hydrotherapy and are usually situated close to the volcanic mountains or plains. Thousands of people visit and drink or swim in their waters because of their health giving properties.

Mineral springs have three different origins: surface level, deep level or a mixture of both. In the first the surface water dissolves the underground chemicals and materials carrying them to the surface. The temperature of such springs is usually between 35 and 40 degrees celsius. The second category of spring flows from the volcanic ground. The third category includes springs whose waters are a mixture of both surface and deep level waters.

More than 369 springs have been recorded in Iran. A large number of them have medical applications for several types of illnesses (A Mesbah, 1999). There are even reports regarding the presence of the radioactive element radon in the springs of the Ramsar region in northern Iran (Mowlavi, A.A. et al., 2009, 45, 3:269-272). It has one of the highest background radon levels in the world. However, there are several other hot springs in other parts of Iran which contain radon and are suitable for curing congenital pains, but were possibly unknown to people in ancient times (D.S Gahrouei., M. Saeb, 2008:49-54; Dabbagh. et.al., 2008 1:91-94). These hot springs were probably not easily accessible to the ancient people. In Sarain of Ardabil Province archaeological excavations (A. Chaichi., Archaeological excavation report, submitted to the Institute of Archaeology, Tehran, Iran 2002) found an Anahita temple located in the old part of the city. Several mineral springs have been reported from Lorestan Provenance where only women are allowed to visit and use its waters. There are also several hot springs in Kharaghan, where there are pre-historical settlements and some Saljuki pillars, 95 Kilometers away from the Qazvin-Hamadan highway.

The Khorha archaeological site is located within the ancient site of Mahalat, 262 kilometres southwest of Tehran, which was probably part of a religious complex which belongs to the Seleucid Parthian period. There are five hot springs with radon gas and lime soil in this region (Beitollahi, M. et.al. , 2007.4:505-508).

Newly excavated archaeological sites in Sarain of the Ardabil province (K. Hadad et al., 2008, 130:309-318), located 20 kilometers away from Ardabil city, have nine springs which were called the Anahita complex belonging to the Parthian period. The springs have hydrotherapic properties.

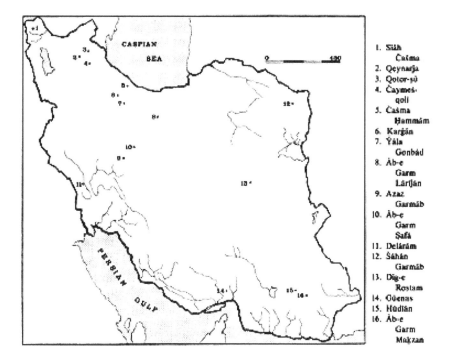

Figure: Sites of some major Thermal Springs in Iran.
Image reproduced here with kind permission from Iranica,
www.iranica.com/ articles/ ab-e-garm-warm-water.

Discussion and conclusion

The Goddess Anahita, who appeared in the religious beliefs of the Iranian people in the Achaemenian period, and who remained as a respected deity until the Islamic conquest, was considered the protector of the rivers and the empire. Her temples were constructed alongside springs and rivers, as well as in settlements and other areas.

In the later periods of the Parthian and Sassanian periods, the Magians changed their attitude towards the chemical and physical features of hot springs. Hence they built many Anahita temples alongside hot or mineral springs, which had hydrotherapic or medical applications. It seems that hot and mineral springs gained importance in the Parthian and Sassanian periods, not only because some of these springs had hydrotherapic usages, but also because of the association of Anahita with water. There are no written documents about these hot and mineral springs or their relationship with Anahita temples, however it is clear that Zoroastrianism was the state religion and that all Kings of the period claimed to be blessed by the divine light called *Xvarenah* in Avestan language.

The principle of *Xvarenah* (stemming from an Avestan word, *huar*, meaning shining) or *Farrah*, means divine light in the Persian language. *Farrah* is a divine light and once it shines on a person's heart, he will be eligible to become a king. In fact, it is the shining of this light which makes a person a king; in addition to a just and successful king. It is the power of this light that grants spiritual perfection to the recipient, who is raised by God to guide the people (Pour-Davood, 1964). Hence, the concept of *Farrah* is the metaphysical and philosophical dimension of government and status of the king, which is a legitimizing factor. Ardeshir I, the founder of the Sassanian Dynasty, was a priest of the Istakhr temple of the Goddess Nahid. The Narseh relief at Naqsh-i Rustam, shows the investiture of King Narseh and Ardeshir by the goddess Anahita.

When someone is perceived to have the divine light, it means that he enjoys such attributes as monarchy, piety, sagacity, nobility and spiritual prominence. This very close association of state and religion called for reliance on religious symbols, including the temples of Anahita, to foster and strengthen the kingdom. Taking into account that the goddess Anahita was a protector of the waters and the kingdom itself, it is logical to conclude that both political and religious considerations were behind the construction of Anahita temples. Nonetheless, more excavations and research are needed to shed light on the characteristics of these temples in ancient Iran.

Further Reading:

Beitollahi., M. et al (2007) *Radiological studies in the hot spring region of Mahalat, Central Iran.* In *Radiation Protection Dosimetery*, vol 123.4:505-508

Chaichi. A. (2002) *Archaeological excavation report, submitted to the Institute of Archaeology.* Tehran: Iran

Colpe., C. (1993) *Development of Religious Thought.* In The Cambridge History of Iran, vol 3.2, Yarshater, E. (ed). London: Cambridge University Press

Dabbagh, R. et al (2006) *Discovery of the second highest level of radioactive mineral spring in Iran.* In *Journal of Radioanalytical and nuclear Chemistry* vol 269.1:91-94

Gahrouei., D.S. & Saeb, M. (2008) *Annual Effective dose measurement from consumption of Dimeh springs in the highest altitude region of Iran.* In *Int.J.Radiation*, vol 5.1:49-54

Hadad, K. et al (2008) *U-Series concentration in surface and ground water resources of Ardabil province.* In *Radiation Protection Dosimetry*, vol 130:309-318.

Kambakhsh, S. (2008) *Archaeological Excavation and Research at Anahita temple and Taq-e Gara, Kermanshah* (2 volumes). Tehran: Publisher Institute of archaeology

Mesbah, A. (1999) *Cheshmeha Ab Garm va madani Iran.* Tehran: University of Tehran press

Mowlavi, A.A. et al (2009) *Dose evolution and measurement of radon concentration in some drinking water sources of Ramsar region in Iran.* In *Isotopes in Environmental and health studies*, vol 45.3:269-272.

Pour-Davoud, Bahram Farahvashi (ed.) (1964) *The Yashts, Vol. 2*. Tehran: University of Tehran Press. The *Yashts* (*Yašts*) are a collection of twenty-one hymns in Younger Avestan. Each of these hymns invokes a specific Zoroastrian divinity or concept.

ANĀHITĀ'S WATER RITUAL IN MAHĀYĀNA BUDDHISM

by Dr. Masato Tōjō

Abstract

There is a water ritual in Mahāyāna Buddhism. It is a famous ritual performed at the temple of Tōdai-ji in the Nara Prefecture of Japan. Its Iranian origin was pointed out by the late Japanese researcher Dr. Gikyō Itō (1909-1996), who was the 17th head priest 住職 (jūšoku) of temple Myō'on-ji 明恩寺 of the Honganji sect 本願寺派 of Šingonšū 真言宗 (Esoteric Buddhism) as well as an Iranologist (a well-learned scholar of Persian language).

This article consists of seven sections. In section 1 the water ritual is introduced. In section 2 the legend about the origin of this ritual is introduced. In section 3 the monk who incorporated this water ritual into the ritual system of Tōdai-ji is introduced. In section 4 the theory advocated by Dr. Itō is introduced. In section 5 common elements between this water ritual and the characteristic features of Mithra and Anāhitā are pointed out. In section 6 the motivation (reason) behind the incorporation of this ritual into the ritual system of Tōdai-ji is considered. In section 7 as a concluding remark, it is suggested that the incorporation of Anāhitā's water ritual into the ritual system of Tōdai-ji should be considered in the context of the movement to re-organise Buddhism as Vairocana (=Mithra-Aditya)-ism.

1. Water Ritual of Tōdai-ji

Tōdai-ji 東大寺 was the central administrative temple for the provincial temples 国分寺 (kokubun-ji) in the Nara period (710-794 CE), and is now listed in the UNESCO World Heritage Sites as *'Historic Monuments of Ancient Nara'*. Nara 奈良 is the ancient capital of Japan (710-783 CE), famous for the world's largest bronze statue of the Buddha Vairocana (14.98 m in height).

There is a water ritual called *'Šu-ni-e'* 修二会 in Tōdai-ji. It is performed from 1st of March to 14th of March. In the ritual, eleven monk-ascetics called *'Rengyōšū'* 練行衆 enter the February time Hall 二月堂 to confess sins and errors of the past year for the people, as well as to pray for the peace and safety of the nation, their prosperity and the happiness and for a rich harvest to the Eleven-faced Kwan-non 観音 (female form of bodhisattva Avalokiteśvara). When they enter February Hall, a group of men called *'Dōji'* 童子, which means *'boys'*, walk in procession carrying torches (6 meters long) in front of them.

At 2:00 am on 13th of March, the water ritual called *'Omizu-tori'* お水取り is performed. This is a ritual to gather water (kōzui 香水) from a well called *'Wakasai'* 若狭井. The water is dedicated to Eleven-faced Kwan-non. This ritual has been performed continuously since 752 CE through to the present day without interuption. A purification ritual by fire 別火 (*'Betubi'*) is performed in preparation to Šu-ni-e by the eleven monks.

On 15th of March, eight monks perform the Dattan ritual 達陀の行法 (Dattan-no-gyōhō). They wear the dattan caps 達陀 and run round the Hall, scattering about fire and water. They are considered to be the avatars of gods (angels) in Tušita Heaven (the Sun sphere) 兜率天. One of them (the fire god) sets aflame a huge torch (60 kg weight). They then pass through the shower of falling sparks from the torch fire. The eight monks put their dattan caps on the heads of infants who came to see the ritual, and these infants are said to grow healthy without illness.

After the ritual the water (kōzui 香水) is then given to laymen for healing.

2. The Legend of the Origin of this Ritual

There is a cave called *'Dragon's cave'* 龍穴 (Ryūketsu) at Mt. Kasagi 笠置山, and it is said to be a tunnel (gate) to Tušita heaven (the Sun sphere) 兜率天 where Miroku (Mithra) 弥勒 presides. According to *The Record on the Origin of February Hall* 二月堂縁起 (Nigatsudō-engi, 1545 CE), one day Jicchū 実忠, who was a monk of Tōdai-ji, entered this cave and came out into Tushita heaven. He saw gods (angels) performing the water ritual for Kwan-non there. After returning to this world, he established the water ritual which we call *'Omizu-tori'* お水取り of Tōdai-ji.

3. Jicchū 実忠 (726-? CE)

Jicchū was a high ranking monk (priest), the second highest monk in Tōdai-ji. He was the head (principal) of the religious academy 大学頭 (daigaku-no-kami) and ranked in šuri-bettō 修理別当 of Tōdai-ji. *'Šuri-bettō'* is an official title for a monk (priest) who is responsible for architecture, construction and maintenance of temples. He was said to have much knowledge about Indic and Iranian religions and cultures. He incorporated Šu-ni-e into the ritual system of Tōdai-ji in 752 CE.

As the head of the religious academy, he appointed Kūkai 空海 (774-835 CE) to the position of the highest monk (bettō 別当) of Tōdai-ji in 810 CE. Kūkai became the founder of the Šingon (Manthra/Mantra) sect 真言宗 of Esoteric Buddhism and was one of few Japanese monks who could read and write in Sanskrit. He studied abroad in China from 804 to 806 CE and during his stay in China he was initiated into Esoteric Buddhism to become an *'ācārya'* 阿闍梨 (805 CE). He visited Persian temples 波斯寺 in Chang'an 長安 the capital city of the Tang dynasty 唐 (618-907 CE), at the time there were at least six Persian temples in Chang'an (some were Zoroastrians, others were Manichaeans). The most important doctrine he learned is *'Dainichi- Miroku-dōtai'* 大日弥勒同体, which advocates that Mahāvairocana 大日 is identical with Miroku 弥勒 (Tōjō. *Zen and Mithraism*, 4.1). He frequently became one with Miroku in meditation and dissolved into Mahāvairocana. It is written in his will *'Goyuigō-nijyūgokajō'* 御遺告二十五箇条, *"I will reborn into Tušita Heaven where the realm of the Sun sphere Miroku presides)"*.

4. A Theory by Dr. Itō

These are the points of the theory advocated by Dr. Gikyō Itō 伊藤義教 in his book *A Consideration on the Coming of Persian Culture to Japan* ペルシア文化渡来考 (1980):

(1) Jicchū 実忠 was an Iranian. His name *'Jicchū'* is a transcription of the Iranian word *'Jud-čihr'*, which means *'foreigner'* in the Persian language (Ch. IV:7).

(2) Jicchū created the legend about the origin of the water ritual (Ch. IV:6).

(3) Jicchū incorporated Anāhitā's water ritual into the ritual of Tōdai-ji, and made it its Spring Equinox (Now-ruz) ritual, presenting a syncretism of Kwan-non and Anāhitā. (Ch. IV:6).

(4) There is an aqueduct which draws water from *'U-no-se'* 鵜の瀬 (in the upper reach of River Onihu (Onyū) 遠敷川, about 2 km south-southeast to Wakasahiko shrine 若狭彦神社) to Tōdai-ji and the total length of this aqueduct is 90 km. This aqueduct must be a Japanese version of the Iranian kanaat. According to his theory, U-no-se and Tōdai-ji is connected by the concept that water comes from the north, running two kanaat under the ground, and emerges from the well of February Hall on Tōdai-ji on Now-ruz (New Year's Day). (Ch. IV:6).

(5) The original word of *'Onihu (Onyū)'* is *'Nāxīd'* 那歇 which is the Sogdian form of *'Anāhitā'*. (Ch. IV:6).

(6) There were exchanges of knowledge about Anāhitā between Jicchū and Kūkai. (Ch. IV:7).

(7)He identified the original word of *'Dattan'* as the Iranian word *'widardan'*, which means *'to pass through'*. Dr. Itō wrote that it is a purification ritual, of Iranian origin, of passing through fire. (Ch. IV:12).

5. Points to be considered

The water ritual of Tōdai-ji has several parallels (common elements) with Mithra and Anāhitā of Iran , as well as the Roman Empire. The followings are points to be considered:

(1) Both Cautes and Cautopates of Roman Mithraism bear torches.

(2) Mithra is the Sun God and the saviour (saosyant). The Sun is his throne and the chariot. Miroku is the Messiah Buddha, he presides over the Sun sphere.

(3) Roman Mithras is closely linked with caves. Mithras was born in a cave. The Roman Mithraeum is a cave-temple. Parthian kings emerged as kings from the coronation ceremony just like Mithra was born in a cave.

(4) Miroku sits on a chair. This is a well-known Hellenistic characteristic of him.

(5) The dattan cap is likely to be the Phrygian cap of Mithra.

(6) Mithra has eight judges (ratus) (*Mihr Yašt* 10.45). Eight gods are incarnated into eight monks in the Dattan ritual.

(7) The ancient Indic Mitra is associated with the ordeal by fire. Zoroastrianism has fire ritual.

(8) The goddess Anāhitā is a goddess of water, and presides over rivers, springs and lakes.

(9) Mithra and Anāhitā are closely connected in various ways, for example child and mother in the legend of Lake Hamun (Nabarz. *The Mysteries of Mithras*, 2005:5-6) and in the Virgin-mother legend of the ancient Russian apocrypha (Milkov. *A Story of Persian Goddess Aphrodite*).

(10) In Manichaean scripture (*Chinese Hymn-scroll*), Kwan-non (male) is identified with Sraoša.

(11) It is highly probable that Jicchū knew Mithra was the Sun God of Central Asia, as he was an Iranian. It is also highly probable that Jicchū and Kūkai, having read the astrological scripture *Sukuyōkyō* 宿曜経* which Kūkai brought back and in exchanging knowledge, found or reconfirmed that *'Dainichi-nyorai'* 大日如来 (Mahāvairocana, Great Sun Buddha), *'Miroku'* 弥勒* and *'Mī(Mir)'* 密 are all variations of the name of Mithra the Sun God (see 7) as both they were both familiar with the Persian language.

(12) This water ritual reminded me of the Mithraic meditation story for Nymph degree in Dr. Payam Nabarz's *The Mysteries of Mithras* (2005). Šu-ni-e and Dr. Nabarz's meditation story both feature water and fire.

Sukuyōkyō 宿曜経 (*The Scripture about the Lunar Mansions and the Seven Planets*)

'Suku' 宿 means the lunar mansions (manzils), *'yō'* 曜 means the seven planets and *'kyō'* 経 means scripture (sutra). Therefore *Sukuyōkyō* means *the Scripture about the Lunar Mansions and the Seven Planets*. The monk who brought *Sukuyōkyō* to Japan is Kūkai 空海. This is a Buddhist scripture (sutra) on astrology, and is the most important and fundamental astrological scripture in Japan. Its content is a dictation of what an Esoteric Buddhist monk Amoghavajra 不空 (704-774) said, as recorded by his disciple. Amoghavajra was born in Samarkand with an Indic father (Brahmin of north India) and Sogdian mother. Therefore there is no Sanskrit original. It gives detailed explanation on the planets, dragon's head, tail, twelve signs, twelve houses, manzils (twenty eight lunar mansions), aspects, week-day and divination techniques used in Central Asia. It gives a complete table of correspondences for the planets, the Persian gods and the Hindu gods (Table 1). It is written

that these are the gods worshipped by the Persians living in Central Asia.

Table 1. Seven Week-day Gods in *Sukuyôkyô*

Week-day	Planets	Persian Gods	Indic Gods
Sunday	Sun	Mithra (Mir) 密 (蜜)	Aditiya 阿儞底耶
Monday	Moon	Mah 莫	Sōma 蘇摩
Tuesday	Mars	Verethraghna 雲漢	Anga-raka 鴦哦羅迦
Wednesday	Mercury	Tyr 咥 (滴)	Budha 部陀
Thursday	Jupiter	Ohrmizd 温勿司 (鶻勿欺)	Brihaspati 勿哩訶婆跛底
Friday	Venus	Anāhitā 那歇 (那頡)	Sukra 戌羯羅
Saturday	Saturn	Kēwān (Kiyān) 枳院 (鷄緩)	Shanaishwalaya 賖乃以室折羅

There is an important description in the chapter 8 of *Sukuyōkyō*. It goes as follows:

末摩尼常以密日持斎.

亦事此日爲大日.

此等事持不忘.

Here are the English translations of these three Chinese sentences:

Mār Mānī always keeps abstention from eating fish and meat on Mithra's day.

Also (he) serves for Mahāvairocana on this day.

(He) keeps (retains) not to forget such a service like this.

Here are the word-for-word translations of these three sentences:

Table 2. 1 The word-for-word translation of the first sentence

末	摩尼	常	以	密日	持	斎
Mār	Mānī	always	On	Mithra's day	keeps	abstention from eating fish and meat

Table 2. 2 The word-for-word translation of the second sentence

亦	事	此	日	爲	大日
Also (And)	(he) serves	this	day	for	Mahāvairocana (i. e. Mithra-Aditya)

Table 2. 3 The word-for-word translation of the third sentence

此	等	事	持	不	忘
This	such	service	(he) keeps (retains)	not to	forget

Sukuyōkyō is used with *the Almanac of the Seven Luminaries (Ch'i-yao-li)* 七曜暦. It is stated in *the Almanac of the Seven Luminaries (Ch'i-yao-li),* discovered in Tung-huang 童貫, that Mithra's day 密日 is particularly auspicious and it will become more so by the wearing of white clothes and the riding of white horses. White was of course the prescribed colour of ceremonial garments among the Manichaeans. For them Mihr (Mithra)'s-day (Sunday) was a holiday. They wore white garments and worshipped Miroku (Mithta) on Mithra's day. Therefore they wrote ' 密' large with red ink on the calendar not to forget the day. This custom was retained also in China and Japan. In *Sukuyōkyō* and *the Almanac of the Seven Luminaries (Ch'i-yao-li),* Chinese character ' 密/蜜' (mī) is used to transcribe Persian *'Mir/Mihr'* (see Table 1). Manichaeans are considered to be largely responsible for the dissemination of astrology and table 1 (Išida. *Spring of Chang'an (ancient capital of China),* p171; Liu. *Manichaean in the Later Roman Empire and Medieval China,* p232).

Note: It is also written in *Sukuyōkyō* that Sunday is the first day (Yek šambeh 曜森勿), Monday is the second day (Douh šambeh 娑森勿), Tuesday is the third day (Seh šambeh 勢森勿), Wednesday is the fourth day (Chehar šambeh 掣森勿), Thursday is the fifth day (Penj šambeh 本森勿), Friday is the sixth day (Šeš šambeh 數森勿) and Saturday is the seventh day (Haft šambeh 翕森勿). It should be remembered that the first day of the week is not Ohrmizd's day (Thursday), but Mihr's day (Sunday).

"Miroku" 弥勒

' 弥勒' is the name of the Messiah Buddha of Buddhism, and is pronounced *'Mi-lə'* in modern Chinese (The pronunciation of /ə/ is the same as /i/ of *'girl'*). In ancient days it was pronounced *'Mi-l'ək'.*

This (Mi-l'ək) is the transcription of Middle Persian *'Mihrak'*, a variation of Mithra's name (Imoto. *Influence of Iranian Culture to Japan*). Therefore some researchers and Mithraists of Japan now claim that the correct pronunciation of ' 弥勒' is Mithra (Mihr), not Maitreya. There is another transcription of Mithra's name. It is Mī(r) ' 密' and/or Mī(Mir) ' 蜜'　that are transcriptions of Iranian 'Mi(h)r'.

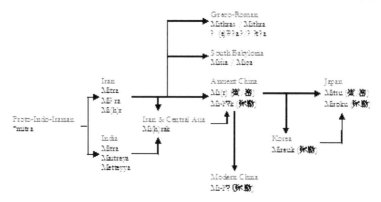

Fig 1 Propagation of Mithra's name

Miroku's Sanskrit (Pāli) name is Maitreya (Metteyya). Both *'Mithra'* and *'Maitreya (Metteyya)'* are derived from the proto Indo-Iranian *mitra*. The earliest Buddhist scripture which mentions Maitreya (Metteyya) are the following two Pāli Canons:

- *Sutta Nipata* (The Scripture Collection) スッタニパータ4:7, 5:3 (C4th-1st BCE)

- *Digha Nikaya* (Collection of Long Discourses) 長阿含経26 (verses: before 268 BCE, addition: 250-150 BCE) (Nakamura)

It is hard to say whether the Iranian Mithra was incorporated into early Buddhism as Maitreya (Metteyya), or Maitreya (Metteyya) was incorporated into Buddhism at its beginning. Either way, it can be said that Maitreya (Metteya) was so strongly Greco-Iran-Mithra-lized in Central Asia that his Chinese name - both Mi-l'ək 弥勒 and Mī(r) 密/蜜 - was derived from his Iranian name Mi(h)r(ak).

6. Consideration on the motivation of Jicchū

What kind of reason was there for Jicchū to incorporate Anāhitā's water ritual (Šu-ni-e) into the ritual system of Tōdai-ji? Why didn't he think of it as a pollution of Mahāyāna Buddhism? Dr. Itō gave no answer to this question. He just wrote that the water ritual (Šu-ni-e) is an original contribution of Iranian Jicchū (Ch. IV:7). In order to find indications for the motivation of Jicchū, I present the following points for consideration:

(1) The water ritual (Šu-ni-e) became one of the most important rituals of Tōdai-ji, and no one thinks of it as heretical or polluted. According to the tradition, Jicchū has a high reputation for making a great contribution to Mahāyāna Buddhism.

(2) Jicchū was the principal of the religious academy, and was the most learned scholar of the Kegon 華厳 doctrine, which claims there is a Universal Buddha from whom everything has born. The name of the Universal Buddha is Vairocana 毘廬遮那, whose other names include *'Dainichi-nyorai'* 大日如来 (Mahāvairocana, Great Sun Buddha) (Tōjō. *Zen and Mithraism*, 4.1). According to Kegon doctrine, Shakyamuni Buddha (Prince Gautama) is an avatar of Vairocana. This implies that Mahāyāna Buddhism is a teaching of Vairocana (Dainich), not a teaching of Shakyamuni Buddha (Prince Gautama).

(3) In *Sukuyōkyō*, Mithra is identified with Indic Aditya. Early Aditya had seven faces (Varuna, Mitra, Aryaman, Bhaga, Anśa (Aṃśa), Dhātṛ (Dakṣa), Indra), he later came to have twelve faces (Aṃśa, Aryaman, Bhaga, Daksa, Dhātr, Indra, Mitra, Ravi, Savit, Sūrya (Arka), Varuna, Yama). Mitra is always one of his faces. It is therefore highly probable that Jicchū and Kūkai inferred that Dainichi (Great Sun Buddha) is identical with Mi(h)r 密 –Aditya 阿儞底耶 of *Sukuyōkyō*, and Miroku 弥勒 with Mitra being a face of Aditya.

(4) The Sassanid dynasty had fallen in 642 CE to the Islamic invasion, however at the time of Jicchū and Kūkai (7th to 8th century CE) the Simorghian religion, which embraced Ahura Mazda worship as a branch, was still strong in Central Asia. Manichaeism was also vigorous there. There is no reference to Miroku in Zoroastrianism, but there is an important doctrine in Manichaeism in which Miroku is the spirit (Christ) of the Sun God Mithra. There is a mention of Manichaeism in *Sukuyōkyō*. Considering these points, it is highly likely that they (Jicchū and Kūkai) knew of the Manichaean doctrine (theosophy) regarding Miroku and Mithra. For more on the syncretism of Buddhism and Simorghian religion, see the appendix.

(5) Esoteric Buddhism is called *'Mikkyō'* 密教 in Japanese, and Jicchū and Kūkai knew that the Chinese character Mī (Mir) 密 means Mithra, therefore for them Mikkyō 密教 must have meant kyō 教 of Mi 密, i. e. the teaching (教) of Mithra (密). For more regarding the syncretism of Buddhism and Simorghian religion, see the appendix.

(6) In the origin legend of Šu-ni-e, the gods performed Anāhitā's water ritual in Tušita heaven (the Sun sphere) 兜率天 which is also where Miroku's realm is.

(7) Tōdai-ji was a temple constructed with all of Japan's might. It was a temple to show national prestige. Jicchū thought it appropriate to make Anāhitā's water ritual its spring ritual.

Considering these points, I think it possible to say the following:

(1) For Jicchū, Vairocana, who is the Lord Buddha of Mahāyāna Buddhism, was identical with Mithra-Aditya. Miroku is a face of Him and His last avatar.

(2) Therefore it is natural for Jicchū to incorporate Anāhitā's water ritual (Šu-ni-e) into the ritual system of Tōdai-ji. For Jicchū it was not pollution, but a great step forward for the perfection of the religion of the Lord Buddha of Mahāyāna Buddhism, i.e. Vairocana (Mithra-Aditya).

(3) Jicchū must have thought it honourable and auspicious to accept the Great Goddess Anāhitā into Mahāyāna Buddhism by making a syncretism with Kwan-non. For Mahāyāna Buddhism is a religion of Vairocana (Mithra-Aditya).

(4) Jicchū's intention of making such a legend that Anāhitā's water ritual was performed in Tušita heaven is to illustrate (prove) its importance and value to Japanese monks. This is because everything that is performed in Tušita heaven is very precious and auspicious for Buddhists, especially so for Miroku/Mahāvairocana worshippers. (Almost all Japanese Buddhists at that time were Miroku worshipper.)

7. Concluding Remarks

Mahāyāna Buddhism was born in the area which encompasses North-west India, Pakistan and Afghanistan. From its birth it was under the strong influence of Iranian culture, especially Mithraism. It is revealed by Chinese researchers that Mahāyāna Buddhism in Central Asia (Bezeklik, Kizil, Dunhuang, Uyghur kingdom, etc.) is Manichaean Buddhism. Jicchū's incorporation of water ritual into the ritual system of Tōdai-ji should be considered in the context of the broad syncretism of Buddhism with Mithra worship (including Manichaean Mithra worship) which took place every where along the silk-road through which Mahāyāna Buddhism came to Japan.

Appendix

The following facts will provide more information for consideration regarding the syncretism of Simorghian religion and Buddhism which occurred in Central Asia. (The term *'Simorghian religion'* means both (a) the ancient Iranian religion which predates Zoroastrianism and (b) the religions of the Medes, Saccas (Scythians), Parthians, Magusaeans and Armenians, which retain the tradition of the ancient Iranian religion).

(1) Mithra worship was prominent in the Indo-Greek kingdom of Bactria (180 BCE - 10 CE). Zeus-Mithra of Ai-Khanum is its example. Under the influence of Mithra worship, Buddha Maitreya and Amitābha developed in Parthian time (C2nd BCE - C2nd CE). Mahāvairocana developed in Sassanid time. There was Maga-Brahmin's Mithra-Surya worship in the area (Afghanistan, Pakistan and north-west India) where Mahāyāna Buddhism was formed (*Bhavishya Purana* 133; Tōjō. Zen, *Buddhism and Mithraism*, pp. 117-118). They (Maga-Brahmin) immigrated into this area in 1st century BCE.

(2) The cave temple of the 1st century found in Kara-Tepa (Syr Darya Province of Uzbekistan) is an archaeological attestation of Iranian religion and Buddhism in Bactria. Many Zoroastrian elements are incorporated into its statues and wall paintings. There is a depiction of a syncretic divinity *'Buddha-Mazda'* with a fire halo, who has features of both Ahura Mazda and Buddha. The temple layout is typical of Iranian temples, where processions of priests performed the main Iranian ritual of walking around the sanctuary. (Berzin. *Historical Sketch of Buddhism and Islam in Afghanistan and Buddhists*).

(3) In the Sassanid time (during the 2nd half of the 3rd century CE), a Zurwanite Zoroastrian high priest Kirder persecuted Buddhism (Buddha-Mazda worship) in Afghanistan (Bactria) and gave the order for the destruction of Buddhist monasteries. Buddhism soon recovered after his death, but the worship of Buddha-Mazda was never revived. (Berzin. *Historical Sketch of Buddhism and Islam in Afghanistan and Buddhists*).

(4) In Bactria (C3rd to C7th CE), the state religion of the Sassanid dynasty, i. e. the Zurwanite Zoroastrianism was less powerful than Simorghian religion (including Mithraism) and Manichaeism who were tolerant of the syncretism. (Berzin. *The Historical Interaction between the Buddhist and Islamic Cultures before the Mongol Empire*).

To summarize above along the timeline, Mithra's syncretism began in about 2nd century BCE. There developed Zeus-Mithra (180

BCE - 10 CE), Mithra-Surya (C1[st] BCE), Maitreya and Amitābha (C2[nd] BCE - C2[nd] CE). The syncretism of Mithra was widely accepted among the multi-ethnic society of Central Asia. There was no record of persecution and suppression of this syncretism. In 1st century CE, there also appears another movement to develop a syncretism of Ahura Mazda (Buddha-Mazda). But this syncretism was destroyed by Kirder and ceased to exist in the Sassanid time (second half of the C3[rd] CE). Shortly after the death of Kirder, Mahāyāna Buddhism quickly revived, and it developed Mahāvairocana, who is the culmination of the syncretism of Simorghian religion and Buddhism, and is under the strong influence of Manichaeism. There also is a possibility that some attributes of Ahura Mazda were incorporated into Mahāvairocana.

Further Reading:

Berzin, Alexander (2001) *Historical Sketch of Buddhism and Islam in Afghanistan and Buddhists.* Online Article from the Berzin Archives

Berzin, Alexander (1996) *The Historical Interaction between the Buddhist and Islamic Cultures before the Mongol Empire.* Lightly revised, January 2003, December 2006

Imoto, Eiichi (2006) *Influence of Iranian Culture to Japan.* In *Journal of Iranian Studies,* Vol. 2:1-5; 井本英一「イラン文化の日本への流入」イラン研究第2号2006年, pp. 1-5

Išida, Mikinosuke (1991[1979]) *Spring of Chang'an (ancient capital of China),* Kōdanša-gakujutsu-bunko.

石田幹之助『長安の春』講談社学術文庫, 1991(1979)

Išigami, Zen'ou (1987) *Bodhisattva Miroku – Eternal Tomorrow.* Šūeiša. 石上善応『弥勒菩薩 ——永遠の明日』集英社, 1987

Itō, Gikyō (1980) *A Consideration on the Coming of Persian Culture to Japan,* Iwanami-šoten.

伊藤義教『ペルシア文化渡来考』岩波書店, 1980

Liu. Samuel N. C. (1992) *Manichaean in the Later Roman Empire and Medieval China.* Paul Siebeck

Milkov, Vladimir Vladimirovitch (1999) *A Story of Persian Goddess Aphrodite.* In *Ancient Russian Apocrypha.* St. Petersburg: Russian Christian Humanitarian Institute Мильков, Владимир Владимирович. "Сказание Афродитиана", в *Древнеруские Апокрифы,* Издательство Русскго Христианского гуманитарного института, Санкт-Петербург, 1999

Nabarz, Payam (2005) *The Mysteries of Mithras.* Inner Traditions

Nakamura, Hajime (1958) *Sutta Nipata*, Iwanami-bunko. 中村元『ブッダのことば』岩波文庫, 1958

Tōjō, Masato (2010) *Zen Buddhism and Mithraism.* In *Mithras Reader - An academic and religious journal of Greek, Roman, and Persian Studies*, Volume 3, ed. Nabarz. Web of Wyrd Press

Sassanid stucco discovered in the Barz-e-qawela in Lorestan province of Iran

by Behzad Mahmoudi, Amir Mansouri, Dr Kamyar Abdi, Dr Gholamreza Karamian, Farhang Khademi Nadooshan

Abstracts

The recent survey and excavation conducted in spring of 2009 and in the autumn of 2010 has brought to light a site that has been found to belong to the Sassanid period. The site seems to be from a local ruler of the Sassanid dynasty, which in addition to coins shows a Sassinid stucco found in pieces as part of the excavation. It has characteristics which is similar to that of Anahita.

In this article, we are trying to show the similarities of the Sassanid stucco with other stuccos and how to recognise it.

Keywords: Sassanid north, west of Iran, Stucco, Anahita

Introduction

'Anahita', 'Anahid' or 'Nahid' is the goddess of water and fertility in ancient Iran; many characteristics of this goddess are similar to the goddess Ishtar, the Mesopotamian goddess of love and war, both being associated with the planet Venus. Possibly Ardavi sura Anahita, like Mitra, were amongst the goddesses who were worshipped among the people of Iran and its neighbours before Zoroaster. The long Fifth *Yasht* called *Aban Yasht* is the most important text that relating to Anahita.

The Old Persian version of *An-Ahita*, which in middle Persian is *Anahid*, is translated in modern Persian *Nahid* as *'not polluted'* and *'innocence'*. *Sura* and *Anahita* both have a common character which translates as *'able'* and *'clean'*, and *Ardavy* which had a special place and from linguistics points of view is the female character which meaning *'moist'* (Goddess of water).

This name amongst the Indo Iranians has been called Sarasvati; (Goddess from which water is coming). Indeed, a river in central India is named after this goddess. Furthermore, the ancient name of the Rakhj region, its capital which has several large rivers in the Qandahar, and in Pakistan is also derived from that of this goddess. In Persian culture, it is called *Harah Vati*, being the symbol of a big river which emerged from Mount Hera and flows to the Vourukasa Sea (*Encyclopaedia Iranica*).

Before Islam, during the reign of Artaxerxes II (404-359 BCE) of the Achaemenid Empire, were the first time that Mitra and Anahita are recorded as being mentioned after Ahura Mazda in an inscription. The Seleucids mixed the Iranian goddess with that of the Greeks and a goddess with Iranian character was worshipped by them (Khademiet al, 2009:1-2).

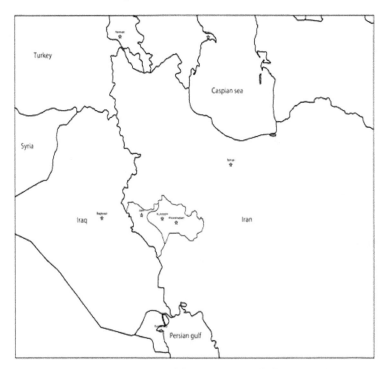

Pic 1: Map of Iran and Lorestan and Ilam province

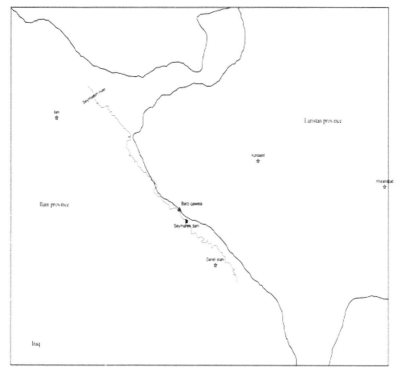

Pic 2: Location of Seymareh dam and Barz-e-qawela site in Lorestan and Ilam province

Anahita in the Parthian period

The Parthians worshipped Anahita amongst the Iranian goddesses in Kangavar which was one of important temples of Anahita in the Parthian period. In the Sassanid period, Anahita took a high position. Papak the father of Ardeshir, the founder of the Sassanid dynasty was also the priest of the temple of Anahita in the city of Istakhr, which is where Ardeshir was crowned.

Research Background

Sir Arul Stein carried out archaeological surveys in the fertilized plain of Tarhan between 1935 and 1936 for the first time. Then in 1938, and after 1938 at Kuhdasht, Delphan, and Tarhan (Valley of Seymareh and Kashkan river) (Stein,1938:313-342 & Schmidt,1989:XIV). From 1962-1964, Dutch and Iranian archaeologists carried out surveys at the Shah Abdagh, Halilan, Tarhan and Kuhdasht. (Mortensen, 1975:41).

Between 1971 and 1974, Hamid Izad Panah surveyed all of the above mentioned regions and noted additional places which were in need of investigation. Ahmad Kabiri and Mohammad Mehyar visited the village of Koonani Kuhdasht in 1981 and reported an open survey. Additionally Mehdi Rahbar and Nusrtaulah Motamadei also surveyed the area (pic1).

Then after a gap, in 2007, Rasul Sayden discovered a number of historical monuments in the basin of the Seymareh dams and following this many more prehistoric, historic and Islamic sites came to light. Between 2008 and 2009, Amir Mansouri repeatedly surveyed the area and in his surveys several plasters of stucco in the site of *Barz-e-qawela* were found as well as engraved potsherds (pics 3 & 4).

Pic 3: view at north (pic by Author).

Archaeological site under study

The *Barz-e-qawala* site which is situated in the basin of the Seymareh River in the region of Koonani (taheh Rahan) is situated 70 kilometers from the city of Khoram Abad, between the Kuhdasht road and a 100 meters further south of the *Barz-e-qawala* site (pics 3 & 4). This site is situated at 47 degree and 9 second 112 second east and in 33 degree and 20 second and 175 minute of north and height of 637 meters over water level and south of the village (Garkhashaou) and 2 kilometers far from Seymareh dam. It was discovered in 2009 by Amir Mansouri, and the base of his research at the archaeological site of Barz-e-qawela is extended to an area of 10000 hectares. In the course of the excavation work several architectural remains and works were discovered (pics 5 & 6).

Pic 4: view at south (pic by Author).

Pic 5: (left) picture of trench, local discovered stucco during survey (pic by author).
Pic 6: (right) picture of trench, local discovered stucco during excavation (pic by author).

 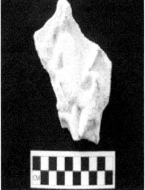 

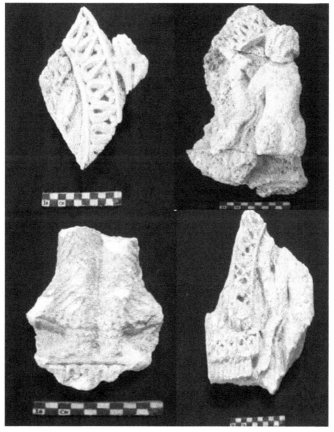

Pics 7: pieces of plaque stucco Anahita goddess before reconstruction (pic by author).

Although the function of the building is unknown to us today; it had a central hall with several rooms of various dimensions around it. The measurements of the mud bricks are 40cm x 40cm and the thickness between 10cm and 12cm. The plaster which was used consists of a mixture of clay with silicate, lime powder and sand. It is probable that this building had an entrance gate with gravel niche at the northern side.

Research methodology

During the surface archaeological survey of the Seymareh basin in the Koonani zone and Tarhan in 2008 and 2009 some Parthian and Sassanid sites were discovered.

This survey was done with the view of of finding human settlements in the region and finding out about distribution in the Sassanid period. During the surface survey, many Sassanid potsherds and other cultural material were found, all all of which were documented. Remarkably many pieces of plaster, Parthian and Sassanid potsherds were found on the surface of the site. The archaeological survey of Iran agreed to do excavations during the autumn of 2010 at the archaeological site of *Barz-e-qawela.*

Archaeological evidence show that plaster architecture during the Parthian and Sassanid periods in the royal family was in vogue. In the Sassanid period plaster was used for covering the walls and it has also been used for both decoration engraving and moulding. Both stucco and plastering were prevalent, and the stucco was used for human figures, depicting themes such as hunting, entertainment, court reception, vegetable figures, flowers, date trees, grapes and geometrical signs such as the swastika,. Additionally the broken cross, animal figurines such as the boar, bear, duck, as well as ritual engravings were created using moulding techniques.

From these sites 33 pieces of stucco decoration were found which were then divided to five categories: human, animal, vegetable, geometry, and decoration related architecture.

Human figurine

Female figure with clothes, the lower parts are covered with clothes, partly are covered with clothes, partly of lower part of female figurine is covered, and other classes of female figurine with covering clothes found on the surface of site?(pic7, pic 8, pic 9).

Animal figurine

A bird sited on a frieze, winged animal, figure of a bird on the plaque, figure of a peacock, figure of wings, boar figures, monkey figures.

Vegetable figures

Lotus figure, fruit of pine tree, figure of flower with five leaves, six leaves, pomegranate, branches, leaf, and trees figurine.

Geometrical sign

Broken crosses, cross on the wall, spring cross with three leaves, basket figurine.

Architectural design

Pieces of plaster working with design base, plaster working possibly from surface of building.

Pic 8: Drawing of plaque stucco Anahita goddess (pic by author).

Pic 9: the plaque stucco Anahita goddess after reconstruction (pic by author).

Discussion

One of remarkable parts of stucco from surface of a site is the figure of a female on the plaque, which after conservation may be described as Anahita. This female figure covered with cloths is young and beautiful with handsome face and a bowed brow, eagle noise, big eyes, small mouth with embossed crenate and long hair which is very similar to the *Avesta* in part 30 of *Aban Yasht*, (Dastkhah, 2006:309, 320).

There is a similarity between the findings of female figures at Tape Damghan and Haji Abad Fars, which is in the Hajji Abad. The figurines and plaques were used as the wall decoration in the temple of Anahita. It is noticeable that the mentioned figurines have the same hairstyle as the Goddess Nike at Taq-i Bustan in Kermanshah.

Also in the tile decoration of Bishapur which paints the figure of a female standing from artistic view white, clothes there is a design typologically in the niche comparable with a silver pitcher (Zeipel, 2001:316). These are kept in the Metropolitan museum, which show a young girls in the niche with the arc decorated with herb and geometry sign, in the right hand keeping a bird similar to falcon and in left hand lotus which is very similar to discovered site and was the vogue theme in the Sassanid period similar to the goddess Anahita (Azarnoush, 1994:126).

Conclusion

The discovered site contains ceramics finds which help us for carrying out comparative studies, which show it belongs to the Sassanid period. Several other stuccos have also been found in this site, the most remarkable of which are the stucco of women, of course in comparison to the other stuccos found in other archaeological sites of the Sassanid period shows that the depiction of Anahita in the Sassanid period has been adopted from a style which was common between written documents and artistic style. It is better to say the arts in the Sassanid period were a function of Zoroastrian religion.

Like the entire Anahita temple, this site is situated beside the river and a small mineral spring, possibly the medicinal application was one of miracles of Anahita. Sign and artistic figurines applied on the plaster plaques in the site are of significance; possibly they were related to the Goddess Anahita, which are comparable with written documents of *Aban Yasht* in the *Avesta*, with high similarity between written documents and stucco which shows a symmetrical relation with the aesthetic pint of view. Possibly in the western part of Seymareh there were places for worshipping of Anahita because of permanent water in the river and mineral water in two hundred meters far from the site.

With attention to the series of stucco mouldings and structure of building in the architectural traces of site, it is evident that the builder used the chalk for covering the structure, and possibly surface of building were covered using plaster by moulding.

Remarks

We are thankful to Dr Nabarz for encouraging us and giving more time to present this article. And Farhang Khademi Nadooshan for his guidance.

Further Reading:

Azarnoush, Masoud (1994) *The Sassanian Manor house at Hajiabad, Iran.* University of Pennsylvania publication.

Boyce, M & Chaumont, M. L & Bier, C 1989, *ANAHID*, in *Encyclopaedia Iranica.*

Dastkhah, Jalil (2006) *Avesta: the ancient Iranian hymns & texts.* Golshan publication. (Persian language)

Khademi, Farhang & et al, (2012) *Hot and mineral springs and Anahita: a short study in Parthian and Sassanian period.* under press, Vol IV.

Mortensen, Peter (1974) *A Survey of Early Prehistoric Sites in the Holailan Valley in Lorestan.* In *Proceedings of the Second Annual Symposium on Archaeological Research in Iran.* Tehran, 1974

Schmidt, Erich & et al (1989) *The Holmes Expeditions to Luristan.* In *Journal of Near Eastern Studies, Vol. 1.*

Stein, Mark Aurel (1938) *An archaeological Journey in western Iran,* In *The Geographical Journal,* Vol.92.4.

Zeipel, Wilfred (2001) *7000 years art of Iran.* National museum of Iran publication. (Persian translation)

WOMEN IN ANCIENT ELAM (ACCORDING TO ARCHAEOLOGICAL & HISTORICAL EVIDENCE)

by Maryam Zour, Saman Farzin, Babak Aryanpour

Abstract

Ancient Elam is the name of land in the southwest of Iran which, based on today's political geographical territories, includes the districts of Khouzestan, Fars, and parts of the provinces of Kerman, Lorestan, and Kordestan during the third, second, and first millennia BCE. Despite many religious and cultural similarities between the civilizations of Elam and Mesopotamia, Elam's religion had highly distinctive features distinguishing it from that of Mesopotamia. One of these was these was the special respect held towards the role of women and the special position allocated to them among the gods. This supremacy was so much that goddesses held superior positions in the pantheon of gods, and women held elevated positions in political and social affairs. Even the throne was attainable for them; to the point that one could deem the society of ancient Elam as a matriarchal one. By studying the remaining archaeological documents related to this civilization such as inscriptions, statues, engravings, the dishes, etc, this study aims to examine and explain the significance and role of women in the religious, political, artistic, and social affairs of that time in the society.

Key words:

Women's position, ancient Elam, cultural similarities, matriarchy, role of women, social, political

Introduction

It is certain that Elam's civilization marks the beginning of urbanization in the south-western districts of our country, and the existing documents show that Elamite society in this period had an attitude and structure based on the superiority of women. This argument is based on the religion of Elam's civilization; religion and religious attitudes indicate individual and social viewpoints and methods (Mohammadi Far, 1996:215). According to the researchers of Elam's history, this nation's religion is based on two main principles: first, a type of unusual sanctity of and respect towards eternal femininity and second snake worship (Hinz, 1992:47).

Political Geography

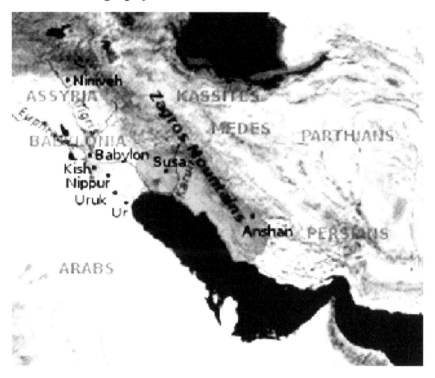

Map 1:
(Elamite Empire and Neighboring (wikipedia.org)

The Elamites descended from the mountains surrounding Susiana (Susa) plain from north and east (Girshman, 1970:39), and they spread along the watery plains of Karoon River to the mountains of the Eastern Plateau (Koch, 2006:12). Based on today's districts of political geography, ancient Elam included the territories of Khouzestan, Fars, and parts of Lorestan and Kourdestan (map1). Archaeological studies have not succeeded in identifying the complete geographical territory of any ancient cultural regions of Iran, and comments on the matter are limited to mere speculations and suppositions (Majid Zadeh, 1991:1). Various beliefs are held about the race of Elam's natives. Some believe the early natives of this land were Abyssinian; a race spread along the coasts of the Persian Gulf all the way to India, from which the Sumerian race was also derived. We can name Diolafoa, De Morgan, and Sykes as some of the supporters of this theory. Another group considers the early residents to be Afro-Asiatic, who were related to Indian Dravidian. These, in fact, considered the natives to be from the Mediterranean race. Finally, the third group believes the early natives of Elam were from the Asian or Aryan race with no relation to the Indu-European or Semitic race (Sarraf, 1993:12). There is no precise information as to how these societies started to form or about the beginning of their history. However, what is certain is that urbanization began in the early fourth millennium in Susiana plain, which is alongside the Mesopotamia plain (Amieh, 1993).

Names of Elam's civilization during periods of history

The Elamites themselves would write the name of their country as HAL-TAM-TI which can also be read as HALTAMPT. HAL here means land, and TAMPT means enlightened and master. This application indicates that the Elamites saw their land as *'the superior land'* or *'the land of God'*, although this is not certain (Hinz, 1992:25). But the Sumerians and Acadians referred to the Elamites using the sign NIM, which was related to the concept of *'highland'*; this was a correct word since not only did the land of Elam include the Susa plain with Karkhe, Dez, and Karoon rivers, but also the mountainous regions and the high plains of north and northeast of Susa plain. Probably dating back to the 27th century BCE, the oldest source in which the name of Elam was mentioned is related to the Sumerian kings and speaks of En-Men-Barage-Si, the half legendary king of the first dynasty of Kish, who invaded Elam and took plenty of loot (Majid Zadeh, 1991:5). Also, it has been mentioned sporadically in the *Old Testament*, the *Holy Book of Prophet Aramaya* and the *New Testament* (Shishe Gar, 2003).

Political history

The government of Elam was basically a government of autonomous tribes or a federal government for want of a better phrase (Amieh, 3:1993). These independent tribes included:

1. Susiana in the north of Khouzestan

2. Awan, which included the north and northeast of Khouzestan plain and had mountainous regions

3. Anshan, which was applied to the eastern and southeastern region of Mal-Amir Bakhtiari (Malian).

4. Parsumash which probably included the current town of Masjid Soleyman (Baghban Kouchak, 1396:8).

When the central government had no importance or became impotent, these tribes would start living their independent lives, and once the central government gained back its strength, it would succeed in unifying these autonomous governments into one (Amieh, 1993:3). Moreover, with regards to the classifications of different periods of Mesopotamia (Old Babylonia, Middle Babylonia, and New Babylonia) or Assyria (Old Assyria, Middle Assyria, and New Assyria). Elam, too, is divided into 3 periods of:

- Old Elamite period, c. 2700 BCE – 1600 BCE (earliest documents until the Eparti dynasty);

- Middle Elamite period: c. 1500 BCE – 1100 BCE (Anzanite dynasty until the Babylonian invasion of Susa);

- Neo-Elamite period: c. 1100 BC – 539 BC (characterized Assyrian and Median influence. 539 BCE marks the beginning of the Achaemenid period).

It is important to know that the period before the Old Elam Period is called ProtoElamite, the reason for which is the use of ProtoElamite characters (Mohammadi Far, 1996:16).

Position of women in the pre-Elam Period

As mentioned before, the structure of Elam was based on the superiority of women, a subject explained in this paper. But first, we should answer the following question: *"Did women gain reverence and elevation in Elam overnight or was there an old background to it?"* In response, it could be said that it was at the end of the Stone Age when the distribution of workload between men and women was created; men would attend to hunting while women and children would gather fruit and plants, and as far as Efimenko was concerned, the tools used by the Neanderthals belonged to both men and women. Sharp-pointed objects were used by men as knives, and women used tools of scraping and cutting (Guardian, 1975:62). Women, who had discovered and invented farming system, managed to domesticate animals gradually and use them, in addition to food, as workforce, which was a turning point in man's life. In primitive societies, the bulk of the economic developments were in women's hands, not men. While men were thoroughly obsessed with hunting by using their old ways, women were improving farming and creating thousands of domestic arts. (Durant, 1975:51). Women were the guardians of fire and perhaps the inventor and creator of pottery, and would grab a stick and go in search of edible roots of plants or gather wild fruits. Hence, there appeared a lack of balance between men and women, and perhaps this was the base of the superiority of women in some primitive societies. In such societies, women would manage the tribe's affairs and reach sanctity, and would also be the one who played the key role in keeping the family bonds. (Girshman, 1970:10). With time, the mother of the family would gain a significant role and be responsible for providing services to the family members and raising children, the mother would appear to be the element on whose innovation and power the discipline and the existence of the family was dependant, and the father would be in a secondary position (Durant, 1975:51). And thus, with the advantages gained by women in economic, domestic, educational, social and political affairs, there began an age in mans' history called the Age of Matriarchy (Childe, 1967:51). What is written above is a summary of the position of women until the early urbanization period.

Women's position in Elam's religion

The superiority of women in the gods' hierarchy

Having studied the tablets and the seals, we aim to discuss the position of goddesses in this section. First, it should be mentioned that despite the similarities between the religions of Mesopotamia and Elam, the latter had entirely distinct features. One of these was the special respect constantly held by the Elamites towards sorcery, magic, the powers of the underworld, and the element of women, in addition to snake worship. (Majid Zadeh, 1991:150) The oldest written document about the religion of the Elamites comes from Susa excavations; a clay tablet, dating back to the period of Hita, the 11th king of *Awan* dynasty reigning between the years 2270 to 2240 BCE (fig.1) This Elamite king was the contemporary counterpart of *Naram-Sin*, the king of Akkad in the south of Mesopotamia (Sarraf, 2004:7).

George Cameron was the first person to bring up the theory that the contemporary counterpart of *Naram-Sin* in this treaty is Hita a king of whom we have nothing except a name in the Elamite kings roster.

The treaty begins with these words: *"O' thou! The goddess of Pinikir and the good gods of the skies! Hear these words!"* (Hinz, 1992:88) Here, the names of 37 Elamite gods are on 6 pillars, but what draws attention is the name of Pinikir, the mother goddess. The existence of mother goddess's name at the top of the Elam gods hierarchy indicates the value and importance of mothers in the Elamite society of the late third millennium BCE (Sarraf, 2005:7) (fig. 1).

Figure 1 (Sarraf, 2005:7)

Pinikir and other goddesses

In Elam, the most elevated god, who was actually separate from the other ones, was a goddess named Pinikir, and all the documents indicate that she was the great mother goddess. It is for this reason that some of the scholars deem Pinikir as the very goddess Kiririsha. The name of this goddess has not appeared in this treaty; this may have been due to the fact that Kiririsha was merely a nickname for Pinikir, which cannot be that simple since with regards to a few documents, Kiririsha's hometown was in the southeast of Elam, and her main residence was in Lian (Boushehr) in the Persian Gulf (Majid Zadeh, 1991:50), while the main residence of Pinikir was in Susiana and Goddess Parthian in the eastern mountains of *Anshan* (Hinz, 1992:50). It is of note that countless clayish statues known as the naked goddesses holding their breasts with two hands are the embodiments of Pinikir and Kiririsha. (Majid Zadeh, 1991:50) (fig. 2).

As mentioned earlier, there existed a great number of gods in Elam, who were related to thunder, fertility, the guarding of palaces, the Moon, victory, the Sun, fate determination, love, water, mountain, fire, precipitation, weather, rainfall, growth, etc. Among the gods, there were countless goddesses who had a particular role each. For instance the goddess of Menzat, Ninkarak, the goddess of harbours and docks; Naride, the goddess of victory; Ninhursag, the goddess of mountain and the mother of all children; Ishnikarab, the goddess of prayer; Upurkupak, the goddess of light, etc (Sarraf, 2005:14). Therefore, it could be inferred that goddesses enjoyed an elevated status in Elam's religion and among its gods.

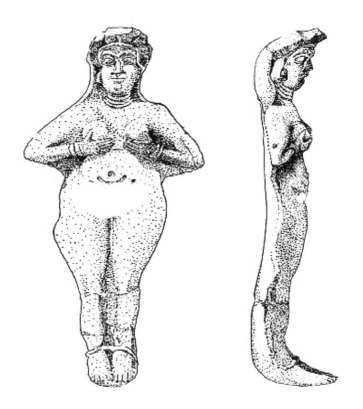

Figure 2 (Mohammadi Far, 1996:280)

The seals and the pictures of women as goddesses

The similarity between the cylindrical seals discovered in Susa and the Sumerian seals is so much that it is very difficult and in some cases impossible to tell the difference. The biggest factor distinguishing them from one another is the religious issues, in which women play an important role. The superiority of women in Elam's religion and the allocation of the highest position available among gods to the great goddess has caused the pictures of goddesses to be far more ubiquitous on the Elamite seals than on the ones from Mesopotamia (Majid Zadeh, 64:1991). One of these is a cylindrical seals dating back to 2400 BCE, in which the activities of the goddesses of Elamite gods hierarchy and hence the superiority of women in Elam's religion are depicted. The seal has been encircled around the ball-shaped entry of the pitcher twice. (fig. 3).

Figure 3 (Majid Zadeh, 1991:122)

The engravings have been carved onto the seal in two rows. In the top row on the left, an inscription in Sumerian characters introduces the seal owner, a goldsmith. In here, an engraving of a goddess while hunting is shown, who is standing on two hounds, holding an arrow with her right hand, and preparing herself to shoot down a wild goat standing on its two legs, having turned its head towards the hunter. The goddess's hat resembles the hat worn by a goddess on the moulded bricks of *Inshushinak* temple belonging to Kutir-Nahhunte and Shilhek-Inshushinak in Susa. (fig.4) In another image, a goddess in a long dress is sitting on two lionesses squatting with their backs turned on one another, and a man with a short skirt is approaching her (Majid Zadeh, 1991:70).

Figure 4 (Majid Zadeh, 1991:70)

That goddess is probably Ishtar, for the sign of Ishtar can be seen on her shoulders, and she is sitting on two lionesses which are her symbols (Graves, 1959:58). On her right, the disk of the Sun, the disk of the Moon, and an octagonal star have been engraved, which are most probably the symbols of the gods of the Sun, the Moon, and the goddess of Inanna-Ishtar. In the third image on the right, we can see the engraving of the demonic figure Griphon with his wings spread, and on his left a scorpion with a human torso and on his right a monkey-looking creature is squatting. In the last image on the very right on the top row, a half-cow half-human creature and a human figure with long tress are facing each other. There are three images in the bottom row. On the left, the sitting goddess of the top row reappears but only on one lioness, and a woman, probably another goddess, with a long skirt and long tress is sitting before her holding a triangular object, which can be the symbol of a temple. Between these two, there is the trinary symbol of the Sun, the Moon and the Octagonal star. On the right, there is another image of a goddess sitting on the back of a lioness but has no decoration or sign. Two naked female servants with long tress are fanning her with a palm leaf. In the middle image, the famous subject of the war between vicious animals on the one hand and human and gods on the other is depicted, which dates back to the second period of ancient dynasties in Mesopotamia and continues until the Akkadian Empire and after that. In here, two lions have attacked a cow, and a holy creature, who has a head decorated with cock's comb, is attacking one of the lions with a dagger, and a half-man half-cow creature has come to his aid from behind by grabbing the lion's tail. The naiveté of the images in this part, the combed back hair of the half-man half-cow, and the full face of the cow showing a human face with a long beard are comparable with similar images of the third period of ancient dynasties. The end of the goddess's hair has been braided upright instead of being naturally laid down on her shoulders, and in this respect has absolute similarity with the hairstyle of an engraved goddess on limestone, found in the excavations of Mari Palace, dating back to the ruling period of Zimri-Lim. The goddess sitting on the back of the lions could be the very Nurundi goddess depicting the relation with lions (Majid Zadeh, 1991:70). It should also be mentioned that the goddess appears in Seals, depicting mythological images of offering gifts, granting staffs, and ceremonial or royal rings (Jouzi, 1993:148), which once again illustrates the importance and value of women as a goddess. (fig. 5).

Figure 5 Granting the power of Goddess present at the scene

The Greatest Festival

Although our information about religious celebrations of Elam is very limited, it seems that the Elamites had a great many religious celebrations. In the discovered archaeological documents, at least two of the big religious celebrations of Elam have been mentioned. (Sarraf, 2005:8) The most important festival or celebration of them seems to be *'the guardian of the capital festival or celebration'*. It is obvious that in the ancient days of Susa, there existed an Acropolis which had a sanctuary including the various temples of gods, out of which Inshushinak temple was the prominent one, and the guardian of the capital was probably applied to Pinikir or perhaps later to the goddess Kiririsha (Hinz, 1992:68). This festival would start in the first month of Fall, and sheep would be sacrificed in the goddess's holy garden named Goshum (Majid Zadeh, 1991:55). Another celebration was the Tugah celebration. This religious celebration, which was for the sanctity of the god Shimot, was held every year on the 25th of February (which in the Persian calendar coincides with Ordibehesht). In this ceremony, oxen were sacrificed for the god Shimot (Sarraf, 2005).

The Religious Organization and presence of women

Considering the existing documents, we intend, in this section, to study the presence of women in the clerical system of that time and know of their position. As we know, there has existed a district related to temples in all periods (Majid Zadeh, 1991:55). Since the Elamites were a type of tribe with many gods, in order to run their religious affairs and familiarize the people with their religion, they had an extensive clerical system consisting of monks and nuns. On the top of this system was the chief monk, who was called Pashi-shurabu in Elamite written documents; he managed all the religious affairs in the entire country of Elam (Sarraf, 2005:4), undoubtedly he had great influence in the court, and often accompanied the ruler in wars (fig.6). The control of vast lands of temples and other sacrifices offered to gods was in monks' hands, and the ordinary monks, who worked in temples attending to religious affairs under the supervision of the chief monk were called Shuten (Hinz, 1992:70). In addition to the chief monk and the other monks, some nuns were of service in Elam's clerical system (Sarraf, 2005). These nuns, the same as their colleagues, attended to the tasks at hand (Hinz, 1992:73), and they were called Mortatbiti, and played an important role in economic (Majid Zadeh, 1992) and religious (Sarraf, 2005) affairs (fig.7). As an instance of their role in economy, we can mention the selling deed of a land by a businessman accompanied by a nun, in which the fingerprint of the nun is still clear. Also, it has been stated in a transcript that they had requested some barley and had attained it (Majid Zadeh, 1992:55). Unfortunately, our knowledge of them comes from the official receipts of the Old Babylonian Period, and the only thing that these receipts prove is that Pinikir's or Kiririsha's servants – the nuns - possessed estates, and gained profit from them. (Hinz,

1992:73) As for their religious activities, we can mention the script discovered in Haft Tappeh, which is related to the Tepti-Ahar kingdom (1350–1500 BCE). He speaks about the nuns' duties as such: *"When the night falls, four nuns must enter the temple; in order to prevent them from pulling anything valuable off (the statues and hide it), their feet must be tightly strapped; they must lie at the foot of Lamason and Kiribati. The ruler, the chief of police, the chief monk, the temple guardian, and the temple monk must lock them in; (guarding nuns) must keep the lights on, and beg Lamason and Kiribati for their support of the king when the day comes, break the seals, and set about their own way"*. (Hinz, 1992:75) In addition to the nightly guarding of Elamite temples, the nuns directly participated in holding religious ceremonies, too. This participation was to the point of leading the prayers, who had the intention of conducting religious affairs, into the temple and for the Elamite gods. Moreover, Elamite nuns attended to gathering oblations (Sarraf, 1991:4).

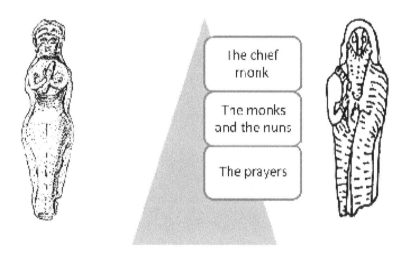

The chief monk

The monks and the nuns

The prayers

Figure 7 (Mortatbiti)   *Figure 6 (Pashi-shurabu)*

Women on the throne

Whether women have ever ruled is a question which might arise; in what period and how? Despite the insufficiency of our information, we can witness that women did rule and reached the throne in ancient Elam. As mentioned, unfortunately, we do not have much information about the Elamite queens; i.e. only two political statues (queen statues) have been discovered and studied. One of these statues belongs to Napirasu, Ontashgal's wife (fig.8), and the other is that of Tepti-Ahar queen (Mohammadi Far, 1996:175). They were discovered in Haft Tappeh and date back to the Middle Elam Period in the years 1450 – 1100 BCE (Reiner, 1973:87).

Figure 8 Queen statue Napirasu (Sarraf, 2005:188)

Figure 9 (Sarraf, 2005:178)

However, to explain how women have managed to reach the throne, we can refer to the Apart dynasty. According to their tradition, after Apart who founded the Apart dynasty, his son Silhaha inherited the throne as he was the prince of Susa. He ruled the dynasty for a long time, yet he ruined his father's reputation so badly that neither he nor his father was known as the founders of the Apart dynasty in history. The third character who had a conspicuous role in the early years of their domination was Silhaha's sister who was appointed as the grandmother of the dynasty (Hinz, 1992:108). In the later days, the people deemed worthy of the throne were those descending from the pedigree of Silhaha, a woman called *'the kind mother'* in Elamite transcripts. King *Shiro Kido* had no son and reigned without having an heir to the throne for a while when suddenly, in an unprecedented move, he appointed his mother, i.e. his maternal pedigree, to the throne, which was the first time in the history of Elam that a woman had reached the official position of the throne (Majid Zadeh, 1991:15). In another transcript, we read that Eshnunna, who was an old ally of Elam in those days, joined Navrain Gotium Mountains of Kordestan, and this queen granted him ten thousand men. At any rate, women had a significant role in politics and ruling, and this was not limited to only the ancient Elam (Hinz, 1992:112). For instance, in the Sassanid dynasty, two of Khosro Parvize's daughters, Pourandokht, and Azarmidokht, reached the throne (*Brosius*, 2010:17)(fig.9).

Women in society

In addition to household affairs and their role in them, women of those days had a significant role in society and were as active as men. Studying a few seals and engravings, we intend to mention parts of their activities in this part. The seals of the third millennium provide helpful information about various lifestyles and activities of the people of Susa. Some information is as follows: the landscape of the Susa plain is cut by some rivers around which there are reeds, and fish are swimming all about them. Buffaloes, wild goats and shookos (a kind of wild goat) are seen under pine, spruce and cedar trees. Different kinds of animals gaze around the meadows or run away from the lions. In one landscape, the Elamite, naked or dressed in clothes made of lion's fur, are seen armed with a bow, an arrow and spears and accompanied by their dogs, and shepherds are leading goats into stables. The stables are made of brick, and there is a tall tower at their entrance; the herd undoubtedly belonged to the court or a temple. Men, holding three-pronged forks, are working on farms, and women, dressed in long skirt, are picking fruit (Majid Zadeh,

19916:6). Also, in pottery workshops, where stone-made dishes are being made, artisans are smoothing the plates by rubbing them against one another while another person is polishing the pitchers' handles. In workshops, we can also see women who are sitting on small wooden seats or on the floor, busy producing wool. Women offer help in farming; we see them in long robes working in palm groves (Hinz, 1992:30). Spinning was an important profession of women, which can be seen in engravings and seals. The best instance of such works exists in an engraving on a black stone, dating back to the New Elam Period. (Taheri, 1994:159) This work, in the size of 13*1 meters, has been found in Susa, and is currently being kept in the Louvre Museum (Musée du Louvre) (Porada, 1978:84).

Also, one of the most important discovered artifacts of the Middle Elam Period, is the engraving (Ontashgal) in Sosa Castle. The stone's surface is divided into four rows, and the engravings in each scene lay on the outline. This is a very old method in Mesopotamia, which was invented by Cyrus the Great, the founder of the Achaemenian dynasty and was continued until the Chaldeans were toppled. Two serpents, which have surrounded the engraving as the framework, would probably reach each other in the top curve of the engraving. In the top row Ontashgal is standing in front of Inshoshinak, and has reached out his hands towards the god in order to be granted the staff (probably a cane in the shape of a snake or ring). The oldest work of this kind dates back to the ancient Babylonia, in which Zimrilim, the ruler of Mari, is receiving a similar staff and ring from Inshoshinak; therefore, it is very probable that this engraving was in the commemoration of Ontashgal's accession to the throne of Elam. What is important is that below this image of Zimrilim, there is another image in which two goddesses, holding a dish each, are depicted. Jets of water have erupted out of these dishes which reach one another. In the Ontashgal engraving, too, we see two goddesses in the third image from the top, whose skirts are a display of a mountain, and the water streams of 6 dishes have reached one another. In the second row on the top, Ontashgal reappears, though with two women this time. While being chased by his wife, Napirasu, on the right, he has moved his forearms upright and is moving towards another woman named Outik, who is also moving towards him. This woman is probably the king's mother or the temple chief nun, and depicts the Inshoshinak. The presence of women in this formal ceremony, illustrates, once again, the position and importance of Elamite women and their active participation in social and governmental affairs (Majid Zadeh, 1994:73).

Female Musicians

Praying was usually accompanied with music and sacrifice in Elam, (Hinz, 1992:68) especially before Elamite gods, for whom music was accompanied with gospels, (Sarraf, 2005:6) and there were musicians constantly present. The question at hand is whether or not women had a hand in music in ancient Elam. It should be mentioned here that the oldest artist figurines are those of women rather than men. Although male artist figurines are greater in number and richer in variety, they are historically newer. Another point to mention is that we can see the advent of female musicians, some clothed and some naked, in the *Simash* Period. Also, naked and clothed male and female musicians can be seen in the Sokol Mokh Period; hence, it could be concluded that there were both female and male musicians and artists in ancient Elam (Mohammadi Far, 1996:219). Considering the moulded plaques, it can be said that women played the tar and the harp, (Taheri, 1994:160) and considering the Figurines, tambourine (Mohammadi Far, 19961:80). From the category of female tambourine players, we can mention the clothed female tambourine player of the Simash Period discovered in Sosa, who is holding the tambourine with both hands in front of her face; the slim face and the slim neck are two features of this work, a similar work to which has been discovered in Tello (Bisi, 57:1980). From the category of female harp players, we can mention the Kidin-Hutran bronze chalice discovered in Arjan (Behbahan, Iran). Dr. Ali Zadeh believes this work belongs to the New Elam Period. The scenes of Kidin-Hutran chalice include:

1. A formal reception in front of the royal tent and the carriage of the hunted animals to the court

2. The scene of king's immediate return to the court and the exertion of force against the rebels

3. Granting gifts

4. The victory celebration

Before anything, it is better to Rock relief the Kul Farah, engraving, in which three Elamites are playing the harp and the flute. The first person's harp is triangular, copies of which could be seen in the hands of two players in the 4th image of Arjan. Among the players in both of the scenes (the chalice and the engraving), there is also a flute player, which depicts the harmony among the musicians in both scenes. The studies done by professor B. Hroda on different types of harps seen on the New Assyrian engravings illustrate that triangular harps were played by women in Assyria. (fig.10)

Figure 10 (Assyrian musicians) (Sarraf, 1993:45)

Perhaps the discrepancy and lack of harmony among the three musicians' clothing is due to the fact that two of them wearing long dresses are Elamite women, who are playing triangular harps, and the third person wearing short clothes is a male musician, who is holding another type of harp. (Sarraf, 1990:44) (fig.11)

Figure 11 (Elamite musicians) (Sarraf, 1993:46)

Incestuous marriage

In the Middle Elam Period, the gods of Inshoshinak and Houmban and the goddess of Kiririsha formed a triangle, the ranking of which based on importance is as follows: Houmban – Kiririsha - Inshoshinak or Houmban - Inshoshinak - Kiririsha (Majid Zadeh, 1991:53). Although demoted, this goddess was never removed from the category of Elam's superior gods (Hinz, 1992:51). The point worthy of attention and importance is the fact that in this trinity, the goddess Kiririsha had been titled as the *'the great spouse'*. This shows that she was married to not only Houmban but also Inshoshinak. Here one would automatically think of the relationship among the tricorn rulers in the royal family, (Hinz, 1992:51) which was one of the Elam's features, i.e. incestuous marriage, which was probably the cause of the high death rate in the royal family. It should also be mentioned that royal incestuous marriage was the fruit of the two features of the succession rules in the royal family of Elam: marrying the late king's widow and the marriage between sisters and brothers. The widow was occasionally the sister of them both. Around the year 710, prince Heni in Mal Amir called princess Huhin *'his beloved wife and sister'* (Majid Zadeh, 14:1991). This type of marriage took place due to the fact that the legitimacy of kingdom was only through the maternal side. (Majid Zadeh, 14:1991)

Conclusion

As mentioned earlier, since the ancient days, women were of importance and were active as much as men or even more, and would even sacrifice their lives protecting themselves and their family. The same as the earth and rain, they were symbols of reproduction and rejuvenation, and were considered sacred. The attitude of women being superior to men reaches its peak in the Elam Period to the point that we even witness the superiority of goddesses to gods. Women participated in all social, political, religious, artistic, etc activities and even reached the throne and ruled. Moreover, the legitimacy of the male kings was only through the maternal side, which was the cause of incestuous marriages; an act no limited only to Elam's period, but also in the later ones having political reasons as their cause rather than religions. In addition, women took part in religious ceremonies, and held responsibilities such as being the temple nuns in the clerical structure. When it came to societal tasks, women were as active as men in many professions such as spinning, farming, pottery, etc. and were also highly skilled in arts such as playing the harp, the tambourine, and the tar. Contrary to the common belief, the role of women was far more important and conspicuous in the primitive civilizations of mankind, and it was only with the passage of time that the matriarchal system gave way to the patriarchal one. However, women were never devalued throughout history to the point that we witness the valuable and significant role of women and even their ruling in periods of patriarchal systems. In the end, it can be said that women held a very high position in Elam, and one of Elam's religious features was the element of women, who were worshipped by all. This sanctity and purity of women enabled them to be influential and active in all aspects of life.

Further Reading:

Persian:

Agajdan, A. (1975) *The History of the Ancient World, volume 1* (translated by Sadegh Ansari and others). Tehran: Andisheh Publications

Amie, Pier (1993) *The History of Elam* (translated by Shirin Bayani). Tehran: Tehran University Publications Institute

Baghabn Kouchak, Gholam Ali (1996) *The Archaeological Comparison and analysis of the Religion and Religious Architecture of Elam Civilization with Mesopotamia Civilization.* Counselling professor: Ali Asghar MirFattah, M.A. thesis. Tarbiat Modarress University

Childe, Gordon (1967) *History* (translated by Ahmad Behmanesh). Tehran: Tehran University Publications

Durant, William (1975) *The History of Civilization* (translated by Ahmad Aram). Tehran: Translation and Publication Institution

Ghirshman, Roman (1970) *Iran, Islam from the beginning* (translated by Mohammad Mo'in). Tehran: Katibeh Educational-Cultural Publications Company

Hinz, Walter (1992) *History of Elam* (translated by Firouz Firouz Nia). Educational and Cultural Publications

Jouzi, Zohre (1993) *The Religion of Elam Regarding Cylindrical Seals (mohr).* Counselling professor: Mohammad Rahim Sarraf, M.A. thesis. Tarbiat Modarress University

Koch, Mary (2006) *Darius of language* (translated by Parviz Rajabi). Karang Publications

Majid Zadeh, Yousef (1991) *The History and Civilization of Elam.* Tehran: University Publication Centre

Mohammadi Far, Yaghoub (1996) *A New Research on the Style and Application of the Human Statues of Elam (from the Beginning to the End of the New Elam).* Counselling professor: Mohammad Rahim Sarraf, M.A. thesis. Tarbiat Modarress University

Prada, I. (1978) *The Art of Ancient Iran* (translated by Yousef Majid Zadeh). Tehran: Tehran University Publications

Sarraf, Mohammad Rahim (1369/1990) *Kidin-Hutran, Bronze Chalice Discovered in Arjan Behbahan.* In *Arjan* special edition, issue 17. The Organization of Cultural Heritage of Iran

Sarraf, Mohammad Rahim (1993) *The Engravings of Elam.* Tehran: Jahad Daneshgahi Publications

Sarraf, Mohammad Rahim (2005) *The Religion of the Elam Tribe.* Tehran, Samt Publications

Shishegar, Arman (2003) *The Discovery of a Tomb from the King Shutrok-Nahunte Dynasty.* The Organization of Cultural Heritage of Iran

Taheri, Mahnaz (1994) *Women's Clothing in Elamite and Achaemenian Periods.* Counselling professor: Mohammad Rahim Sarraf, M.A. thesis. Tarbiat Modarress University

Latin:

Bisi, A.M. (1980) *Les Déesses au Tympanon de la Mésopotamie à Carthage.* In *Assyriological Miscellanies vol 1.*

Reiner Erica (1973) *Inscription from a Royal Elamite Tomb including Excursus: The Names of the Months in Elam.* In *Archiv für Orientforschung* 24:87-102. Berlin/Graz

Graves (1959) *New Larousse Encyclopedia of Mythology.* London, New York

Terrbal: Water or Fire Temple

by Reza MehrAfarin

Abstract

Ardeshir Papakan, the founder of the Sassanian dynasty gave much emphasis to the urbanization process. So, he ordered the construction of a number of cities that most of the early Islamic historians and geographers commented on.

The biggest and the most famous city of Ardeshir was Gour or Ardeshir Khoreh that was located near Firooz Abaad in Fars province. This city in reality is considered to be the seat/capital of Ardeshir, and like some of the Parthian cities, it possessed a circular plan. There was a lofty tower in the centre of the city called Terrbal that was the temple of water goddess Anahita, and, a big palace was constructed in its vicinity taking into account the Achaemenid architectural styles. Apart from descriptions of Islamic geographers about important buildings in this city, archaeologists were also able to find essential information about the installations during archaeological excavations over the past years. This city was founded after Ardeshir's victory over Ardavan V and subsequently a grand fort was named after him (Ardeshir/FiroozAbaad Fort). This was constructed close to the city along the Anahita fountain, so that it could be suitable for the royal dignitaries, especially during the later years of Ardeshir Papakan when he abdicated his rule. Using historical and geographical accounts as well as archaeological remains, this paper tries to identify the actual purpose of the central tower/minaret in the city of Gour, which is as famous as the Terrbal.

Keywords: Sassanian Dynasty, Ardeshir Papakan, Urbanization, Gour City, Terrbal

Introduction

A nobly-born Iranian, Sasan was the head of the Zoroastrian priests at the Anahid (Anahita) temple in the city of Stakhra. After marrying the daughter of a local Persian king, he attached himself to the court. After the death of Sasan, his son Papak assumed his responsibility, and could bring together local Persian fighters who believed in this ancient religion.

Papak had a number offspring, one of them being Ardeshir who played a significant role in Sassanian history. At the age of seven, by the request of his father, Ardeshir was handed over to a local king Darabgerd for military training. Ardeshir succeeded his father and with dominance over small neighbouring rulers, he expanded his influence across the region. Thereafter, Papak when opportunity presented itself revolted against Gochehr, the king of Stakhra, and after killing him he took control of the region's rule (Shipman, 1383:24).

A little before his death, Papak appointed his eldest son Shapour as the king. This can be traced in the inscription of Shapour I on the walls of Kaabe Zartosht that says: *'King Shapour, son of Papak'*. Ardeshir, who was now a deputy commander of Darabgerd, did not pay respect to his brother Shapour. Consequently, Shapour sent an army against him but he ambiguously got killed and hence opened the way for Ardeshir to be crowned as the king in Stakhra.

After coronation and suppression of local rebellions as well as occupation of adjacent provinces, Ardeshir considered himself to be so powerful that he sent an emissary to Ardavan and asked him to determine a place for the final and destined battle. Ardavan proposed the plain of Hormuzgan where the battle took place in 224 CE. The Parthians got defeated and Ardavan was killed on the battlefield. Ardeshir was able to defeat Ardavan three times consecutively and hence; founded the Sassanian Empire. From then onward, Ardeshir came to be known as emperor or *shah-e- shahan* and started conquering the territory which he called Iran (Christensen, 1374:11).

Importance of Urbanization during Ardeshir

Unlike the Parthians who followed a feudal system, the Sassanians founded a powerful centralized administration. In this way, they could control a rebellious and aristocratic government and with a systematic and fruitful planning in irrigation and urbanization affairs, architecture and industry even for the defeat of Roman

Empire; they could extend political dominance in the west and the east (Porada, 1355:277).

The successful consolidation of the Sassanian rule during Ardeshir I itself has been an important factor for the foundation and expansion of cities. At that time, some of the cities by considering of economic, cultural and religious or by military and strategic purposes came into existence or renovated. The Sassanian rule could bring together two axes of religion and centralization hence; declared Zoroastrian as the official religion.

The existence of comprehensive customs and beliefs in Iran could help establish cities during antiquity. These were in two forms: first, reliance and emphasis on worshipping places and giving greater opportunities to them that as a result accommodate other city installations and related networking. The city of Gour which contains a tower in its centre can be counted in this group. The second, impact of religious symbols and social beliefs in the city's planning and networking. This group includes attention to celestial and heavenly bodies, rising direction of sun and moon throughout the year and shape of sun and other related elements. As such, the presence of fourfold entrance in the cities such as Darabgird and Ardshir Khoreh (Mehr gate in the east, Bahram gate in the west, Hormuz gate in the north and Ardeshir gate in the south) are result of these beliefs and thoughts (Varjavand, 1366:5).

Ardeshir Papakan himself was one the founders of several Sassanian cities. Tabari mentions the numbers and names of those cities as: *"Ardeshir founded eight cities that include 1. Ardeshir Khoreh (Gour), 2. Ram Ardeshir, 3. Riv Ardeshir in Fars, 4. Hormuz Ardeshir that is the same as Sough-al Ahwaz in Ahwaz, 5. Beh Ardeshir in the west of Madayen (Seleucian and Ctesiphone), 6. Estabath Ardeshir that is the same as Karkh Mishan in Sawad (present Iraq), 7. Fasa Ardeshir that is the same as the city of Khat in Bahrain and, 8. Buz Ardeshir or Kharreh near Mousel"* (Tabari, 1362:584).

As noticed, despite being engaged in continuous war with Parthians and vanquishing local rulers, and his ceaseless efforts for establishing a permanent Iranian nation, Ardeshir Papakan gave prominence to his new city projects; hence he was successful in establishing a large number of cities. However, not all of those cities enjoy similar importance. The most important and the biggest project of Ardeshir during his early years was the city of Gour (Ardeshir Khoreh) that became his governing seat. Although, this city lost its political importancc during Shapour I, the son and successor of Ardeshir, but it preserved its importance until the end of Sassanian rule and even afterwards as a customary and traditional city, and, often the heirs apparent were coroneted over there with magnificent ceremony and accordance with to Iranian religious tradition.

Gour City

Probably, before building the city of Gour, Ardeshir embarked on constructing a defensive *dokhtar* fort that angered the Parthians. Actually, this fort was the rebellion of Ardeshir, and on the other a symbol of wrath of Ardavan. After concluding small local battles as well as sporadic fighting with Ardavan, he organised the final battle in this strategic fort and sketched yet another plan with his army generals for destruction of the Parthian rule.

After a difficult victory over Ardavan V, Ardeshir felt the necessity of a big and grandeur city, which in addition to safeguarding his newly founded empire could be suitable for a great king like him. Consequently, after acquiring power and consolidating his administrative base, he issued a decree for the city of Gour. With the termination of rebellions at different parts and complete subjugation of Parthia, Ardeshir also issued a decree for the construction of a fort near this city that manifests the peak of his strength and power. Firooz Abaad Palace with its good natural situation, powerful materials, beautiful design and particular grandeur could prove positive for the ambitious desires of Ardeshir.

Gour (Jour) was also called Ardeshir Khoreh; it is the first Sassanian city which is located in the vicinity of the Firooz Abad in the Fars Province. The city was known as Gour (Jour) during the past and at the same time a part of Ardeshir Khoreh state. (Estakhri, 1340:111-113). Estakhri describes its extent and the manner of its foundation: *"Jour was built by Ardeshir. It is said to be a lake. Since Ardeshir put aside his enmity against his enemies, he wished to build a city. Then he decreed to build ways to the extent of water. The city is encircled by a mud wall with four entrances, one called mehr gate towards the east, another towards west as Bahram gate on the right side as Ardeshir gate and on the left Hormuz gate and at the centre a tower called Terrbal that in Persian known as Ivan and Kiya Khoreh where the entire villages and area could be seen. Water was drawn from a nearby mountain which flowed like fountain to Terrbal and then merged with other channels constructed with lime and stone. Now, it has been deserted. Running water is enormous in the city. There is a garden and a theatre at each entrance gate"* (Estakhri, 1340:110-111).

The city is surrounded by a defensive wall, a ditch of about 55m wide and a bricked wall with four actual entrance gates at four axes (Huff, 1969:391). The interior part of the city with a diameter up to about 2km, like a wheel with two real axes from northern to southern entrance and from eastern to western entrances, is divided equally into four sections that cut across each other at the central point. Each of the four sections is further divided equally into five parts. Apart, the interior space of the city has been fragmented with three concentric circles. Consequently, the central diameter reaches up to 450m. A number of round and concentric streets create indirect links of central zone with residential units, work and commercial places (Fig.1).

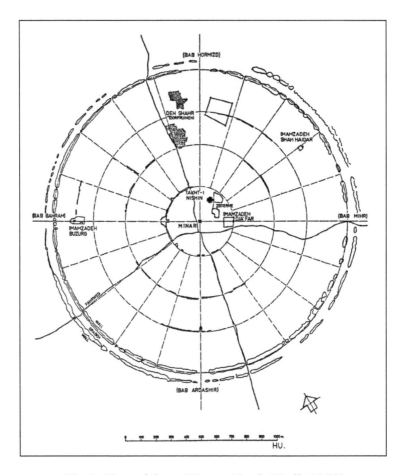

Fig 1, Plan of Gour (Firooz Abad) (Huff, 1368)

Terrbal (Minaret/Tower): It is located in the centre of the city of Gour and has four corners and Ibn-e Hauqal called it *Terrbal* (Ibn-e Hauqal, 1345:287). Ibn-e Balkhi explains: in the middle of the city that looks like a compass point, projected stall known as *Gerdeh* (round) to Iranians and *Terrbal* to Arabs. Above the stall, a shade was built and in the middle a great dome called as *Gumbad Girmaan*. Length of the four walls of this dome is 75m and is made of granite. The great dome is covered with bricks and water from a mountain spread over it like fountain (Ibn-e Balkhi, 1329:138). This structure was built by uneven stones as well as gypsum and lime. There are niches around that have continued as spiral until over the tower (Vandenberg, 1368:50). The lower diameter is more than the upper one and the thickness of each block presently is about 9m and height 30m (Huff, 1368:79). (fig.2)

Fig 2, Terrbal (Flanden & Coast)

About the purpose of the above mentioned structure, different views have been put forward. Flanden, based on local beliefs, names it a fire temple (Flanden, 1356:387). Estakhri who remembers it as Ivan (portico) and Kia Khoreh, notes *"waters were drawn from the mountain, water like fountain comes to Terrbal and then merges with other channel"* (Estakhri, 1340:111-113). Ruether compares this structure with Ziggurats of Mesopotamia and believes that at special occasion, holy fire that was preserved in temples was kindled on the open space of this tower (Ruether, 1977:56). Louis Vandenberg writes: In the open and free environment on the top of the tower, they kindled holy fire and worshippers gathered around it (Vandenberg, 1368:50). Huff believes that this building most probably was the divine manifestation of king Ardeshir. Likewise, he points that this wonderful and unique structure existed as symbolic place in the centre of the empire that is an allusion of establishing the law of Ahura Mazda in the centre of the world. He reiterates that this tower must have had scientific applications in a way that at the time of planning the city, it was employed as a central point for creating a circular shape of the city and later as a watch tower for dokhtar fort in the northwestern mountain (Huff, 1368:79). Sarfaraz rejects the viewpoints of Huff and writes: this building is a symbol of Zoroastrianism and fire on higher and open space during early Sassanian rule that had promised the revival and consolidation of this belief in order to strengthen its own rule. On the other side, this religious issue must be seen in the Zoroastrian law that against Mazdaism, the fire must be placed under the shadow so that the sun does not shine upon it and the rain does not make it extinct (Sarfaraz, 1365:32).

Describing the purpose of this structure, the writing of Forsat al-Daula Shirazi who lived during Qajar and personally visited this building is not devoid of interest: *"Haji Mulla Mohammad is famous as Haji Akhund who was a Sheikh-ul-Islam or a judge mentions that few years ago we asked a person to go on top of the minaret. Finally he climbed the tower with great difficulty. This person reported that he has seen a hole in the middle of it. So, he tied a heavy object on the end of a rope and dropped it about a few meters down in the hole. It was found that the minaret was empty or there was a passage in the middle of it. Some stressed that there were a building and a pool on the summit of the tower. The water was drawn on the top from a nearby mountain"* (Forsat al-Daula Shirazi, 1362:113-114). The external wall and staircases are desecrated and only a four-corner room with 30m high and 9m wide steps in the form of a thin column has remained over there.

Takht Neshin: In the centre of this circular city and about 100m northeast of the minaret, there is a deserted square-shape rock cut building famous as *Takht Neshin*. The interior space of this structure includes a dome on the square altitude surrounded by niches.

Forsat al-Daula who had seen this structure points to a square building that has been constructed a firm ceiling on its four strong bases. Close to this building was a pool made of mortar (Forsat al-Daula Shirazi, 1362:113). Visiting the remains at Ardeshir Khoreh and the place of Takht Neshin, Flanden relate them architecturally to the Achaemenid era. He expressed this opinion based on a black stone column and its architectural style that was placed near Mausoleum of Imamzadeh Jaafar in the suburb of Takht Neshin

(Flanden, 1356:387). About the purpose, Flanden says that the above building does not have the merit of a big palace and hence; it cannot be other than a mausoleum or a temple. Comparing this structure with the mausoleum of the mother of Suleiman (Cyrus Mausoleum) Flanden concludes that the above building would have been the mausoleum of several kings (Ibid). Vandenberg calls it a Chahartaghi that was built on a terrace and holy fire was lit there and only clergies could access to it (Vandenberg, 1368:52). Huff, too, introduces this building as a fire temple and writes: the four-corner cubical structure includes a central chamber with two side openings and this is the feature of the Sassanian architecture that must be considered as a dome on the central chamber and arches on the openings. Outside of this cubical structure, four supplementary parts were added that includes chambers, porticos and counters. He considers Takht Neshin as the same dome mentioned by Ibn Balkhi (Huff, 1368:79). Sarfaraz believes that Terrbal of FiroozAbaad that is famous as Takht Neshin cannot be considered as a temple just based on its cruciform or by considering specific ideology that prevailed in the early of Sassanid era as well as lofty minaret of Firooz Abaad. Relying upon writings that have reached to us, this place from the emergence of Islam till now has been introduced as Terrbal or Takht Neshin i.e. a private palace of Ardeshir. Architectural features and materials also confirm that this building has been an aristocratic and ceremonial place not a religious one. Later, with the growth of power of Kartir in making Zoroastrian an official religion in 4th Century and during the reign of Bahram II such a temple was not built (Sarfaraz, 1365:26). But we know that Sarfaraz was in mistake because all of the past writers such an Ibn-e Balkhi, Estakhri and ibn-e Hauqal stressed that the minaret which is in the centre of Gour is terrbal not Takht Neshin which is about 100m away from the centre of town.

Ardeshir Palace: At about 5km north of the city of Gour, a big two-storey building with three domes is seen where a number of rooms have been remained on the southern part of it that were used as women's section in the past. A narrow passage that leads to second floor has been repaired today. There was a big pool in front of this palace that had fresh running water (Daryaei, 1383:18). This building has also been introduced as the FiroozAbaad temple or Ardeshir Palace.

The whole complex consists of a fountain, a garden and a palace. The walls were made of ruble stones and mortar and their thickness reached up to 4m. Huff believes that Ardeshir began constructing this palace after the defeat of the Parthian king Ardavan V. Ardeshir called himself king after the victory over Parthian. By defeating of Ardavan V no other danger could threaten his palace in Gour. Probably, the mountainous *Dokhtar* fort that was arduous and difficult to receive guests was dropped as dwelling palace and replaced with a big fort along a big and pleasant pool (Sarfaraz & Firoozmandi, 1373:396). The FiroozAbaad Palace that is known locally as Sassanian Palace has often been wrongly called as temple and some emphasize that this place had been a fire temple (Ibid). Forsat ul Daula has called it as a temple (Forsat al-Daula Shirazi, 1362:115). Pirnia believes that the FiroozAbaad structure lacked installations necessary for being a palace (Pirnia, 1369:95).

With reference to the portico, Ruether believes that the role of this portico was distinct from that of the Parthians. At Ardeshir Palace, it was used as a hall or waiting place during official (aristocratic) ceremonies and guests were attended at chambers attached to it (Ruether, 1977:55). Huff believes that the portico was a complex and splendid space that was probably the sitting of the king before the audiences which expanded by sides with halls, the attached porticos and unknown spaces (Huff, 1977:34).

Conclusion

Ardeshir Papakan, founder of Sassanians, for consolidating his power and accomplishing his ambitious goals needed a peaceful and strategic place so that he could organise and protect his small army against the mighty and great Parthians. Consequently, he left Darabgird and Stakhra and preferred the straight of FiroozAbaad that was inaccessible by enemies hence; a small but efficient army could stand firmed against the enemy for longer period. As such, Ardeshir embarked upon constructing a defensive fort at the shallow FiroozAbaad that is famous as *Dokhtar* Fort. After the downfall of Parthians, Ardeshir did not leave the area rather ordered to build a magnificent city with a circular plan based on Parthian style in the fertile plain of Ardeshir Khoreh. The circular plan of the Gour, its networking, different installations and all of the places were influenced by religious and military thought of Ardeshir as well as reflect his power and ambitiousness.

The most standard architectural elements in this newly-founded city is the ceremonial centre and an imperial palace in the centre and adjacent to each other. This system continued afterward and reached to its peak during the Islamic era. Ardeshir who had inherited spirituality from his forefathers linked religion and politics. With the foundation of a splendid minaret at the centre of Ardeshir Khoreh and drawing water to that height, he continued the spiritual ways of his forefathers in worshipping the water goddess Anahita in a new and magnificent form and hence; he founded a large Anahita temple close to his palace. Shapour I, his son and successor also established Anahita temple in other form close to his palace in Bishapour. Close to the minaret that Arabs remembered as Terrbal (minarets and temple), a grandeur palace was built according to Achaemenid materials but, in a new form that became the method of architecture in the Sassanian period and similarly during the Islamic era. In this palace, the imperial power of Ardeshir reached to its zenith.

With the complete establishment of Sassanian government and after consecutive wars, Ardeshir got an opportunity so that he could gradually abdicate in favor of his son, Shapour I. Ardeshir with his aristocracy that he brought from his wealth and power, separated his dwelling from the imperial palace and administrative in order to pray at the end of his life in his splendid palace in the vicinity of Anahita fountain who had bestowed him kingship. Hence; he lived with tranquility remembering difficult days blended with big victories.

Sources:

Christensen, Arthur (1374/1995) *Vaze Dowlat va Darbar dar Dowreye Shahanshahi Sassanian* (translated by Mojtaba Minovi). Tehran: Paxhooheshgah-e olum-e Ensani

Daryaei, Tooraj (1383/2004) *Soghoot-e Sassanian* (translated by Mansooreh Etehadieh & Farahnaz Amirkhani Hasinakloo). Tehran: Nashr-e Tarikh-e Iran

Estakhri, Abu Eshaq Ebrahim (1340/1961) *Masalek va Mamalek* (translated by Iraj Afshar). Tehran: Elmi va Farhangi

Flanden, Uzhen (1356/1977) *Safarnameh* (translated by Hosein Noor Sadeghi). Tehran: Entesharat Eshraghi

Forsat, Aldole Shirazi & Seyyed, Mohammad Nasir (1362/1983) *Asarol Ajam*. Tehran: Farhangsara

Huff, Ditrish (1368/1989) *Firooz Abad* (translated by Keramatollah Afsar). In *Dar Shahrhaye Iran*, vol 3, Kiani, Mohammad Yousef. Tehran: Jahad Daneshgahi

Huff, D. (1969/70) *Zur Rekonstruktion des Turmes von Firuzabad*. Istanbuler, Mitt 19/20

Huff, D. (1977) *Aspect Historie et Archeologiques*. In *Ghala Dokhtar Atechkade*, H. Hugi, Ecolepolytechnique, Federal. Zurich, Avril

Ibn-e Balkhi (1329/1950) *Fars Nameh*. Tehran: Darolfonoon

Ibn-e Haughal, & Mohammad Ben Ali (1345/1966) *Sooratol arz* (translated by Jaafar Shear) Tehran: Bonyade Farhang-e Iran

Porada, Edith (1355/1976) *Honar-e Iran Bastan* (translated by Yousef Majidzadeh). Tehran: Daneshgah Tehran

Pirnia, Mohammad Karim (1369/1990) *Shiveh hay Memari Iran.* Tehran: Moasese Nashre honare Eslami

Ruether, Oscar (1977) *Sassanian Architecture.* In *Survey of Persian Art,* A/U/POP, Vol. 2, third edition with Bibliography and Addenda published

Sarfaraz, Ali Akbar (1365/1986) *Jozveh Doroos-e Bastanshenasi.* Tehran: Daneshgah Tehran

Sarfaraz, Ali Akbar & Firoozmandi, Bahman (1373/1994) *Majmooe Doroos-e Bastanshenasi va Honar-e Iran dar Dowran-e Tarikhi Mad, Hakhamaneshi, Ashkani va Sasani.* Tehran: Qoqnus, Tehran

Shipman, Claus (1383/2004) *Tarikh-e Shahanshahi Sasani* (translated by Faramarz Najd Samiee). Tehran: Sazeman Miras Farhangi va Gardeshgari

Tabari, Mohammad Ebne Jarir (1362/1983) *Tarikh-e Tabari* (translated by Abolqasem Payandeh). Tehran: Asatir

Vandenberg, Louee (1368/1989) *Bastan Shenasi Iran Bastan* (translated by Isa Behnam). Tehran: Entesharat Daneshgah Tehran

Varjavand, Parviz (1366/1987) *Shahr Sazi va Shahrneshini dar Iran.* In *Dar Shahrhaye Iran* Vol 4, Kiani, Mohammad Yousef. Tehran: Jahad Daneshgahi

Part 2

Arts

Figure 17: Anahita statue in snow, photo by Payam Nabarz.

Anahita by Akashnath

Goddess Anahita, painting by Akashnath, 2008.

Iranian Warrior Women by Shapour Suren-Pahlav

Iranian Warrior Women, a reconstruction of a female Achaemenid cavalry unit, Water Colour 55x37cm, 2004.

Anahita by Ana C Jones

Sculptures and painting created by Ana C Jones and used in modern practise.

Altar showing Anahita on the left, Kosmokrator in the middle, Mithras on the right.

Green Anahita

Anahita painting by Ana C Jones 2011.

An Image of Great Goddess Anahita and its Artistic Notes

by Dr. Tōjō Masato

Chairman of Mithraeum Japan Tokyo, Japan

1. An Image of Great Goddess Anahita

2. Date of drawing

1996, summer.

3. Size

36 cm in height, 27 cm in width.

4. Drawing Process

First: by pencil. Second: outline is drawn by pen and ink. Third: scanned and coloured by PC painting tool.

5. Textual references

See bibliography.

6. Commentaries

Here are the points I had considered when I drew this image. Of course these considerations don't exclude other interpretations.

(1) There are Venus, the Sun and the Moon in the sky (from left to right). They are depicted by Babylonian planctary symbols.

(2) The Sun symbolizes Mithra. Venus symbolizes Anahita as Mithra's sister and/or love. The Moon symbolizes Anahita as Mithra's mother.

(3) Anahita holds an Egyptian ankh in her right hand. The ankh is the key of Nile, key of eternal Life. This is an allusion of the followings:

Pattern 1

- Moon/Venus: Anahita-Isis-Mary-Virgin Mother

- Sun: Mithra's logos-Horus-Christ-the Son and Mithra-Ra-Yahweh/Metatron-Father

- Sirius: Tir (Tishtrya)-Sothis-the Star of Bethlehem-the three Magi

Pattern 2

- Moon/Venus: Anahita-Isis-Artemis-Mary-Virgin Mother

- Sun: Mithra-Horus-Christ-the Son

- Jupiter: Aramazd-Osiris-Zeus-Yahweh-Father

- Sirius: Tir (Tishtrya)-Sothis-the Star of Bethlehem-the three Magi

The following legend and scriptures will broaden your imagination:

- *Legend of Lake Hamin* (see Nabarz, 2005:6)

- *Сказание Афродитиана* Персиянина (Story of Persian Aphrodite) (see Мильков 1999:712-934)

- *Revelation of the Magi* (see Landau, 2010)

- *Gospel According to Mathew* 1:18-25, 2:1-2

(4) The fish in the river is an allusion of imagery association of Fish-Christ-Grail.

(5) Astrology and astral symbolism are characteristic features of Roman Mithraism. So, Anahita stands in front of the city Babylon, which was one of the major centres of astrology.

(6) In front of Babylon flows the River Euphrates. For Anahita presides all the rivers of the world (*Ardwi Sur Yasht* 1.4-5). The earth is covered with green and flowers. For she makes the earth fertile (*Ardwi Sur Yasht* 1.1).

(7) Three birds in the sky are simorghs (Iranian phoenix). They bring happiness and fortune.

(8) The image reflects the syncretism of Anahita with Aphrodite, Artemis, Cybele, Ishtar and Isis. Her golden hair symbolizes her syncretism with Greek Aphrodite.

(9) Anahita wears a cloth. Its colour is an allusion of peacock. Peacock, phoenix, simorgh and eagle are equivalent. The cloth symbolizes her aura.

(10) Using Chinese characters (kanji), the Sun, the Moon and Venus are represented as follows (Gakken, 1998:152-156):

- Sun: Hi 日

- Moon: Tsuki 月

- Venus: Myōjō 明星 (Myō 明 means light, Jō 星 means star/planet)

In East Asia, there is a mysterious esoteric tradition about kanji meaning interpretation. According to this tradition, Venus is thought to harmonize the energies of the Sun and the Moon, for Myō 明 = Hi 日 + Tsuki 月. Applying this esoteric interpretation to Anahita, she has the power to harmonize the energies of the Sun and the Moon.

Bibliography

Ananikian, Mardiros H. (1908) *Armenia*. In *The Encyclopedia of Religion and Ethics*, Vol. 1, Hastings, J. (ed). New York: Charles Scribner

Ananikian, Mardiros H. (1925) *Armenian Mythology*. In *The Mythology of All Races*, Vol. VII. New York: Marshall Jones Co.

Darmesteter, James (trans) (1882) *Ardwi Sur Yasht (Aban Yast)*. In *The Zend-Avesta Part II, the Sacred Books of the East Vol. 23*. Motilal Banarsidass Publishers

Gakken (ed.) (1998) *A Book on the Teachings of Tendai Sect of Esoteric Buddhism*. Books Esoterica 21

Gakushukenkyusha (1998) 学研編『天台密教の本』学習研究社, Books Esoterica 21

Herodotus (1997) History 1.131-132. In *Traditions of the Magi, Zoroastrianism in Greek and Latin Literature*, Albert de Jong. Leiden: Brill

Landau, Brent (2010) *Revelation of the Magi*. Harper One

Milkov, Vladimir V. (1999) *Story of Persian Aphrodite*. In *Ancient Russian Apocrypha*. St. Petersburg: Russian Humanitarian Institute

Владимир Владимирович Мильков. "Сказание Афродитиана Персиянина", в *Древнеруские Апокрифы*, Издателство Русскго Христианского гуманитарного института, Санкт-Петрбрг, 1999

Nabarz, Payam (2005) *The Mysteries of Mithras* (Legend of Lake Hamin). Inner Traditions

Russell, James R. (1987) *Zoroastrianism in Armenia*. Harvard University Press

Strabo (1997) *Geography* 15.3.13-15. In *Traditions of the Magi, Zoroastrianism in Greek and Latin Literature*, Albert de Jong. Leiden: Brill

PHOTOS OF THE TEMPLE OF ANAHITA AT BISHAPOUR

by Rahele Koulabadi

Part 3
Poem

GREAT LADY ANAHITA

by Katherine Sutherland

Great Lady, as strong and as vast as the seas,
swathed in tides of time and mystery;
the principle of existence – manifest,
awe-inspiring warrior woman, beautiful none the less.

Surging energy, a rushing stream,
of form springing forth from a mountain's dream,
purifier of the cauldron space of all women's' wombs,
bringer of life and the granter of boons.

Giver of Mother's milk
the sustenance of life,
birth supported
nurturing midwife.

Charioteer, powerful, holy and strong,
carried by swift horses, your elemental throng,
rushing, dashing Cloud, Wind Rain and Sleet,
draw you through the skies with dancing feet.

Stellar maiden, from high above the Sun,

hailed and worshipped as the day is begun,

and as each day ends with failing light,

devotees pray for your divine insight.

Honest pleas only reach your sacred ears,

wicked cries fall, as unacknowledged bitter tears,

Oh Anahita, dwelling in every body of water,

rivers, pools and streams are all your flowing daughters.

You are the palace set within the head,

where you lie with roses on a scented bed,

clothed in a mantle of golden light,

beautiful to behold ~ a powerful sight.

Crowned with stars and proud light streaming,

a glorious vision for Magi dreaming,

flowing into our hearts and minds,

Lady of the Green Path of all time.

INDEX

Mithras Reader Vol 1

This edition includes in **Part 1 academic papers:** Continuity and Change in the Cult of Mithra, by Dr. Israel Campos Mendez. Mithra and the warrior group Mithra and the Iranian words and images Introduction to Classes of Manichean, Mithraism and Sufiyeh, by Dr. Saloome Rostampoor. Entheos ho syros, polymathes ho phoinix: Neoplatonist approaches to religious practice in Iamblichus and Porphyry, by Sergio Knipe. Mithraism and Alchemy, by David Livingstone.
Part 2 Arts: 'For example Mithras' part I exhibition by Farangis Yegane.
Part 3 Religious articles: Meeting Mithra, by Guya Vichi. Ode To Mithra, by Guya Vichi. Hymn to the Sun, by Katherine Sutherland. Mithras Liturgy with the Orphic Hymns, by Payam Nabarz.

ISBN-13: 978-1905524099, (Twin Serpents Ltd, 2006).

Mithras Reader Vol 2

This edition includes in **Part 1 academic papers:** Factors determining the outside projection of the Mithraic Mysteries by Dr. Israel Campos Méndez. The Mithras Liturgy: cult liturgy, religious ritual, or magical theurgy? Some aspects and considerations of the Mithras Liturgy from the Paris Codex and what they may imply for the origin and purpose of this spell by Kim Huggens.

Part 2 Arts: 'For example Mithras' part II exhibition by Farangis Yegane. Mithras-Phanes art piece by James Rodriguez. Temple of Mithra in Garni, Armenia, photos by Jalil Nozari. Mithras artistic depiction by Robert Kavjian.

Part 3 Religious articles: MITHRAS SOL INVICTUS Invocation by M. Hajduk. Ode to Aphrodite by Sappho, translated by Harita Meenee. Norooz Phiroze by Farida Bamji. Disappearing Shrines and Moving Shrines by S. David. The Sleeping Lord by Katherine Sutherland. The right handed handshake of the Gods by Payam Nabarz.

ISBN: 978-0-9556858-1-1, (Web of Wyrd Press, 2008).

Mithras Reader Vol 3

Mithras Reader Vol. III

An Academic and Religious Journal of Greek, Roman and Persian Studies

Editor: Payam Nabarz

This edition includes in **Part 1 academic papers:** A Journey to the Hypercosmic side of the Sun by Prof Ezio Albrile. Internet & the Resurrection of a God: the Neo-Mithraic Communities by Israel Campos. Aristotle & the Natural Slave: The Athenian Relationship with India by Robert F. Mullen. The Dawn of Religions in Afghanistan-Seistan-Gandhara & the Personal Seals of Gotama Buddha & Zoroaster by Ranajit Pal. Dacia & the Cult of Mithras by Csaba Szabó. Sun Tzu & the Achaemenid Grand Strategy by Sheda Vasseghi. Zen Buddhism & Mithraism by Masato Tōjō. A new Archaeological Research of the Sassanian Fire Temple of Rivand in Sabzevar, by Hassan Hashemi Zarjabad. The Zoroastrian Holyland of Haetumant by Reza MehrAfarin. **Part 2 Arts:** Kephra by Akashanath. **Part 3 Religious articles:** Into The Looking Glass Tragic Reflections of Life by Lesley Madytinou. Solomon in Olympus: The Enduring Connection between King Solomon & Greek Magic by David Rankine. Orphic Hymn to Aphrodite trans by Harita Meenee. The Athenian Festivals of Demeter by Melissa Gold. The Lioness by Jane Raeburn. Plus many more articles, and artwork.

ISBN-10: 0955685834, (Web of Wyrd Press, 2010).

If you enjoyed this book, you may also enjoy some of the other titles published by Avalonia...

A Collection of Magical Secrets by David Rankine (editor)

Artemis: Virgin Goddess of the Sun & Moon by Sorita d'Este

Defences Against the Witches' Craft by John Canard

From a Drop of Water (anthology, various contributors) edited by Kim Huggens

Heka: Egyptian Magic by David Rankine

Hekate Her Sacred Fires (anthology) edited by Sorita d'Este

Hekate Liminal Rites (history) by Sorita d'Este & David Rankine

Odin's Gateways by Katie Gerrard

The Priory of Sion by Jean-luc Chaumeil

Seidr: The Gate is Open by Katie Gerrard

Stellar Magic by Payam Nabarz

The Book of Gold by David Rankine (editor) & Paul Harry Barron (translator)

The Cosmic Shekinah by Sorita d'Este & David Rankine

The Gods of the Vikings by Marion Pearce

The Grimoire of Arthur Gauntlet by David Rankine (editor)

The Guises of the Morrigan by David Rankine & Sorita d'Este

The Faerie Queens (anthology, various contributors), edited by Sorita d'Este and David Rankine

The Isles of the Many Gods by David Rankine & Sorita d'Este

The Temple of Hekate by Tara Sanchez

Thracian Magic by Georgi Mishev

Thoth: The Ancient Egyptian God of Wisdom by Lesley Jackson

Visions of the Cailleach by Sorita d'Este & David Rankine

Vs. (anthology, various contributors) edited by Kim Huggens

Wicca Magickal Beginnings by Sorita d'Este & David Rankine

Memento Mori (anthology) by Kim Huggens (editor)

*****

These and many more unique and interesting esoteric titles are available from our website, **www.avaloniabooks.co.uk**

You can also write to us,
Avalonia, BM Avalonia, London, WC1N 3XX, United Kimgdom

Lightning Source UK Ltd.
Milton Keynes UK
UKHW031850051022
409984UK00010B/930